PREACHER

Book Five

PREACHER

Book Five

Garth Ennis Writer Steve Dillon Artist

Pamela Rambo Colorist Clem Robins Letterer

Cover Art and Original Series Covers by Glenn Fabry

Preacher created by Garth Ennis and Steve Dillon

PREACHER BOOK FIVE

 DC Comics, 2900 W. Alameda Avenue, Burbank, CA 91505. Printed in the USA. Third Printing.
ISBN: 978-1-4012-5074-4

Library of Congress Cataloging-in-Publication Data

Ennis, Garth, author.
Preacher book five / Garth Ennis ; illustrated by Steve Dillon.
pages cm
Summary: "Preacher Jesse Custer's dark journey to find God, accompanied by his gun-toting girlfriend and Irish vampire buddy, continues as Jesse becomes the sheriff of a troubled Texas town. Then, he decides it's high time to renew his quest to find God and hold him accountable for all of his actions. But before he can continue down that path, he must reunite with his girlfriend, Tulip"-- Provided by publisher.
"Originally published in single magazine form as Preacher 41-54"--T.p. verso.
ISBN 978-1-4012-5074-4 (paperback)
1. Custer, Jesse (Fictitious character)--Comic books, strips, etc. 2. Clergy--Comic books, strips, etc. 3. Vigilantes--Comic books, strips, etc. 4. Graphic novels. I. Dillon, Steve, illustrator. II. Title.
PN6727.E56P7335 2014
741.5'973--dc23

2014018204

Table of Contents

Introduction

I remember bracing for the bullet. One Thursday every month, the morning after the latest issue of PREACHER hit comic store shelves, I'd ready myself for the inevitable letter to arrive on the desk of someone way up the food chain at DC Comics — a letter sent by an irate reader who'd somehow bypassed the "mature readers" label on the cover and taken grave offense at something inside. After that, events would unfold rapidly: I'd get summoned to a meeting attended by a grim-faced HR representative, there'd be an animated discussion of my editorial judgment and moral fiber, and that would be the end of my career in comics.

Remarkably, that day never came. For its 66-issue run, Garth Ennis and Steve Dillon's iconoclastic, neo-spaghetti western was a lightning rod for public opinion, but it ran its full course, didn't outstay its welcome, and ended on its own terms. One of the most celebrated and influential comics of its day, PREACHER owes its success to the insane alchemy of its creative team and the unwavering support of its publisher, but at the root of its popularity lies a dark secret that I'm not sure anyone involved in its creation — myself included — will readily admit.

PREACHER provoked all sorts of reactions, but never indifference. Jesse Custer's walkabout through the American id resonates because the landscape isn't fantasy but funhouse mirror. Jesus de Sade and the Meatman delight because they are totally outlandish and disturbingly feasible. And the fact that Custer's gripe goes right to the top only adds to the fun. When he decides to make the Supreme Architect atone for His sins, who doesn't kinda, sorta cheer? It's an age-old question everyone asks at some point: How the hell did things get this bad, and how the hell did He let 'em?

Asking this question left PREACHER open to charges of sacrilege or cynicism, but both claims are false. Doubt is the crucible in which true faith is forged — this Catholic knows that from experience. And Garth is more pissed-off humanist than jaded cynic. Beneath the sordid surface, PREACHER is a deeply moral tale of good versus evil. Its protagonist and moral centerpiece, Jesse Custer, isn't cut from the cloth of the fuzzy-edged anti-hero that dominates so many alternative comics; he's a highly moral man on a quest to navigate a highly immoral world. Sure, he choked the life out of his half-brother Jody, stomped the shit out of Odin Quincannon and incinerated his demonic Gran'ma, but hotdang if those sumbitches didn't deserve every inch of what they got. Jesse Custer simply had the resolve to do what needed to be done — what Batman should've done a long time ago to the Joker — and we love him for it.

Which brings me to the deep, dark secret of PREACHER's success. Look past the surface of zipper-masked geeks, redneck cannibals and traumatized chickens and you'll see PREACHER for what it really is. Jesse Custer's got a code and a quest. He's got super-powers, a costume, a sidekick, a girlfriend who can take care of her own, a complicated family legacy, and a rogues' gallery that rivals that of anyone who's ever worn a cape or cowl. The familiar tropes are all there, flipping you the bird, daring you to find them. And that's the secret of PREACHER's success: Somehow, some way, two guys from o'er the pond who profess no love for the spandex genre created a work of fiction that defies easy categorization but just might stand as one of the best damn super-hero comics of all time.

— Axel Alonso
Editor in Chief, Marvel Comics
Former editor of PREACHER

A 17-year comics industry veteran, Axel Alonso got his start at DC Comics' Vertigo imprint, where he edited HELLBLAZER, 100 BULLETS and PREACHER before leaping to Marvel Comics in 2001. Since that time he has overseen many of the publisher's biggest franchises — including Spider-Man, Hulk and the X-Men — and edited some of its most talked-about series — including Truth, Rawhide Kid *and* X-Statix. *In 2011 he was promoted to Editor in Chief of Marvel Worldwide, Inc. Besides comics, his passions include basketball, hip-hop, 8-year-old shooting guard Tito Alonso, and preparing for the inevitable Zombie Apocalypse.*

PREACHER

Book Five

SHERIFF
SALVATION, TX
POP. 1626
GLENN FABRY 98

"I'm talkin' about a little fart of a town an' some bad boys need slappin' down, an' a sheriff could use some help doin' it."

SIX MONTHS LATER
THERE COMES A TIME, SKEETER OL' BOY...
WHEN YOU JUST PLAIN RUN OUT OF AMERICA.

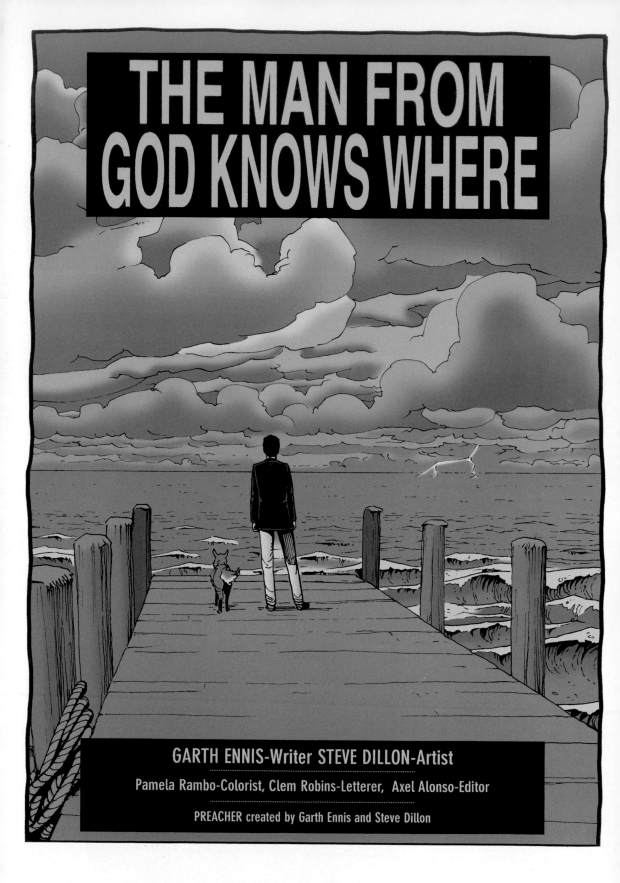

THE MAN FROM GOD KNOWS WHERE

GARTH ENNIS-Writer STEVE DILLON-Artist

Pamela Rambo-Colorist, Clem Robins-Letterer, Axel Alonso-Editor

PREACHER created by Garth Ennis and Steve Dillon

SIX
MONTHS
EARLIER:

SALVATION TX.
POPN. 1626

S DINER

JODIE'S BAR & G

COMIN'?
WUFF!

LONE STAR'N A SHOT.

SURE, DUDE.

YA-HARR, JIM-LAD!

C'MON, DAVY, LEAVE HIM BE...

DUDE, THE GUY'S TRYNNA--

DAMN THIS HOOK, JIM-LAD! WENT TO SCRATCH ME EYE AN' NOW LOOK AT ME, YA-HARR! AN' WHEN I WENT TO TAKE A LEAK--

SHOULDN'T YOU HAVE A HAND UP YOUR ASS?

HUH?

I ALWAYS HEARD MISS PIGGY HAD A HAND UP HER ASS.

DAVY--!

OH, CAP'N BLACKBEARD'S A *COMEDIAN*...

WALK AWAY, BOY.

WHO THE *FUCK* ARE YOU CALLIN'--

bud

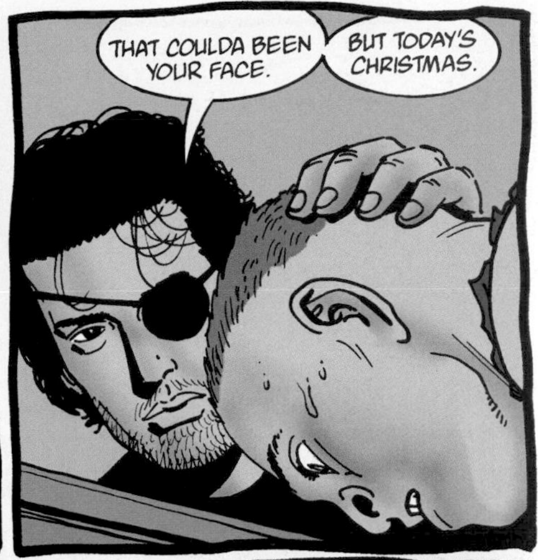
THAT COULDA BEEN YOUR FACE.
BUT TODAY'S CHRISTMAS.

THANKS, DUDE.

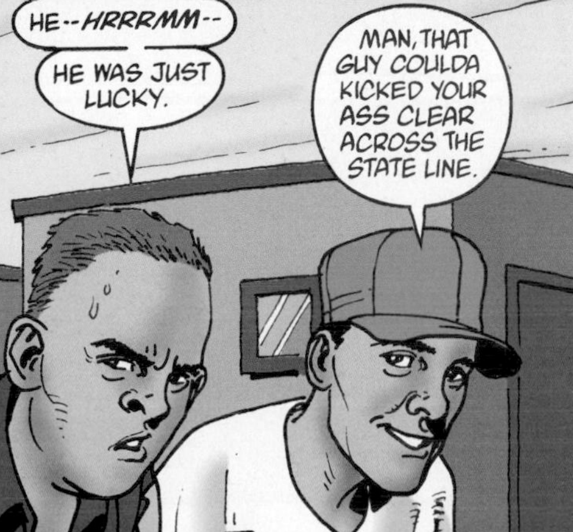
HE--*HRRRMM*--
HE WAS JUST LUCKY.
MAN, THAT GUY COULDA KICKED YOUR ASS CLEAR ACROSS THE STATE LINE.

HEY! CYCLOPS!!
SHERIFF

C'MON, HONEY, GIVE US A LOOK AT IT!
WHAT THE FUCK ARE YOU, FROM STAR TREK OR SOMETHIN'?
THEY LET YOU OUT FOR THE DAY, EYEBALL? HAW!
FUCKIN' MUTATED BITCH--
PLEASE! STOP IT! STOP IT!

WHY CAN'T YOU JUST LEAVE ME ALONE?!

LORIE--?

WHAT THE FUCK DO YOU WANT?

SORRY, MISS--
SORRY--
WON'T DO IT AGAIN, EVER--
SWEAR TO GOD--

YOU OKAY, LORIE? MISS BOBBS?
I AM NOW, THANK YOU...UM...
PARDON ME, BUT DO I KNOW YOU?

LONG TIME AGO YOU DID. JESSE CUSTER.
YOUR BROTHER BILLY-BOB'S FRIEND? WHEN WE WERE KIDS?
UM...

JESSE...?
BUT--BUT YOU LOOK SO DIFFERENT! I'D NEVER HAVE RECOGNIZED YOU IN A MILLION YEARS!
YEAH, WELL, I HAD A LITTLE ACCIDENT...

NO, I MEAN YOU LOOK COMPLETELY DIFFERENT! YOU'RE LIKE A NEW MAN!
I MEAN YOU WERE TALL EVEN THEN, WELL OVER SIX FEET, AND YOU WERE SO GOOD-LOOKING...

AND YOUR EYES USED TO BE BROWN, DIDN'T THEY? AND YOUR HAIR--WHAT HAPPENED TO ALL THAT BEAUTIFUL SHINY BLACK HAIR YOU HAD?

UH, WELL, LONG AS I'M HERE, LEMME GIVE YOU A RIDE HOME...
OH, BUT I LIVE JUST RIGHT AROUND THE CORNER--
IT'S NO TROUBLE.

WE CAN'T JUST STAND BY AND--
I SAID: LEAVE IT.
BUT HE BEAT THE HELL OUTTA THEM RIGHT IN THE STREET!

DIDN'T HE, THOUGH.

MA'AM.

HMMMM.

NO, MY DADDY WAS MAD ABOUT IT FOR A LONG TIME, PROB-ABLY STILL IS. BUT I REMEMBERED YOU AND BILLY-BOB FROM WHEN YOU WERE LITTLE KIDS. I KNEW YOU'D NEVER DO ANYTHING TO HURT HIM...
MEANS A LOT TO HEAR YOU SAY THAT, LORIE. EVEN NOW.

HE CAN STAY IN THE TRUCK...
NO, HE'S FINE. HE'S A SWEET LITTLE GUY.
WUFF!

IT WASN'T TOO LONG AFTER THAT I LEFT HOME, ACTUALLY. I WANTED TO GO TO COLLEGE AND STUDY FOR A BUSINESS DEGREE, BUT ...WELL, YOU'VE SEEN HOW PEOPLE CAN BE. THERE WEREN'T TOO MANY PLACES WANTED ME AROUND CAMPUS.
BUT I TAUGHT MYSELF A LOT FROM BOOKS AND THINGS. AND JODIE HELPED ME GET THROUGH THE TESTS--IT'S AMAZING, REALLY. JODIE KNOWS JUST ABOUT EVERYTHING.

JODIE, HUH?
YES, COME IN AND SAY HELLO!

GOD *DAMMIT*, LORENA...YOU EVER GOING TO LEARN ANY CONSIDERATION FOR MY *FUCKING HANGOVER*...?

WHO'S THIS?

JODIE, I'D LIKE YOU TO MEET JESSE CUSTER.
EVENIN', MA'AM.

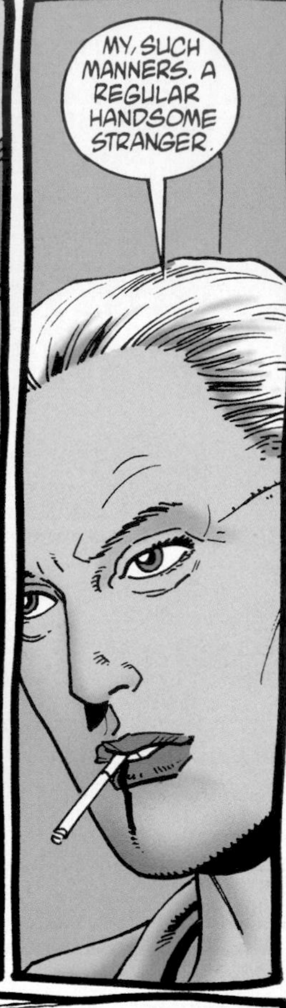
MY, SUCH MANNERS. A REGULAR HANDSOME STRANGER.

SOME OF THOSE AWFUL QUINCANNON MEN WERE GIVING ME TROUBLE AGAIN, JODIE. JESSE SAVED ME-- HE REALLY TAUGHT THEM A LESSON, HONESTLY!

KNIGHT IN SHINING ARMOR, TOO. WELL, I GUESS THAT DESERVES A DRINK...
I'LL MAKE SOME TEA.

GOT SOME-THING STRONGER THROUGH HERE. THE MUTT YOURS?
YEAH.
HE BETTER NOT SHIT ON THE CARPET.

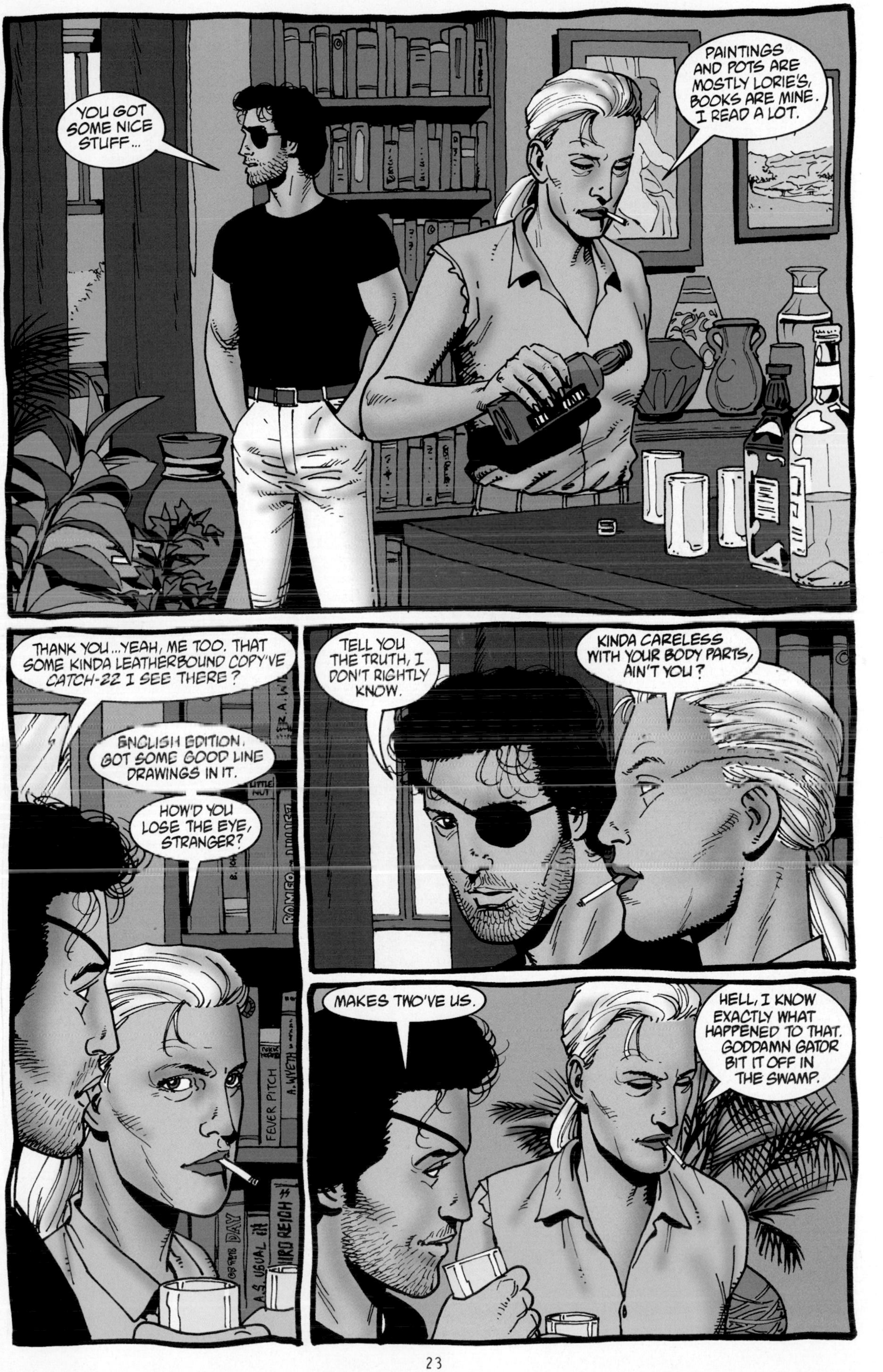

YOU GOT SOME NICE STUFF...
PAINTINGS AND POTS ARE MOSTLY LORIE'S, BOOKS ARE MINE. I READ A LOT.

JODIE... HEY, THAT PLACE ON THE MAIN STREET YOURS? BOY BEHIND THE BAR CALLS FELLAS *DUDE* WITHOUT CHECKIN' IF THEY OBJECT OR NOT?
MINE AND LORIE'S. I RUN IT, SHE DOES THE BOOKS. THAT GIRL'S A MATHEMATICAL GENIUS, I TELL YOU.
WHERE DO YOU KNOW HER FROM, ANYWAY?

WE KINDA GREW UP TOGETHER--ME AN' HER BROTHER, ANYHOW.
FUNNY THING WAS, SHE DIDN'T SEEM TO RECOGNIZE ME. NOT ONE BIT.
THAT'S BECAUSE OF HER EYE CONDITION.

SOMEONE OR OTHER'S SYNDROME, I DON'T KNOW THE EXACT DETAILS. BASICALLY, THE EYES --WELL, THE EYE--SOMETIMES IT SENDS THE WRONG INFORMATION TO THE BRAIN. YOU LOOK AT ONE THING, BUT YOU SEE SOMETHING ELSE ALTOGETHER.

HERE WE ARE... JESSE, ARE YOU IN A HURRY TO GET SOMEWHERE?
NO...
WELL, WE HAVE A SPARE ROOM UPSTAIRS. WHY DON'T YOU STAY HERE TONIGHT AND THEN MAKE A FRESH START IN THE MORNING?

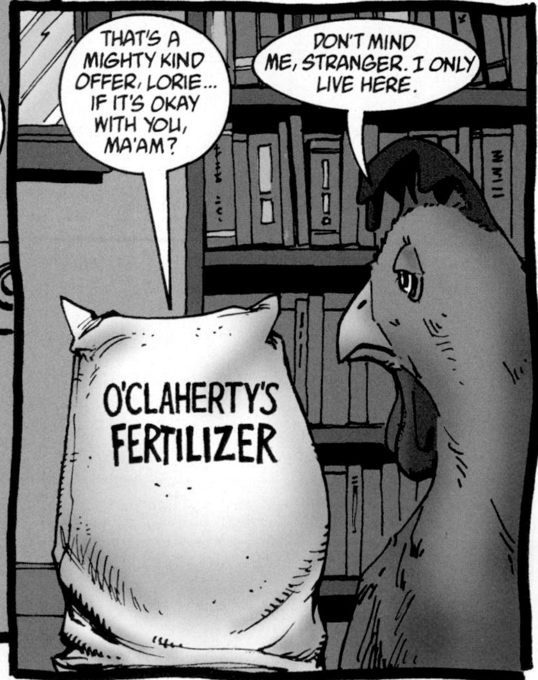
THAT'S A MIGHTY KIND OFFER, LORIE... IF IT'S OKAY WITH YOU, MA'AM?
DON'T MIND ME, STRANGER. I ONLY LIVE HERE.
O'CLAHERTY'S FERTILIZER

...THEN WHAT?
NO.

AM I IN A HURRY TO GET SOMEWHERE...

AM I SHIT.

AIN'T ABOUT TA GO... QUITTIN' ON ME, ARE YA, PILGRIM?

HELL, NO, I AIN'T ABOUT TO QUIT ON YOU. ANY TIME NOW I'M GONNA CHOKE DOWN THIS BIG OL' SHIT SANDWICH I BEEN SERVED AN' SHOULDER MY GOD-DAMN BURDEN AGAIN, KEEP ON TRYNNA ACCOMPLISH THE IMPOSSIBLE.
ANY TIME NOW.

AN' WHAT THE HELL IS THAT SUPPOSED TO MEAN?
MEANS I CAN'T KEEP ON DOIN' THIS WHEN THERE'S SO MUCH I AIN'T SURE OF. LIKE WHAT THE HELL HAPPENED TO MY EYE? WHY CAN'T I REMEMBER ANYTHING AFTER THE PLANE?

AN' HOW COME I GOT FUCKED SO BAD, BY THE PEOPLE I LOVED THE MOST?

I JUST DUNNO HOW TO FIT IT IN MY HEAD.
CASS, GODDAMMIT, I SAVED HIS ASS AN' HE SAVED MINE TWICE EACH, EASY--HOW THE HELL'D HE DO SOMETHIN' LIKE THAT? HE'DA BURNED UP LIKE A FUCKIN' CRISPY CRITTER, I HADN'T STOPPED HIM...

AN' TULIP, JESUS, TULIP... I DON'T EVEN WANNA *THINK*...
I FEEL LIKE PUKIN'. SWEAR TO GOD.

THIS WHAT I GET? TRY TO BE A GOOD GUY, TRY TO DO RIGHT BY FOLKS--IS THIS MY FUCKIN' *REWARD*?

WELL NOW, PILGRIM... I DON'T RECALL NOBODY SAYIN' *NOTHIN'* ABOUT NO *REE-WARD*.

POINT.

AW, FUCK THIS SELF-PITYIN' BULLSHIT.

I DUNNO.
COULD BE ALL I NEED'S TO SHIFT DOWN A GEAR.

HOW COME THERE AIN'T NO SWIMMIN' POOLS IN MEXICO? 'CAUSE ANYONE CAN SWIM'S ALREADY OVER HERE ANYHOW!
HAW! 'KAY, HOW COME MEXICANS EAT REFRIED BEANS?
'CAUSE THEY COULDN'T GET 'EM RIGHT THE FIRST TIME!
HA HA HA!

WELL, HOW 'BOUT THIS ONE--
THAT BOY GONNA SIT THERE AN' TAKE THAT?
HECTOR? SURE.

THEY RAG ON HIM FROM TIME TO TIME, JUST TO REMIND HIM OF HIS PLACE. HE SMILES AT THEIR JOKES, HE GETS TO HANG OUT WITH THEM.
FUN BUNCH LIKE THAT, I GUESS IT'S WORTH THE ABUSE...

DON'T KNOCK IT. HECTOR'S A LITTLE SLOW, DOESN'T KNOW TOO MANY PEOPLE. AND THOSE DICKS ARE PRETTY GOOD TO HIM, MOST OF THE TIME.
HELL, SOMETIMES IT'S EVEN HIS TURN TO GO HOME WITH CORA.

HAAAWWW!
LUCKY DOG.

NICE LIGHTER, STRANGER--MM--
THEY'RE HARMLESS. THEY WENT TO HIGH SCHOOL TOGETHER, DRIFTED AWAY, REALIZED THEY DIDN'T KNOW SHIT ABOUT SHIT AND DRIFTED BACK. NEVER UNDERESTIMATE THE STRANGELY MAGNETIC PULL OF THE TOWN OF SALVATION, ESPECIALLY TO THOSE AS IGNORANT AS SIN.
MOST NIGHTS, CORA TAKES HOME WHICHEVER ONE TREATS HER NICEST. I ACTUALLY THINK IT'S KIND OF SWEET.

I SWEAR. TEXAS, HUH?
YOU MEAN HECTOR? SHIT, AROUND HERE, THAT'S PROGRESS. HE WAS BLACK HE WOULDN'T EVEN BE IN HERE.
FUCK COMMUNISM

YOU DON'T MEAN--
NO, OF COURSE I FUCKING DON'T MEAN. BUT THEY WON'T COME IN. THEY CHOOSE NOT TO, THEY HAVE THEIR OWN PLACES.

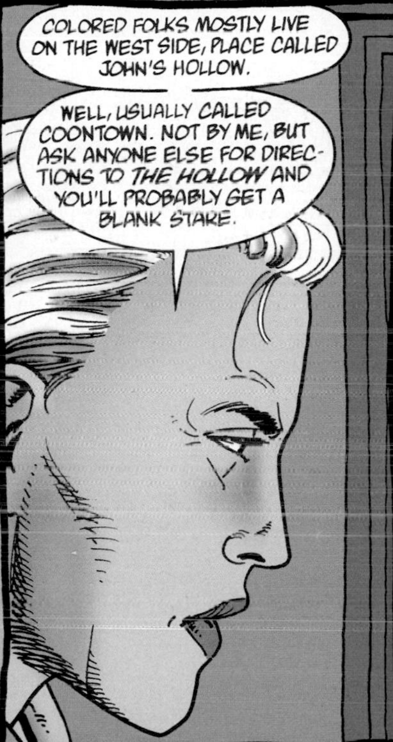
COLORED FOLKS MOSTLY LIVE ON THE WEST SIDE, PLACE CALLED JOHN'S HOLLOW.
WELL, USUALLY CALLED COONTOWN. NOT BY ME, BUT ASK ANYONE ELSE FOR DIRECTIONS TO *THE HOLLOW* AND YOU'LL PROBABLY GET A BLANK STARE.

BUT NOT YOU.
I PREFER TO JUDGE PEOPLE BY WHAT'S IN THEM, NOT HOW THEY LOOK.
MY HALO'S IN THE MAIL, IN CASE YOU WERE WONDERING.

NO, I HAPPEN TO AGREE WITH YOU. WHAT I SAW OF THIS PLACE THIS AFTERNOON DIDN'T EXACTLY LIGHT MY FIRE.
OH, THOSE QUINCANNON ASSHOLES-- NO, THEY'RE NOT LOCAL. THEY WORK AT THE MEATPACKING PLANT DOWN THE ROAD.
FUCKS ARE ALWAYS COMING INTO TOWN, GIVING PEOPLE SHIT. I DON'T LET THEM IN HERE.
GODDAMN WORTHLESS TRASH, PICKIN' ON THE GIRL LIKE THAT. I SHOULDA STUCK AROUND AN' WALED ON 'EM SOME MORE...
OH, I DECLARE. JUST CAN'T STAND SEEIN' A WOMAN IN PAIN, MM?
LITTLE WEAKNESS OF MINE.
WHAT WAS THAT YOU WERE SAYIN' ABOUT HALOES...?
I GUESS THEY'VE GOT US SAINTS SURROUNDED, HUH?
I MEAN I COULD GO OVER THERE AND BAWL THOSE PISSANTS OUT FOR BEING NASTY TO HECTOR, AND THEY'D JUST GO SOMEWHERE ELSE AND KEEP AT IT. HE WOULDN'T THANK ME. THEY'RE THE ONLY FRIENDS HE'S GOT.
YOU CAN'T CHANGE THINGS. YOU CAN WATCH OVER THEM, MAYBE STOP THEM GETTING WORSE...
BUT NOBODY'S TRYING TO SAVE THE WORLD, STRANGER.
NOBODY'S DUMB ENOUGH
ON THE HOUSE.

HOWDY.

EVENIN'.
I WAS WONDERIN' IF I COULD JOIN YOU FOR A MOMENT?
SURE.

YOU'RE THE SHERIFF, AIN'T YOU?
THAT I AM. JIM BEWLEY'S THE NAME.

JESSE CUSTER.
RIGHT. WELL, MISTER CUSTER...AH... WHAT IT IS, I SAW THAT LITTLE SET-TO YOU HAD WITH THEM BOYS TODAY? IN THE STREET?

YOU COME TO TAKE ME IN?

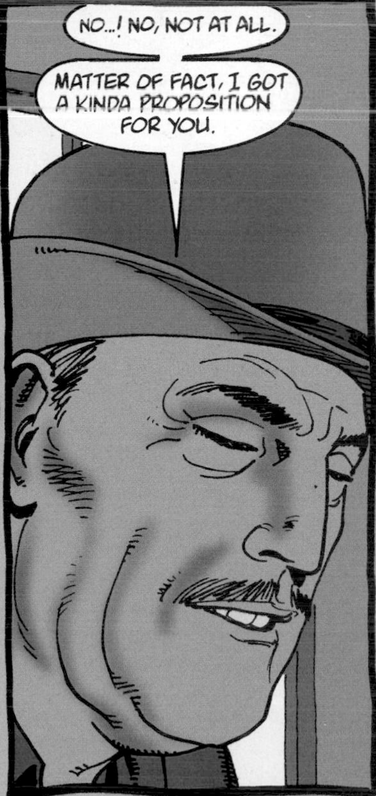
NO...! NO, NOT AT ALL.
MATTER OF FACT, I GOT A KINDA PROPOSITION FOR YOU.

...SO YOU SEE EVEN FOR A, A NORMALLY PEACEFUL LITTLE TOWN LIKE SALVATION, WE DO HAVE SOME PUBLIC ORDER PROBLEMS...
NAME I KEEP HEARIN' IS QUINCANNON.

OOOHH, NO, MISTER CUSTER. LEMME MAKE IT REAL CLEAR THAT MISTER QUINCANNON IS A RESPECTED BUSINESSMAN, A GENUINE OL' FASHIONED GENTLEMAN. THAT PLANT OF HIS HAS BROUGHT A LOT OF MONEY INTO THE COUNTY, A LOT OF JOBS...
BUT, TRUTH TO TELL, SOME OF THE MEN HE'S HIRED IN DO LEAVE A LITTLE TO BE DESIRED. AND THAT'S WHERE WE GET THEM PUBLIC ORDER PROBLEMS I MENTIONED.

SEE, THE TROUBLE IS, THERE'S REALLY ONLY ME TO KEEP A LID ON THINGS, YOU KNOW? AN' WELL, I AIN'T AS SPRIGHTLY AS I ONCE WAS--
DIDN'T I SEE YOU HAD A DEPUTY WITH YOU THIS AFTERNOON?

CINDY?
HELL, MISTER CUSTER, SHE'S REALLY ONLY THERE TO KEEP THE LOCAL NIGRAS HAPPY...WE GOTTA BE SEEN TO BE IMPARTIAL--IF YOU GET MY DRIFT?

EVER HAVE ANY KLAN TROUBLE ROUND HERE, SHERIFF?
DAMN, NO!

WE NEVER HAD ANYTHING LIKE THAT AROUND HERE, NOT WHILE I BEEN SHERIFF! I MEAN IN THE OLD DAYS, SURE--BUT THAT'S TRUE OF EVERYWHERE, AIN'T IT?
LET'S BE SURE WE'RE ON THE SAME PAGE HERE, MISTER CUSTER: I'M TALKIN' ABOUT A LITTLE FART OF A TOWN AN' SOME BAD BOYS NEED SLAPPIN' DOWN, AN' A SHERIFF COULD USE SOME HELP DOIN' IT. NOTHIN' MORE.
GO ON.
WELL, LIKE I SAY, I SAW HOW YOU DEALT WITH THEM FOUR TODAY, YOU SEEM TO ME LIKE A MAN WHO KNOWS HOW TO HANDLE HIMSELF.
AN'...LOOK, DON'T GET MAD, BUT I COULDN'T HELP OVERHEARIN' SOME OF WHAT YOU SAID TO JODIE IN THERE. I THINK MAYBE YOU MIGHT BE ABLE TO HELP ME OUT WITH THIS PROBLEM I BEEN TALKIN' ABOUT...
HELL, MISTER CUSTER, WOULD YOU BE INTERESTED IN BEIN' MY DEPUTY?
NO.
BUT I'LL BE YOUR GODDAMN SHERIFF.

GLENN
FABRY 90

"Work the shaft... Work the shaft..."

WORK THE SHAFT...
WORK THE SHAFT...
QUINCANNON MEATS inc

EXIT
CRADLE THE BALLS...

CRADLE THE BALLS...

NOW...

SAY THE NAME...

SAY THE NAME

...MORNIN', BOYS.
MORNIN', MISTER QUINCANNON.

THE MEATMAN COMETH

GARTH ENNIS-Writer STEVE DILLON-Artist

Pamela Rambo-Colorist, Clem Robins-Letterer, Axel Alonso-Editor

PREACHER created by Garth Ennis and Steve Dillon

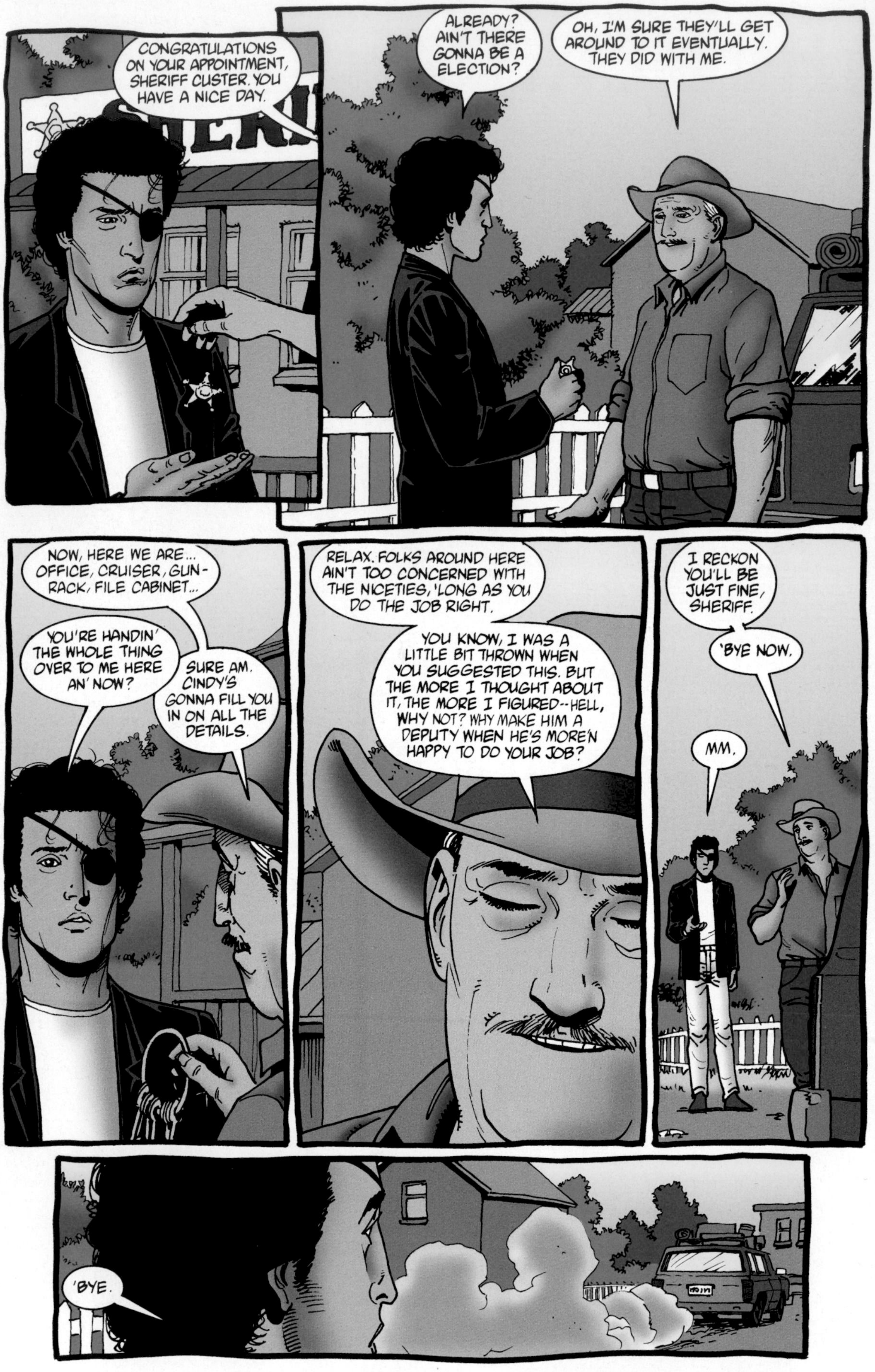

CONGRATULATIONS ON YOUR APPOINTMENT, SHERIFF CUSTER. YOU HAVE A NICE DAY.

ALREADY? AIN'T THERE GONNA BE A ELECTION?

OH, I'M SURE THEY'LL GET AROUND TO IT EVENTUALLY. THEY DID WITH ME.

NOW, HERE WE ARE... OFFICE, CRUISER, GUN-RACK, FILE CABINET...
YOU'RE HANDIN' THE WHOLE THING OVER TO ME HERE AN' NOW?
SURE AM. CINDY'S GONNA FILL YOU IN ON ALL THE DETAILS.

RELAX. FOLKS AROUND HERE AIN'T TOO CONCERNED WITH THE NICETIES, 'LONG AS YOU DO THE JOB RIGHT.
YOU KNOW, I WAS A LITTLE BIT THROWN WHEN YOU SUGGESTED THIS. BUT THE MORE I THOUGHT ABOUT IT, THE MORE I FIGURED--HELL, WHY NOT? WHY MAKE HIM A DEPUTY WHEN HE'S MORE'N HAPPY TO DO YOUR JOB?

I RECKON YOU'LL BE JUST FINE, SHERIFF.
'BYE NOW.
MM.

'BYE.

WUFF!
RECKON SO, HUH?

ME TOO.

GOOD MORNING, SHERIFF.
HUH? OH. MORNIN'.

MY OH MY...! DIDN'T TAKE YOU LONG, DID IT?
IMPECCABLE REFERENCES. YOU KNOW HOW IT IS.

TRADITION DEMANDS YOU START CLEANING THIS PLACE UP. RUN THE BAD GUYS OUT OF TOWN ON A RAIL, FALL IN LOVE WITH THE TOWN BEAUTY, ACQUIRE A DRUNKEN BUT AMUSING SIDEKICK.
HOW ABOUT IT, STRANGER?
OPEN

THAT'S SHERIFF STRANGER TO YOU.
SEE YOU LATER, JODIE.

YOU MUST BE CINDY...
DEPUTY DAGGETT. YOUR OFFICE IS THROUGH HERE.
SHERIFF

WELL I'M--
I KNOW WHO YOU ARE.

I WAS HOPIN' YOU MIGHT DRIVE ME 'ROUND A LITTLE BIT LATER ON. SHOW ME THE AREA. INTRODUCE ME TO FOLKS.
I'VE GOT ALL THIS TO GET THROUGH. MAYBE THE DAY AFTER TOMORROW.

AIN'T WE GOT A SECRETARY FOR THAT?
NO. WE'VE GOT ME. APPARENTLY.

WELL THAT'S NO GOOD. YOU'RE A LAW OFFICER, YOU AIN'T GOT TIME FOR THIS BULLSHIT.
HIRE A SECRETARY. TAKE IT OUTTA MY SALARY.
MIND IF I SMOKE?
UH...NO...

YOU TWO WAIT HERE WITH THE CAR.

...SO OUR JURISDICTION RUNS AS FAR AS THE RIVER HERE, AN' THEN OUT TO THE COUNTY LINE HERE. IT AIN'T MUCH TO SPEAK OF.

NOPE...

SHERIFF CUSTER?

ODIN QUINCANNON.
WHY DON'T YOU HAVE YOUR GIRL HERE MAKE SOME COFFEE, AN' ME AN' YOU CAN HAVE A LITTLE TALK?

EVER HEARDA KNOCKIN'?

HEH!
ONCE.

NOW OL' ODIN BROUGHT A LOT OF DOLLARS INTO THIS COUNTY, YESSIR. LOT OF JOBS TOO. AN' FRANKLY I EXPECT THE RESPECT THAT'S DUE TO ME.

MY MEN ARE REGULAR PATRONS OF SALVATION'S SERVICES. THEY GOT PLENTY OF MONEY TO SPEND, AND LOCAL LAW ENFORCEMENT HAS TO BEAR THAT IN MIND WHEN DEALIN' WITH ANY HIGH SPIRITS THAT MIGHT ARISE. SAME PRINCIPLE APPLIES TO THE LIBERAL INTERPRETATION OF CERTAIN REGULATIONS AT THE PLANT, BOTH ENVIRONMENTAL AN' SAFETY-ORIENTED.

SUMMIN' UP, THEN: YOU DO YOUR JOB NICE AN' QUIET AN' HANDLE EVERYTHING RIGHT HERE AT LOCAL LEVEL, NO NEED TO GO NO HIGHER...

WAAAAKK--!
JESUS CHRIST!
SON OF A BITCH, HE'S SEVENTY-FIVE YEARS OLD!
THAT'S OKAY--
I HIT YOUNG FUCKS TOO--
SHIT--
WHAT THE FUCK--

UNNH
NOW YOU JUST--
SAFETY.
HUH--?
SAFETY'S ON.
BUTTTUUUUHHH
STOP THIS AT ONCE!!
...AN' WHO MIGHT YOU BE?
RIFF
I AM MISS OATLASH.
AND YOU HAVE JUST BOOKED YOURSELF A SEAT IN HELL.

I AM MR. QUINCANNON'S LAWYER AND I CAN ASSURE YOU, SHERIFF, THAT YOU HAVE MADE THE BIGGEST MISTAKE OF YOUR SHORT AND POINTLESS CAREER!
THIS OUTRAGE OF YOURS IS AN ABUSE OF POLICE AUTHORITY OUTSTRIP-PING THE KING BEATING, AND FOR IT I INTEND TO HOUND YOU THROUGH EVERY--
NO!!

HE'S MINE! MINE! AN' WE'RE GONNA DO HIM MY WAY!
SIR, YOU REALLY SHOULDN'T SAY THOSE THINGS--
SHUT UP, DAMN YOU! ODIN QUINCAN-NON SAYS WHAT HE LIKES!
YOU'RE FUCKING DEAD, CUSTER! YOU HEAR ME?!

YEAH, YEAH, WHAT-EVER. YOU ASSWIPES SCRAPE THIS OL' BUZZARD UP AN' GET HIM OUTTA HERE. I DON'T WANNA SEE ANY'VE YOU IN THIS TOWN AGAIN.
FOR FUTURE REFERENCE, SHORTY: THE LAW IN SALVATION AIN'T FOR SALE NO MORE.
NOW GIT.

I HATE A FELLA TALKS ABOUT HIMSELF IN THE THIRD PERSON...

JODIE--MM--
I GOTTA TELL YOU, THIS IS ABOUT THE BEST DAMN CHEESEBURGER I EVER ATE...
REALLY?
UH-HUH. AN' THAT AIN'T BULL-SHIT, NEITHER. YOU'RE TALKIN' TO A BURGER CONNOISSEUR.

WELL, THANK YOU. I DO A PRETTY GOOD SZECHUAN LOBSTER STIR-FRY WITH CHILI SAUCE TOO, BUT THERE'S NOT A LOT OF CALL FOR THAT AROUND HERE.

MM.
YOU'RE QUITE A WORKER YOURSELF, AREN'T YOU, STRANGER? I SAW WHAT HAPPENED TO QUINCANNON AND HIS BOYS.

SHORT SHARP SHOCK. GETS 'EM USED TO THE NEW REGIME.
ANYHOW, THEY WERE NOTHIN'. I FIGHT PUKES LIKE THAT ON MY DAYS OFF FROM KICKIN' ASS.

MM-HMM.
DO YOU MIND ME ASKING WHAT THE HELL YOU THINK YOU'RE DOING HERE, EXACTLY?

WELL...
I GUESS YOU COULD SAY I GOT THIS JOB I GOTTA DO. AN'...UP 'TIL RECENTLY ANYHOW, IT LOOKED LIKE I WAS MAKIN' SOME PROGRESS ON IT.
THEN BAM-- WHOLE MESS GOES TITS-UP ON ME. ALL OF A SUDDEN I CAN'T TELL WHO'S RIGHT AND WHO'S WRONG, WHO I CAN COUNT ON, HELL, JUST ABOUT EVERYTHING DOWN TO THE WAY THE GODDAMN WORLD WORKS. AN' THAT'S SOMETHIN' I USED TO THINK I WAS SURE OF.
SO UNTIL I FIGURE ALL THAT OUT AN' COME UP WITH SOME ANSWERS SATISFY ME, THAT JOB'S GONNA HAVE TO STAY UNDONE.
THAT ISN'T REALLY WHAT I ASKED...
NO. WELL, LET'S JUST SAY I SAW A OPPORTUNITY TO MAKE MYSELF USEFUL 'TIL I COME UP WITH THEM ANSWERS.
I SEE. AND IS THIS HOW YOU USUALLY KILL TIME, STRANGER?
HMH.
WOULDN'T WANT FOLKS THINKIN' I WAS SOME KINDA FREELOADER NOW, WOULD I?
AN' YOU CAN CALL ME JESSE.
OH, I THINK I LIKE STRANGER JUST FINE.

SO TELL ME ABOUT BEWLEY...
MM?
I'M TRYNNA FIGURE OUT WHY HE WAS SO QUICK TO HIRE ME.
WELL, I DON'T KNOW ABOUT THAT. I HATED THE SON OF A BITCH.
HE WAS JUST A YES-MAN, REALLY. EXCEPT...
YOU PROBABLY KNOW QUINCANNON WAS PAYIN' HIM OFF, AN' SURE ENOUGH HE ALWAYS DID WHAT HE WAS TOLD. BUT I HAVE TO ADMIT, BEWLEY WAS FAIR WITH FOLKS. HE DID HIS BEST TO SOLVE DISPUTES AN' SUCH SO NO ONE FELT PUT OUT, AN' HE TURNED A BLIND EYE TO STUPID LITTLE THINGS, GOT THE COURTS TO GO EASY ON FIRST OFFENDERS...
I MEAN EVEN IN JOHN'S HOLLOW, WHERE I GREW UP, WE'D DRIVE OVER THERE AN' HE'D DO A REAL GOOD JOB POURIN' OIL ON TROUBLED WATERS, AN' THEN ON THE WAY HOME WITH ME *RIGHT BESIDE HIM IN THE CAR,* HE'D SAY--
"MAYBE *NOW* THEM NIGGERS'LL BEHAVE THEMSELVES."

9 LOUIS TARGET CS.
HEY...!

PRACTICE, IS ALL. YOU SHOOT MUCH?
NO, BUT I KNOW 'BOUT GOOD SHOOTIN'...SO WHAT WAS HIS DEAL WITH QUINCANNON, EXACTLY?

JUST TO IGNORE THE PLANT WORKERS WHEN THEY CAUSE TROUBLE IN TOWN, WHICH THEY DO PLENTY OF. MAKE SURE THEY DON'T HAVE TO GO TO COURT. THEY AIN'T EVEN LOCAL, THEY MOVED DOWN FROM HOUSTON, MOST'VE 'EM...
ALL BEWLEY HAD TO DO WAS LOOK THE OTHER WAY--WHICH WAS GOOD, 'CAUSE THAT'S ALL FOLKS IN SALVATION EVER DO, REALLY.

YEAH?
IT'S JUST THAT KINDA PLACE. YOU AIN'T LEFT BY THE TIME YOU'RE TWENTY-FIVE, YOU'RE STUCK.
YOU LET YOURSELF GET STUCK, YOU'RE PROBABLY THE KINDA PERSON'LL LOOK THE OTHER WAY IF IT MAKES LIFE EASIER ON YOU.

THAT INCLUDE YOU, DEPUTY DAGGETT?
OH, YOU CAN CALL ME CINDY.
IF YOU LIKE.

WANT TO TRY?
DAMN, IT'S BEEN A WHILE...
YOU'LL BE OKAY. NO, I WANTED TO LEAVE, I REALLY DID...

BUT JUST WHEN I WAS ALL SET TO GO IN THE ARMY, MY MOMMA GOT DRUNK AN' BROKE HER BACK FALLIN' OFF THE PORCH. POPS IS DEAD, MY BIG SIS KIM'S MARRIED--THAT SORTA PUT ME BEHIND THE EIGHTBALL.
I LOOK AFTER MOMMA MOST'VE THE TIME. KIM COMES OVER WHEN I'M ON DUTY, WHICH AIN'T TOO OFTEN. BEWLEY DIDN'T EVEN NEED A DEPUTY--I'M ONLY HERE 'CAUSE--
HE TOLD ME. FUCK HIM.

I NEED A DEPUTY, CINDY. I AIN'T TOO HOT AT LOOKIN' THE OTHER WAY.
YEAH...I WAS GOIN' TO ASK, DO YOU HAVE A LOT OF EXPERIENCE IN LAW ENFORCEMENT?

GRAND THEFT AUTO. NEVER GOT CAUGHT.
WHAT?

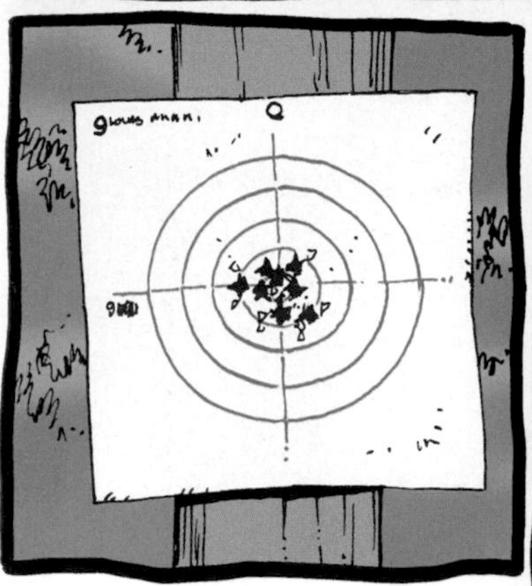

...JESUS CHRIST, WHO THE HELL TAUGHT YOU TO SHOOT?

SADISTIC FUCKIN' MADMAN I USED TO KNOW.
LONG STORY.

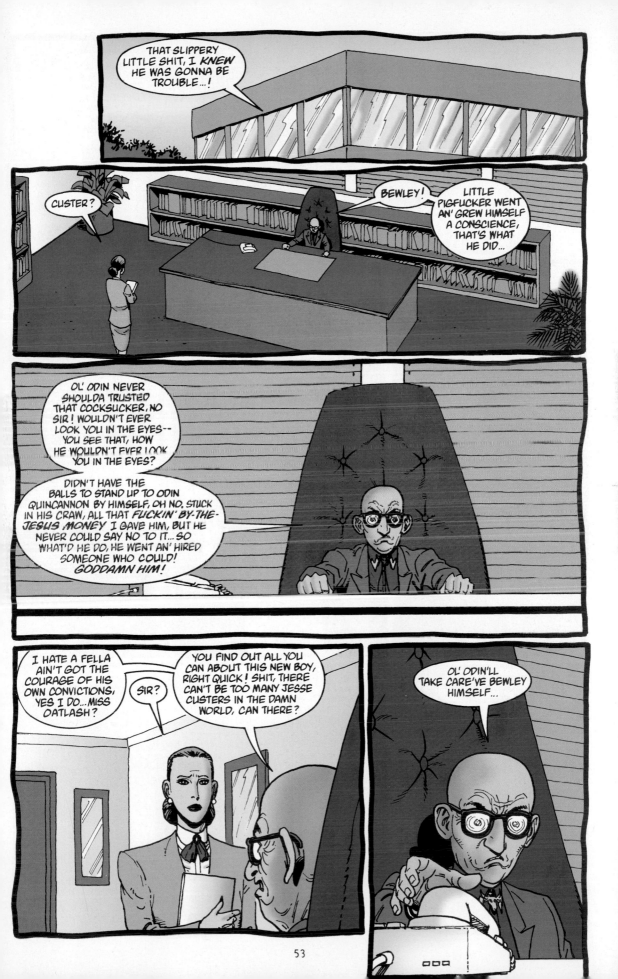

OL' ODIN NEVER SHOULDA TRUSTED THAT COCKSUCKER, NO SIR! WOULDN'T EVER LOOK YOU IN THE EYES-- YOU SEE THAT, HOW HE WOULDN'T EVER LOOK YOU IN THE EYES?

DIDN'T HAVE THE BALLS TO STAND UP TO ODIN QUINCANNON BY HIMSELF, OH NO, STUCK IN HIS CRAW, ALL THAT *FUCKIN' BY-THE-JESUS MONEY* I GAVE HIM, BUT HE NEVER COULD SAY NO TO IT... SO WHAT'D HE DO, HE WENT AN' HIRED SOMEONE WHO COULD! ***GODDAMN HIM!***

YOU DON'T HAVE TO MOVE, JESSE. YOU'RE MORE THAN WELCOME TO STAY.
THANKS, LORIE, BUT THERE'S A LITTLE ROOM IN BACK OF MY OFFICE. I RECKON I'LL BED DOWN THERE'N GIVE YOU TWO BACK YOUR PRIVACY.

OF COURSE, YOU'RE THE TOWN SHERIFF NOW, AREN'T YOU? WITH YOUR OSTRICH AND EVERYTHING!

MY OSTRICH...OH YEAH, RIGHT, MY OSTRICH. YEAH.
LISTEN, LORIE, SOMETHIN' I WANTED TO ASK YOU ABOUT...
MM?

WHAT'S JODIE'S STORY?

I MEAN WHO IS SHE EXACTLY, YOU KNOW? WHERE'S SHE COME FROM?
OH, WELL THAT'S QUITE A TALE...

SHE HASN'T HAD IT EASY, I'LL TELL YOU THAT. WHEN I MET HER SHE'D ONLY JUST GOTTEN OUT OF A MENTAL INSTITUTION.

SHE TOLD ME SHE WAS FOUND IN THE SWAMPS YEARS AGO, A LITTLE BIT EAST OF HERE. SHE'D LOST HER ARM AND SHE WAS RAVING, COMPLETELY CRAZY, ALL SHE KNEW WAS HER NAME. SHE WAS SHOUTING IT OVER AND OVER. "JODIE! JODIE! JODIE!" LIKE THAT... IT SOUNDS LIKE IT WAS AWFUL FOR HER.
SHE DOESN'T KNOW WHAT HAPPENED BEFORE THAT. OR MUCH AFTER IT, EITHER. SHE'S GOT ALL THESE GAPS, SHE STILL FORGETS THINGS--I THINK THAT'S WHY SHE WAS IN THE INSTITUTION...
WHY DO YOU ASK, ANYWAY?
I DUNNO. I JUST CAN'T FIGURE HER, I GUESS.
I MEAN SHE SEEMS SO TOUGH, YOU KNOW? HELL, SHE IS TOUGH. BUT SHE'S GOT A LOTTA CLASS ALONG WITH IT.
SHE'S SMART, TOO. NOT JUST QUICK, BUT SOPHISTICATED. SHE SPEAKS REAL WELL, REAL REFINED-- EVEN WHEN SHE'S CUSSIN'. AN' YOU ONLY GOTTA LOOK AROUND THIS PLACE TO SEE SHE'S GOT THE KINDA TASTE COMES FROM A EDUCATED BACKGROUND.
I DUNNO, SOMETHIN' JUST DON'T ADD UP...
I'VE NEVER REALLY THOUGHT ABOUT IT, TO TELL YOU THE TRUTH. I KNOW SHE LIKES YOU, THOUGH.
SHE DOES?
MM. SHE'D NEVER SAY SO--SHE LIKES TO KEEP UP THAT HARD, GRIM SORT OF FRONT.
BUT I CAN TELL.
HMM.
EAST OF HERE, YOU SAID?

LICENSE AN' REGISTRATION, THANK YOU...
AIN'T YOU GONNA TELL ME WHAT IT IS YOU THINK I DONE?
WON'T TAKE A MOMENT.

OKAY? SEE? ONE OF THE GOOD GUYS. NOW, CAN I PLEASE GET GOIN'?

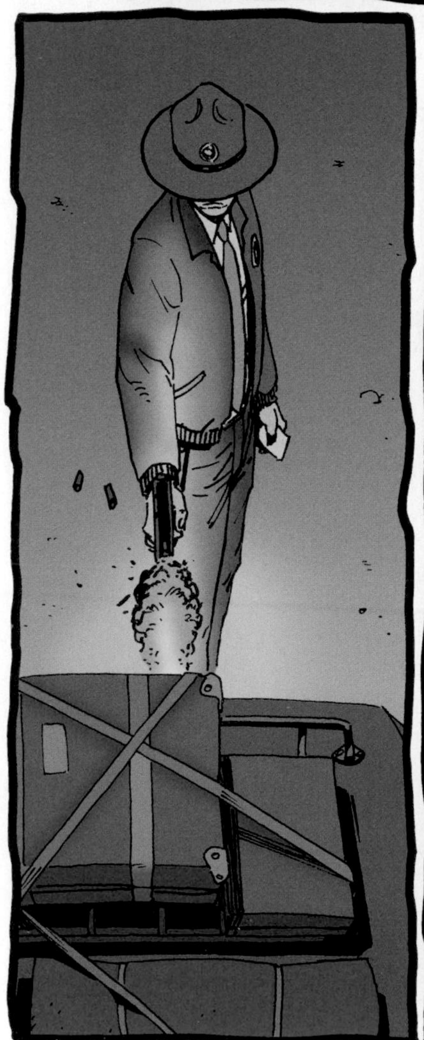

YES, SIR. DONE, SIR.

CLOSED
THE WHOLE TOWN'S TALKING ABOUT YOU, STRANGER. NO ONE EVER STOOD UP TO THAT LITTLE NOSEPICK QUINCANNON BEFORE, MUCH LESS THREW HIM THROUGH A WINDOW.
I HOPE YOU REMEMBER WHAT I SAID TO YOU ABOUT SAVING THE WORLD...

STRANGER?

NOT TALKING?
MM?
STRANGER?

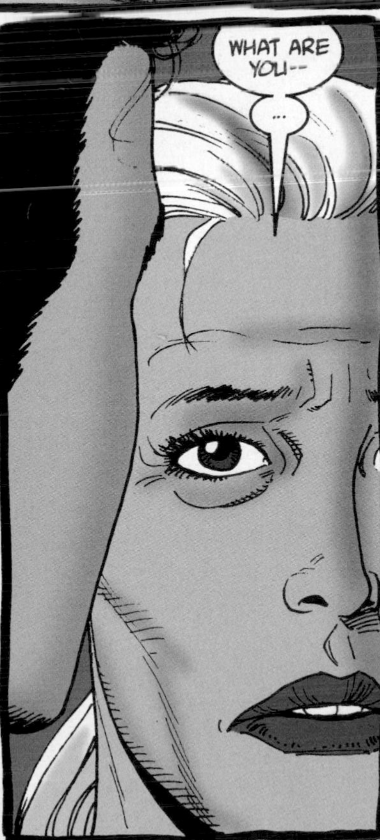
WHAT ARE YOU--
...

MOM?

GLENN FABRY

"I went back. I killed 'em. I choked the life outta Jody an' burned the damn house down. Gran'ma went up with it. They're in hell."

WHAT ABOUT JESSE?

BOY AIN'T NO CONCERN O' YORES NO MORE. HE'S WITH US NOW.

WE GONNA MAKE WHAT WE CAN OF HIM.

FAR ENOUGH.

HELL DO YOU CARE, ANYHOW? I SEEN HOW YOU ARE: ALL YOU DO'S SIT AROUND PININ' FOR YORE SOLDIER-BOY. ONLY THING YOU REALLY WANT IS TO SEE HIS STUPID FAGGOT FACE AGAIN.
WELL GOOD NEWS. YOU GONNA GET YORE WISH.
FUCK COMMUNISM

HE KICKED YOUR ASS QUICK ENOUGH, YOU TWO-BIT BOOTBOY.
HE BEAT YOU DOWN LIKE THE TRASH YOU ARE.

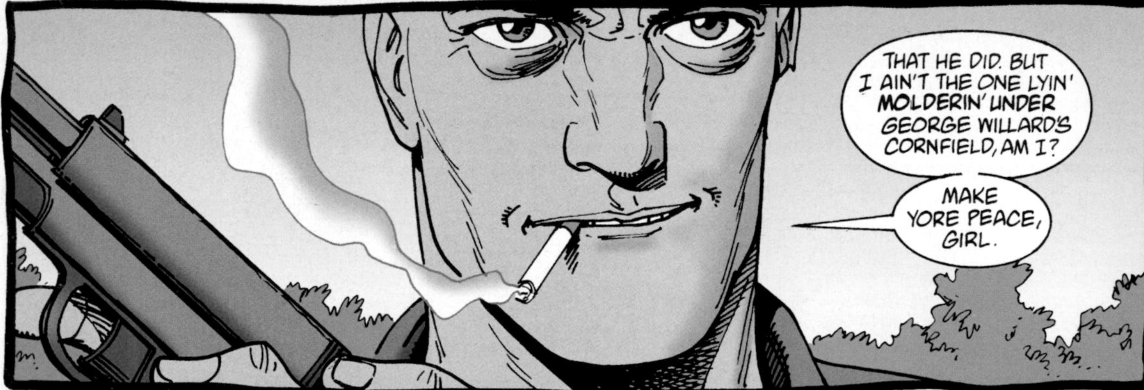
THAT HE DID. BUT I AIN'T THE ONE LYIN' MOLDERIN' UNDER GEORGE WILLARD'S CORNFIELD, AM I?
MAKE YORE PEACE, GIRL.

DO YOU KNOW WHAT MY HUSBAND THOUGHT OF YOU, JODY? WHAT HE SAID TO ME ABOUT YOU?
HUH?

HE SAID YOU WERE BIG, AND STRONG, AND MEAN AS HELL...
BUT YOU WERE ALWAYS SLOW.

AAAWWHH!!

AAAHHH, BITCH!!

FUCKIN' LITTLE-- GODDAMMIT--!

FUCKIN' WHORE!!

CHRISTINA'S WORLD

GARTH ENNIS-Writer STEVE DILLON-Artist

Pamela Rambo-Colorist, Clem Robins-Letterer, Axel Alonso-Editor

PREACHER created by Garth Ennis and Steve Dillon

HOW DID YOU KNOW?
DIDN'T. JUST GUESSED AN' HOPED.

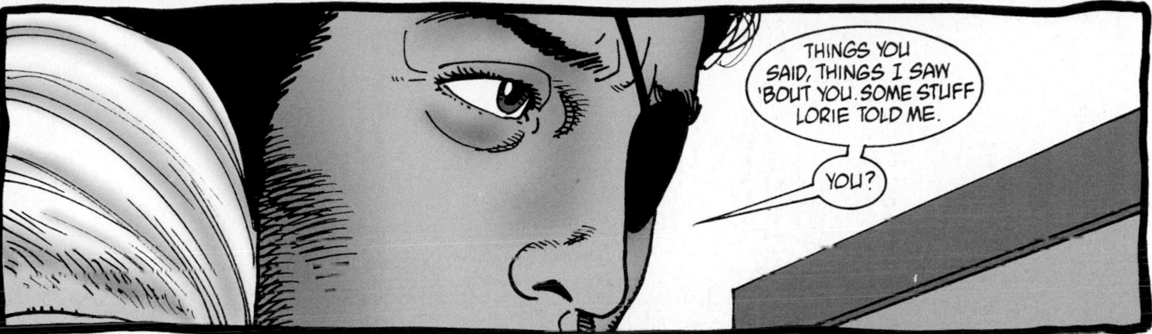
THINGS YOU SAID, THINGS I SAW 'BOUT YOU. SOME STUFF LORIE TOLD ME.
YOU?

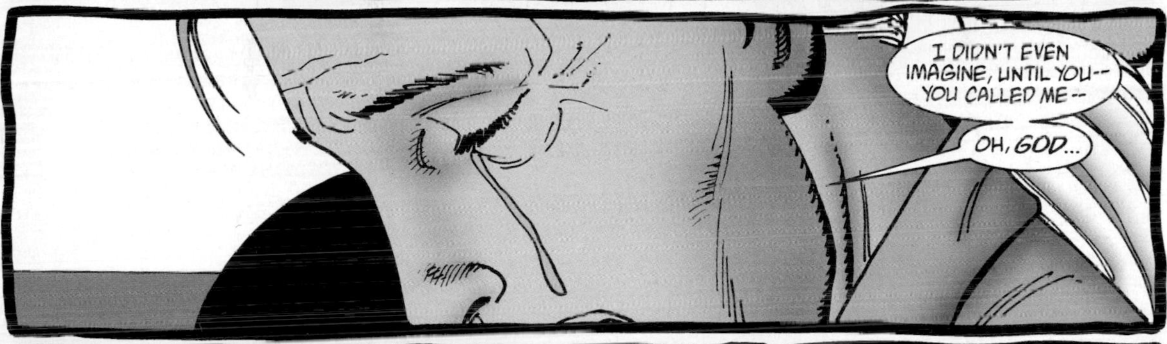
I DIDN'T EVEN IMAGINE, UNTIL YOU-- YOU CALLED ME --
OH, GOD...

JESUS.
THIS IS GOING TO TAKE SOME EXPLAINING. AND I WILL, I PROMISE I WILL.

BUT WILL YOU HOLD ME TIGHT JUST A LITTLE WHILE LONGER?

SURE, MOM.
SURE.

I THINK I'M GOING TO NEED A LOT OF THIS...
YOU AN' ME BOTH. POUR AWAY.
JODY SHOT ME AND I WENT INTO THE SWAMP.
I WASN'T DEAD BUT I DIDN'T KNOW WHO I WAS. I TOUCHED THE PAIN IN MY HEAD BECAUSE I NO LONGER KNEW I SHOULDN'T, AND MY FINGERS WENT IN AND SOMETHING SOFT...YIELDED AND I FELL DOWN SCREAMING WITH KNIVES BEHIND MY EYES.
BUT WHEN I WOKE UP I DID IT AGAIN BECAUSE I COULDN'T REMEMBER NOT TO ANYMORE.
I DON'T KNOW HOW LONG I WAS IN THERE OR HOW FAR I WENT.
BUT I KNOW HOW I REMEMBERED.

UHHH...
UHHH...
UH
EEEYAAAAA
EEEEEEEEE!!
AAAAHHH!
AAIEE!!
THERE!
HOLY
SHIT--

JESUS CHRIST...
OKAY, OKAY NOW, WE GOTTA SPREAD OUT AN' LOOK--
SHE'S HERE!

C'MON, HONEY--JESUS, FUCKIN' HELP! STOP THE GODDAMN BLEEDIN'!
STICK YOUR THUMB IN AN' PINCH OFF THE GOD-DAMN ARTERY! DO IT!
OH CHRIST--OH MY GOD--

JUST THREE BOYS UP FROM HOUSTON ON A HUNTING TRIP. THEY SAVED ME. ONE OF THEM WAS AN ARMY MEDIC IN VIET-NAM, KNEW JUST WHAT TO DO...

HONEY, C'MON, YOU GOTTA STAY WITH ME NOW! DON'T GO TO SLEEP, NO, DON'T DO THAT! YOUR NAME, CAN YOU TELL ME YOUR NAME?
BILL, GET THE BOAT! OH, FUCK!

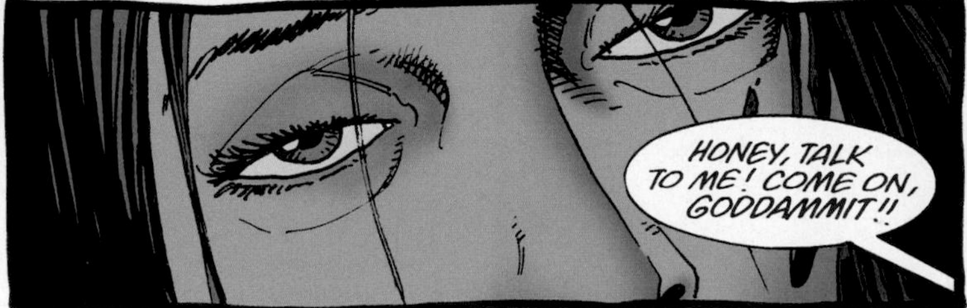

HONEY, TALK TO ME! COME ON, GODDAMMIT!!

JOOOODDYYYY!!!

I DIDN'T SPEAK AGAIN FOR TEN YEARS.

OH... FUCK...
THEY GOT ME TO A HOSPITAL, AND A SURGEON STITCHED ME UP, AND THE POLICE CAME TO ASK ME SOME QUESTIONS, AND EVENTUALLY A SHRINK TOOK A LOOK AT ME, AND NOT ONE OF THEM GOT SHIT...

SO THEY STUCK ME IN THE BIN WITH THE NAME OF THE FUCKER WHO WRECKED OUR LIVES.
JODIE

YOU WANT, WE CAN LEAVE THIS...
NO.
YOU DON'T HAVE TO TIPTOE AROUND ME, JESSE. I'M NOT WEAK AND I DON'T NEED TO BE PRO-TECTED. I'VE HAD FIFTY YEARS OF DEMONS TO TEACH ME THAT.
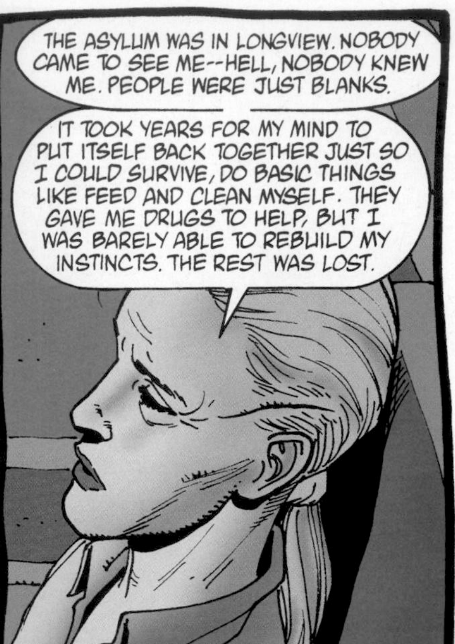
THE ASYLUM WAS IN LONGVIEW. NOBODY CAME TO SEE ME--HELL, NOBODY KNEW ME. PEOPLE WERE JUST BLANKS.
IT TOOK YEARS FOR MY MIND TO PUT ITSELF BACK TOGETHER JUST SO I COULD SURVIVE, DO BASIC THINGS LIKE FEED AND CLEAN MYSELF. THEY GAVE ME DRUGS TO HELP, BUT I WAS BARELY ABLE TO REBUILD MY INSTINCTS. THE REST WAS LOST.

OF COURSE, I DIDN'T NEED THE REST FOR THE STATE TO GET SHOT OF ME--
YOU GET YOUR TICKET AN' YOU GO ANYWHERE YOU WANT, HON. YOU KNOW WHERE YOU GOIN', MMM?
GOOD FOR YOU. YOU ALL GROWED UP NOW...

THEN IT HAPPENED. FOR THE VERY FIRST TIME, LIKE IT WOULD AGAIN AND AGAIN AND AGAIN...

ONE OF THE BLANKS GOT FILLED IN.

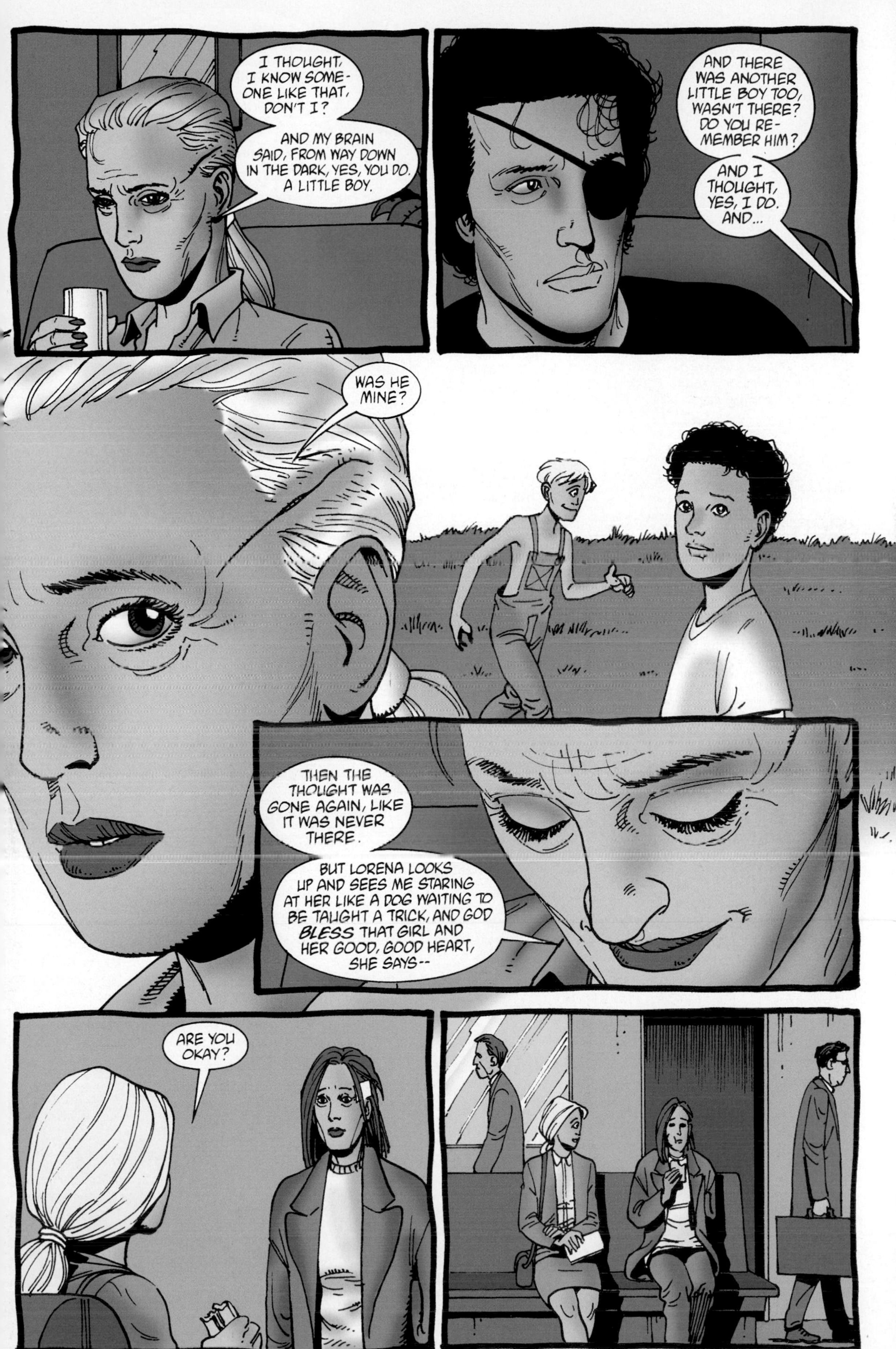
I THOUGHT, I KNOW SOME-ONE LIKE THAT, DON'T I?
AND MY BRAIN SAID, FROM WAY DOWN IN THE DARK, YES, YOU DO. A LITTLE BOY.
AND THERE WAS ANOTHER LITTLE BOY TOO, WASN'T THERE? DO YOU RE-MEMBER HIM?
AND I THOUGHT, YES, I DO. AND...
WAS HE MINE?
THEN THE THOUGHT WAS GONE AGAIN, LIKE IT WAS NEVER THERE.
BUT LORENA LOOKS UP AND SEES ME STARING AT HER LIKE A DOG WAITING TO BE TAUGHT A TRICK, AND GOD *BLESS* THAT GIRL AND HER GOOD, GOOD HEART, SHE SAYS--
ARE YOU OKAY?

FROM THEN ON I STARTED COMING BACK.
I WAS LIKE AN EMPTY SPACE WAITING TO BE FILLED IN, AND THE FILLING CAME SLOWLY, IN BITS AND PIECES. WHO I WAS--THE KIND OF PERSON I WAS--THAT CAME WITH LORIE.
SOMETHING IN ME DIDN'T LIKE HOW PEOPLE TREATED THIS SCARED YOUNG GIRL, SO I KNEW I HAD TO LOOK AFTER HER. AND ONCE I STARTED CARING, I FOUND OUT I COULD BE BRAVE AND DECISIVE AND I WOULDN'T TAKE ANY SHIT, BECAUSE IT WAS A HARD WORLD AND YOU HAD TO PROTECT THE ONES YOU LOVED. I THOUGHT--THIS MUST BE ME.
BUT WHAT I WAS AND WHERE I CAME FROM WAS A MYSTERY, EXCEPT THAT IT WAS SOMETHING BAD.
I KNEW SOMEHOW THAT. I WAS ONLY SO BRAVE. THAT THE BAD THING WAS MORE, MUCH MORE THAN I COULD HANDLE, BECAUSE IT HAD BEEN TOO MUCH FOR ME BEFORE.
THAT IT HAD SMASHED EVERYTHING I'D EVER CARED ABOUT AND COULD DO SO AGAIN AT WILL AND SEND ME BACK INTO THE DARK FOREVER.
SOMETIMES--
SOMETIMES I'D REMEMBER WHAT IT WAS.

IT WAS EASIER MOVING FORWARD THAN BACK BECAUSE IT FILLED UP THE SPACES IN MY HEAD. ANYTHING NEW WAS GOOD: A HOME, A JOB, A BOOK TO READ, EVEN A GODDAMN BOTTLE OF WHISKEY. IT WAS ALL EXPERIENCE.
IT MADE ME A PERSON AGAIN.
SO I'D BE DOING SOMETHING LIKE THAT, MAYBE WORKING ON THE BAR THAT LORIE AND I WENT INTO TOGETHER--SHE PUT IN THE INHERITANCE, I PUT IN THE ATTITUDE--AND IT WOULD HAPPEN.
JODIE'S
THAT TIME WOULD COME BACK TO ME LIKE A LIGHTNING BOLT TO THE BRAIN.
JODY. THE COFFIN. THAT MORNING IN THE CORN. HER.
ANGELVILLE.
JESSE, I SWEAR, I SWEAR TO YOU--I TRIED, I TRULY DID--
MOM, I KNOW--
I'D GET ON A BUS, OR, OR A TRAIN, AND I'D BE HEADING EAST--I KNEW WHERE IT WAS, I KNEW WHERE THE FUCKING PLACE WAS--
I--I--
IT'S OKAY. SHHH.
I WAS LONG GONE BY THEN.
SHHH, NOW.
I'D BE COMING TO GET YOU AND MY FUCKING MIND WOULD GO BLANK AND I'D FORGET ALL OVER AGAIN--!

ALL I COULD DO WAS --COME BACK HERE--
JESUS CHRIST...!
WELL.
HERE'S TO THE MAN WHO THOUGHT TO BOTTLE THIS STUFF, MM?
AMEN TO THAT.
IT WOULD BE SO STRANGE... GETTING OFF A BUS IN THE MIDDLE OF WHATEVER GODFORSAKEN HOLE I'D ENDED UP IN, WONDERING HOW, WHY, WHERE...
IT WAS EASIER MOVING FORWARD. LIKE I SAID.
SO THAT'S WHAT I RESOLVED TO DO, AND IT WORKED. THE BAD THING STOPPED COMING. I THINK I HAD MY LAST... EPISODE, MAYBE THREE OR FOUR YEARS AGO.
ALL I HAD TO DO WAS CONCENTRATE ON BEING ME.
AND THAT'S WHAT I THOUGHT I WAS DOING, WHAT I WAS SO SURE I WAS DOING, SO THAT WHEN I SAW YOU YESTERDAY IT DIDN'T EVEN CLICK.
I HEARD YOUR VOICE, I WATCHED YOU MOVE--AND YOU ARE SO LIKE YOUR FATHER THERE, JESSE, YOU WOULD NOT BELIEVE IT--I EVEN HEARD YOUR NAME...
BUT IT WASN'T 'TIL YOU WALKED IN HERE AND CALLED ME MOM--
THAT I KNEW WHO I WAS.

YOU OKAY?
A LITTLE QUEASY. EVERYTHING COMING BACK LIKE THAT, ALL THE PIECES SLAMMING INTO MY MIND AT ONCE, IT...
I DON'T KNOW. I'VE JUST REMEMBERED MY LIFE, JESSE.
IT THROWS YOU.

I GUESS I'M NOT WHAT YOU EXPECTED, MM?
LAST TIME I SAW YOU THAT SON OF A BITCH WAS HAULIN' YOU AWAY TO KILL YOU. I AIN'T HAD NOTHIN' TO EXPECT MY WHOLE GOD-DAMN LIFE.
YOU'RE MY MOM AN' YOU'RE ALIVE, AN' BY GOD THAT'S ALL THAT MATTERS TO ME.

OH GOD, THAT PLACE. YOU WERE...WHAT WERE YOU, TEN?
THAT PLACE AND THOSE MONSTERS...

AND THAT VICIOUS OLD--
THEY'RE GONE, MOM.

I WENT BACK. I KILLED 'EM.
I CHOKED THE LIFE OUTTA JODY AN' BURNED THE DAMN HOUSE DOWN. GRAN'MA WENT UP WITH IT.
THEY'RE IN HELL.

GOOD BOY.
GOOD BOY.

SAY, YOU KNOW WHAT? I SAW THE PICTURE.
MM?

THE WYETH. YOU REMEMBER.
THEY GOT THE ORIGINAL IN THE MUSEUM OF MODERN ART IN NEW YORK.

YOU SAW IT?
uh-huh.
WHAT WAS IT LIKE...?

IT WAS BEAUTIFUL, MOM. COLORS WERE SO VIVID, MORE'N ANY BOOK OR PRINT COULD REPRODUCE.
IT WAS ABOUT THE SADDEST THING I EVER DID SEE.

SO YOU REMEMBERED.
YOU USED TO STARE AT IT FOR HOURS, BUT I NEVER DID KNOW WHY AT THE TIME. WASN'T 'TIL THE MUSEUM I FIGURED IT OUT.

I FOUND IT IN A BOOK IN THAT HUGE LIBRARY IN ANGELVILLE. I WAS ABOUT TWELVE, JUST STARTING TO UNDERSTAND THAT THINGS WOULD NEVER CHANGE FOR ME...AND I READ ABOUT THE PICTURE...
AND MY GOD, I THOUGHT. MY GOD.

SOMEBODY'S PAINTED MY LIFE.
CHRISTINA'S WORLD

THE GIRL WAS SOME COUSIN OF WYETH'S. SHE HAD POLIO.
I KNOW, MOM.
SHE WAS SO WEAK, AND THIS WAS AS FAR AS SHE COULD GO, THE BOTTOM OF THE FIELD. ALWAYS IN VIEW OF THE HOUSE.
I REMEMBER.

IT CENTERED HER WORLD. SHE COULDN'T ESCAPE IT. IT REACHED OUT AND BROUGHT HER BACK, NO MATTER WHAT...

GOOD MORNING...!
HEY, ARE YOU STILL UP?

OH HI, JESSE, I DIDN'T KNOW YOU WERE HERE! JODIE, I'M GOING TO START BREAKFAST--
HOLD ON A SECOND, LORIE.

THERE'S SOMETHING I HAVE TO TELL YOU. HELL, THERE'S A LOT.
JODIE ISN'T MY REAL NAME.

IT'S NOT?
NO.

IT'S CHRISTINA.
CHRISTINA CUSTER.

THIS IS MY SON.

CUSTER'S DEAD.
I KNOW THAT, MISS OATLASH. THAT'S 'XACTLY WHAT OL' ODIN'S WORKIN' ON.
NO SIR, I MEAN HE REALLY IS DEAD. OFFICIALLY.
THE ONLY JESSE CUSTER I COULD FIND-- PROBABLY THE ONLY ONE IN EXISTENCE, AS YOU GUESSED--USED TO BE A MINISTER FOR SOME OBSCURE LITTLE PRESBYTERIAN-BAPTIST SECT NO ONE'S EVER HEARD OF. HE WAS BASED IN ANNVILLE, SOMEWHERE WEST OF LUBBOCK.
A LITTLE OVER THREE MONTHS AGO HIS CHURCH AND ENTIRE CONGREGATION WERE INCINERATED IN A MYSTERIOUS FIRE. I DON'T KNOW IF YOU REMEMBER, BUT THERE WERE A LOT OF STRANGE GOINGS-ON IN THE AREA AT THE TIME...
NOPE.
THOSE DEPUTIES THAT DIED? THE MASSACRE AT THE BAR?
HELL, SOME NIGGER TERRORIST JUST NUKED OUT MONUMENT VALLEY. I CAN'T BE 'SPECTED TO KEEP TRACK.
THIS HAS TO BE BULLSHIT...SAYS HERE THE BOY WAS FOUND DEAD A WEEK LATER. PULLED HIM OUT'VE A RIVER IN NEW YORK CITY.
WHERE'D YOU GET THIS HERE INFORMATION, ANYHOW?

AN ASSOCIATE OF MINE, SIR. HE WORKS FOR THE BUREAU, IN THEIR RECORDS DIVISION. HE SAYS THEY'VE OFFICIALLY CLOSED THE CASE.
ASSOCIATE? WENT TO GODDAMN YALE TOGETHER, YOU MEAN! S'POSE THAT'S WHERE YOU KNOW HIM FROM!
OL' ODIN NEVER HAD NO FANCY EDUCATION, NO SIR! ODIN QUINCANNON STARTED OUT SO POOR HE HAD TO WIPE HIS ASS WITH HIS HAND!
BUT HE PULLED HIMSELF UP BY HIS BOOTSTRAPS AN' MADE SOMETHIN' OF HIS LIFE, AN' BY GOD HE DID IT ALONE! ODIN CLEANS HIS CRACK WITH SMOOTHEST SILK TODAY, AN' HE DIDN'T GET THERE BY EXPLOITIN' CONTACTS AN' CALLIN' IN FAVORS FROM NO FAGGY FUCKIN' LAW SCHOOL! HE GOT THERE BY HARD FUCKIN' WORK!
WE DIDN'T ATTEND LAW SCHOOL TOGETHER, SIR. WE USED TO COMMIT ACTS OF EXTREME SEXUAL DEVIANCY TOGETHER IN A MOTEL ROOM IN AUSTIN, INCLUDING BONDAGE AND GOLDEN SHOWERS.
THAT'S WHERE I KNOW HIM FROM.
OH. WELL.
SO CUSTER'S OFFICIALLY DEAD, HUH? GOT NO KIN, NO PAST WORTH TALKIN' ABOUT...
THAT'S CORRECT, MR. QUINCANNON.
WELL, I GUESS THERE AIN'T NOBODY GONNA MISS HIM THEN, IS THERE?

JODIE'S B
YOU FIXIN' TO LEAVE THE SIGN LIKE THAT?
OH, I DON'T KNOW. I WAS JODIE FOR NEARLY TWENTY YEARS. NO POINT TRYING TO DENY IT.
SO WHAT NEXT?

NEXT IS GETTING TO KNOW YOU AGAIN, I HOPE. IF YOU'RE GOING TO BE AROUND.
I'LL BE HERE.

THIS THING I STARTED WITH QUINCANNON, I CAN'T RIGHTLY LEAVE TILL IT'S OVER AN' DONE WITH. AIN'T NO WAY THE LITTLE BASTARD'LL LET IT GO ANYWAY.

SAVING THE WORLD?
DOIN' WHAT'S RIGHT.

AH, GOOD EVENING, SHERIFF.
EVENIN'...

AND LORENA TELLS ME IT IS NOW CHRISTINA, IS THAT RIGHT?
LONG STORY, GUNTHER.

I'D LIKE YOU TO MEET MY SON, JESSE. JESSE, THIS IS MR. GUNTHER HAHN.
HOWDY.
A PLEASURE TO FINALLY MEET YOU, JESSE.
PLEASE, DON'T LET ME INTERRUPT YOU. I AM SURE THE TWO OF YOU HAVE LOTS TO TALK ABOUT.
GOOD GUY. I SEEN HIM BEFORE, I THINK.
HE LIVES ON HOLLOW ROAD. GERMAN ORIGINALLY, BUT HE'S BEEN HERE AS LONG AS ANYONE CAN REMEMBER. MUST BE PUSHING SEVENTY BY NOW.
STILL LOOKS PRETTY FRISKY TO ME, THOUGH...
MOM...!
WHAT?
WELL-- I MEAN--YOU KNOW--
KNOW WHAT?
LOOK, YOU CAN'T TALK ABOUT STUFF LIKE THAT TO--YOU KNOW, WITH--
OH WHAT, I'VE GOT TO CLEAN UP MY ACT NOW I'M YOUR MOM?

TIME TO GO HOME, I THINK.
MM? OH, HEY THERE...

YES, YOUR MOTHER IS CLOSING UP FOR THE NIGHT.
MIGHT I TROUBLE YOU FOR A LIGHT, SHERIFF?
SURE.

THANK YOU--MM--
NO PROBLEM. SO I UNDERSTAND YOU CAME FROM GERMANY, THAT RIGHT? THAT BE AFTER THE WAR?

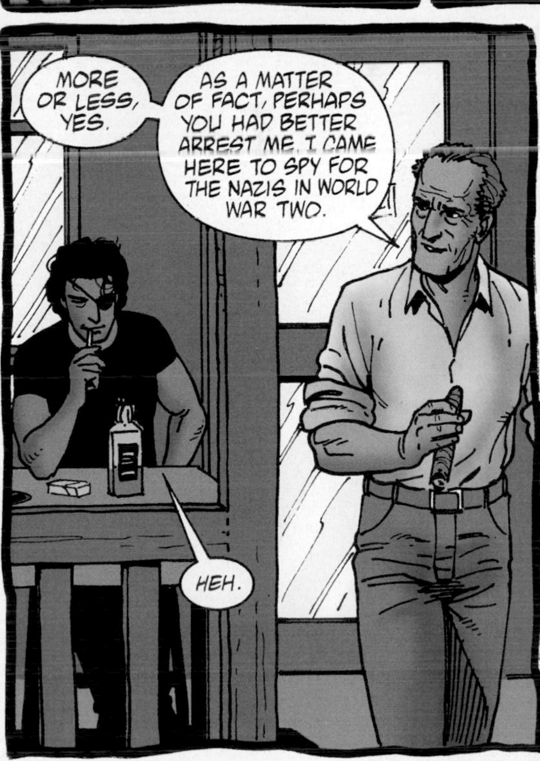
MORE OR LESS, YES.
AS A MATTER OF FACT, PERHAPS YOU HAD BETTER ARREST ME. I CAME HERE TO SPY FOR THE NAZIS IN WORLD WAR TWO.
HEH.

NO, SERIOUSLY.
GOODNIGHT, SHERIFF CUSTER.

GLENN
FABRY
98

"I saw you in there, Jesse. You woulda murdered that man, I hadn't of stopped you."

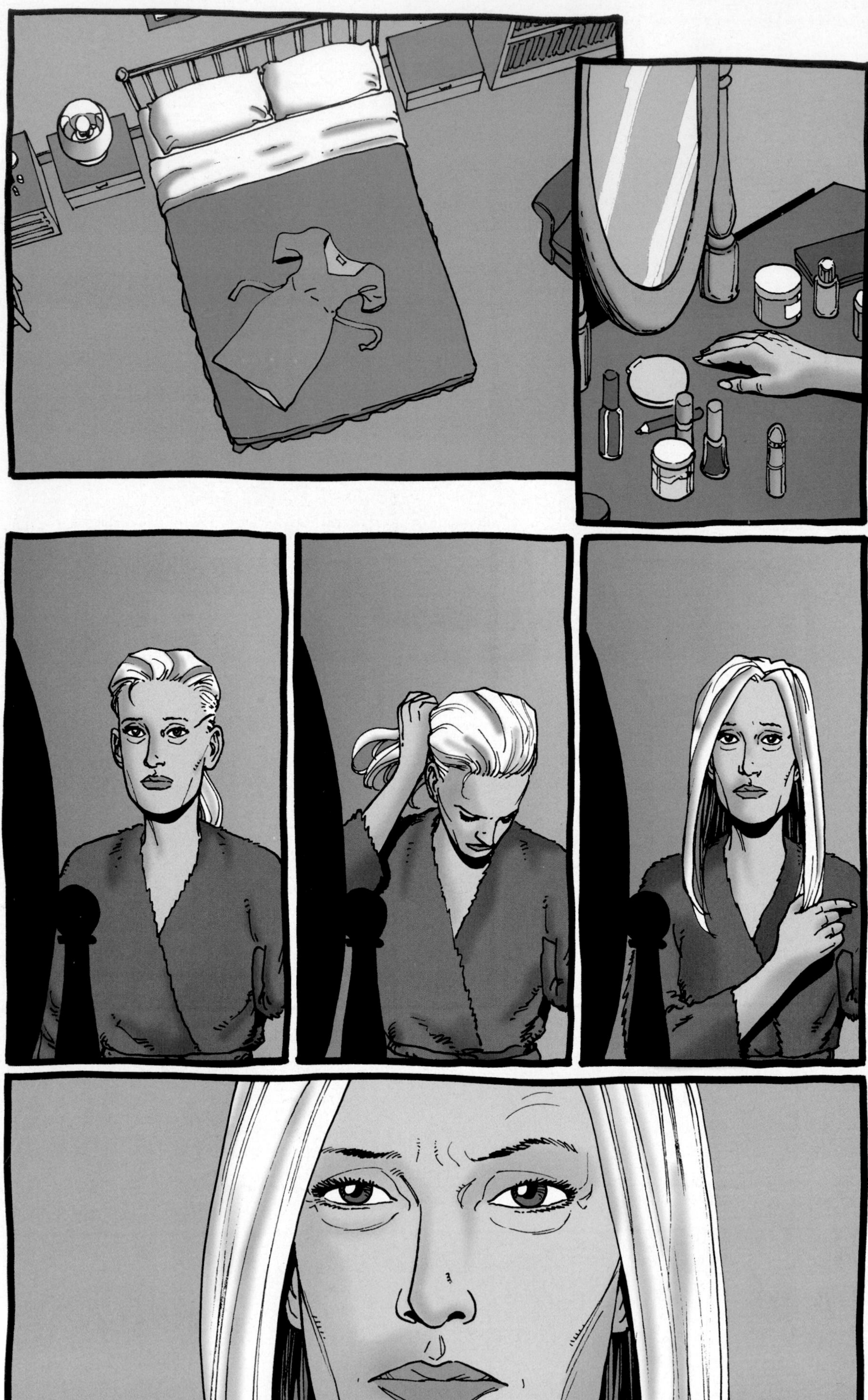

LET'S GO, DEPUTY.
WUFF!

WUFF! WUFF!
WELL, FIRST WE GONNA DRIVE OVER TO JOHN'S HOLLOW AN' PICK UP CINDY, AN' THEN WE GONNA GO MEET SOME FOLKS. KINDA GET TO KNOW THE TOWN A LITTLE BIT.
THEN WE GONNA PICK UP SOME GROCERIES AN' SUCH, AN' SWING BY MOM'S IN TIME FOR LUNCH. HOW'S THAT SOUND?

...MOM'S.
I SWEAR.

GODDAMMIT...

FIRST WE GONNA CALL CINDY AN' HAVE HER BRING OVER THE CRUISER. THEN WE GONNA TAKE A SLEDGEHAMMER TO THIS WORN-OUT PIECE OF SHIT.
THEN WE GONNA GO GRAB A BEER. HOW'S THAT SOUND?

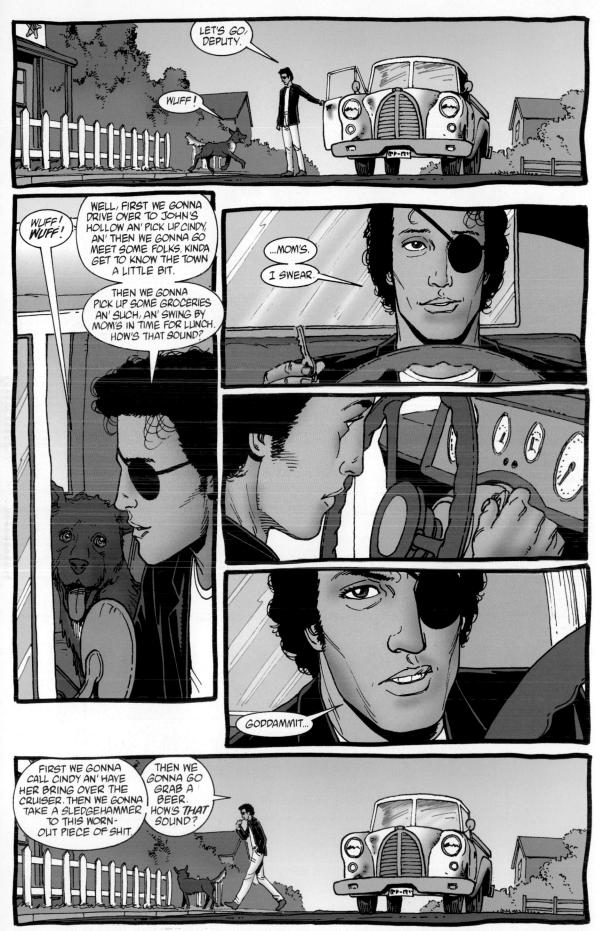

CUSTER'S LAW

GARTH ENNIS - Writer STEVE DILLON - Artist

Pamela Rambo - Colorist, Clem Robins - Letterer, Axel Alonso - Editor

PREACHER created by Garth Ennis and Steve Dillon

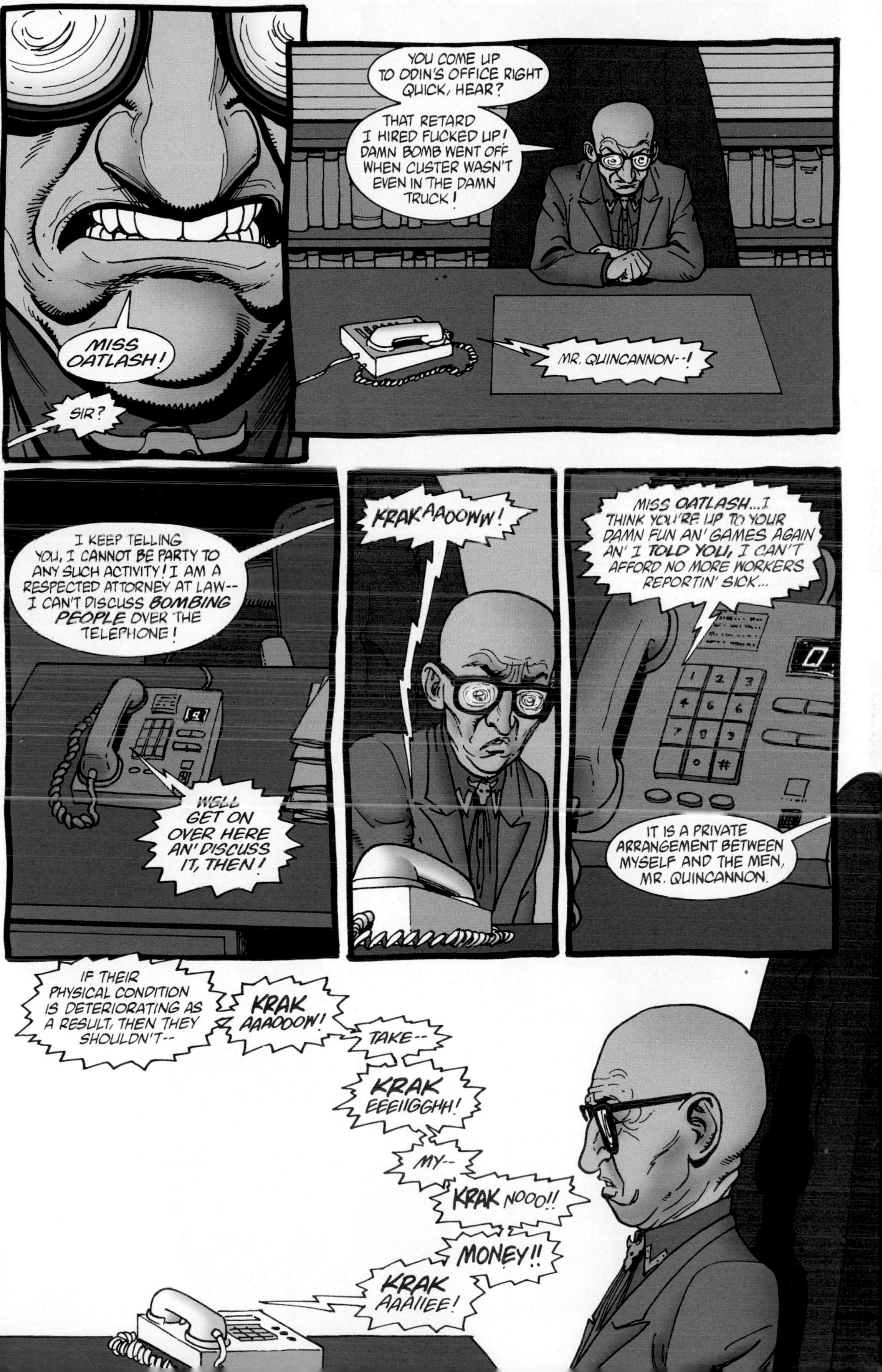

MISS OATLASH!
SIR?
MR. QUINCANNON--!
YOU COME UP TO ODIN'S OFFICE RIGHT QUICK, HEAR?
THAT RETARD I HIRED FUCKED UP! DAMN BOMB WENT OFF WHEN CUSTER WASN'T EVEN IN THE DAMN TRUCK!

NOW.
I'LL BE RIGHT OVER.
THE NEXT ONE OF YOU PIGS GOES CRAWLING TO THE DOCTOR'S OFFICE I'LL STAPLE HIS COCK SHUT, UNDER-STAND?
Y-YES, MISS OUTLASH.
WAIT HERE.
YOU BET, MISS OUTLASH.

YOU CERTAIN IT WAS QUINCANNON?
COCKSUCKER ALL BUT SIGNED IT.

WELL... WHAT'RE YOU PLANNIN' ON DOIN'?
NEVER PLAN A ACT OF VIOLENCE, CINDY. JUST LET IT HAPPEN NATURAL.
HEY, THAT'S THAT SON OF A BITCH SHERIFF...
MOTHER-FUCKER, I'M STILL EATIN' THROUGH A GODDAMN STRAW!
OH SHIT, HE'S COMIN' IN HERE...!

SEE WHAT THAT ASSHOLE CAN DO WHEN I'M READY FOR HIM! HE WAS LUCKY ONCE!
ONCE IS ALL HE GETS!

THIS IS PRIVATE PRUUCCHH

JESSE--
WHERE'S QUINCANNON?
WHAT--WHO--YOU CAN'T--

TELL ME.

DEMOLITION EXPERIENCE MY ASS, THAT GODDAMN HILL-BILLY COULDN'T CHANGE THE BATTERIES ON HIS OLD LADY'S VIBRATOR...
WHAT'S THAT COMMOTION DOWNSTAIRS?
M-M-MR. QUINCANNON?

WHAT THE HELL WAS THAT?!
OL' INJUN TRICK.

I JUST COULDN'T STOP HIM, SIR, HE--IT WAS LIKE--SIR, I'M SORRY, HE'S COMING UP--
WHO IS?!

OH FUCK--

C'MERE, YOU LITTLE PECKERHEAD--
NO! GET OUT! YOU STAY AWAY FROM ME, I'M WARNIN' YOU!
SHERIFF CUSTER, HOW DARE YOU! THIS IS PRIVATE PROPERTY!

SHERIFF CUSTER, I MUST WARN YOU THAT THIS ACTION CONSTITUTES A VIOLATION OF MR. QUINCANNON'S RIGHTS AND IS TOTALLY ILLEGAL!
I AM A WITNESS! THIS IS OUTRAGEOUS!
STOP!!
NO! NOOO! AAAAAH, MOMMY, DADDY, MAKE HIM GET OFFA ME!

OH GOD-- OH CHRIST--
HEEELLLPP!!

HOLY JESUS, STOP!
THE FUCK I WILL--

GODDAMMIT, JESSE! YOU CAN'T DO THIS!
AAAIIIEEEGH!!!

...WHY NOT?

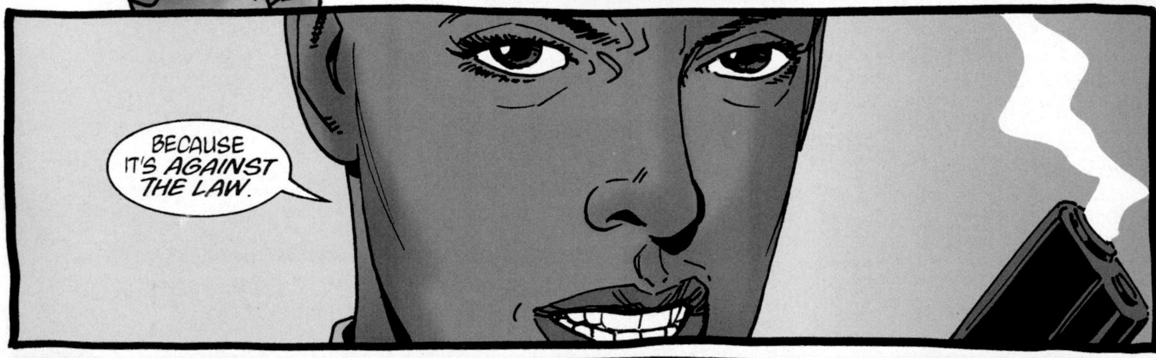
BECAUSE IT'S *AGAINST THE LAW*.

HMMM.

GLURK--!
EXTENSIVE DAMAGE TO ONE SHERIFF'S DEPARTMENT VEHICLE, SHORTY.
GO FETCH YOUR CHECK-BOOK.

ATTABOY.
WORD OF ADVICE, LITTLE MAN: AIN'T NO ONE EVER TOOK A SHOT AT ME AN' WALKED AWAY INTACT BEFORE, 'SPECIALLY NOT NO SAWED-OFF RUNT LIKE YOU. YOU PLAY SMART AN' CALL THIS QUITS, HEAR?
AN' MISS OUTLASH?
YES?
DON'T TRY TO FRIGHTEN ME WITH THE LAW, MA'AM.
YOU AIN'T SCARY.
I, UH...I JUST GOTTA GO TO THE BATHROOM...
ME TOO.

HE AIN'T GONNA QUIT...

NO HE AIN'T. HE'S THE KIND LIKES TO TAKE CARE OF THINGS PERSONAL.
AIN'T NO SATISFACTION IN SENDIN' A MAN TO JAIL WHEN WHAT YOU REALLY WANT IS TO LOOK HIM IN THE EYES WHILE YOU'RE CHOKIN' HIM TO DEATH.

TELL YOU THE TRUTH, I CAN SORTA RELATE.
SO I NOTICED. AN' I THINK IT'S SOMETHIN' WE GONNA HAVE TO TALK ABOUT.

YEAH?
I SAW YOU IN THERE, JESSE. YOU WOULDA MURDERED THAT MAN, I HADN'T OF STOPPED YOU.
NOW I DON'T KNOW HOW YOU'RE USED TO DOIN' THINGS, BUT YOU CAN'T BE YOUR OWN EXECUTIONER HERE. ONCE YOU PUT THAT STAR ON, YOU AGREE TO ABIDE BY THE LAW AN' APPLY IT FAIRLY AN' EQUALLY.

YOU CAN'T JUST KILL ODIN QUINCANNON, EVEN IF HE IS A SON OF A BITCH. YOU CAN'T EVEN MOVE AGAINST HIM, 'LESS YOU GOT PROOF.
PROOF HE TRIED TO KILL YOU. PROOF HE'S PISSIN' ON THE RULES AROUND HERE, MESSIN' UP THE RIVER WITH FILTH FROM HIS PLANT AN' LETTIN' HIS BOYS RUN RIOT IN SALVATION. YOU ACT WITHOUT IT, HE'S GONNA WIN AN' WE'LL BE IN A WORLD OF SHIT THE SMARTEST LAWYER IN TEXAS COULDN'T GET US OUT OF...

AN' WHAT THE HELL WAS THAT SHIT YOU PULLED ON THE RECEPTIONIST? I SWEAR, THAT THING YOU DID WITH YOUR VOICE FELT LIKE NAILS SCRAPIN' DOWN INSIDE MY SOUL!

WELL THAT'S A, KIND OF A HYPNOSIS THING I LEARNED FROM CERTAIN MONK FELLAS, DURIN' MY TRAVELS IN THE ORIENT.
IN MY YOUTH.

AN' LOOK, YOU'RE RIGHT: I WAS OUTTA LINE BACK THERE. I'M USED TO SETTLIN' THINGS MY OWN DAMN WAY AN' THEN DISAPPEARIN' 'FORE I HAVE TO ACCOUNT FOR IT. AN' THAT'S GONNA HAVE TO CHANGE.

I PROMISE YOU I'LL DO MY BEST TO UPHOLD THE LAW. I AIN'T SAYIN' I'LL BE PERFECT--OLD DOG, NEW TRICKS--BUT I'M GONNA TRY TO TAKE THAT BASTARD DOWN LEGAL.
AN' I'LL TRY NOT TO CHARGE IN WITHOUT THINKIN' AN' EXPECTIN' YOU TO FOLLOW ME. YOU'RE MY DEPUTY AN' YOU DESERVE MORE RESPECT THAN THAT, AN' IF I'M TO DO THIS JOB I NEED YOU WITH ME.

NOW HOW'S THAT SOUND?

I GUESS IT SOUNDS OKAY.

"TRAVELS IN THE ORIENT," JESUS CHRIST...

LOAN ME THE CRUISER TONIGHT? I GOT SOMEONE I GOTTA GO SEE.
BUY YOU LUNCH...
YEAH, BRIBERY MIGHT WORK.

IT'S JUST THE ONCE. I'LL GET ME SOME MORE TRANSPORT ONCE ODIN'S CHECK CLEARS.
HELL, YOU GOT ENOUGH FOR TWO TRUCKS HERE.
SO IS THIS YOURS OR THE DEPARTMENT'S, YOU THINK?

WELL, IT'S MADE OUT TO THE DEPARTMENT. AN' WE AIN'T GOT MUCH OF A BUDGET, AFTER ALL.
MY THOUGHTS EXACTLY. SO AS LONG AS YOU'RE SPLASHIN' OUT--

CAN I GET ONE OF THESE?
USA MILITARY AND LAW

DON'T SEE WHY NOT.
KOCH

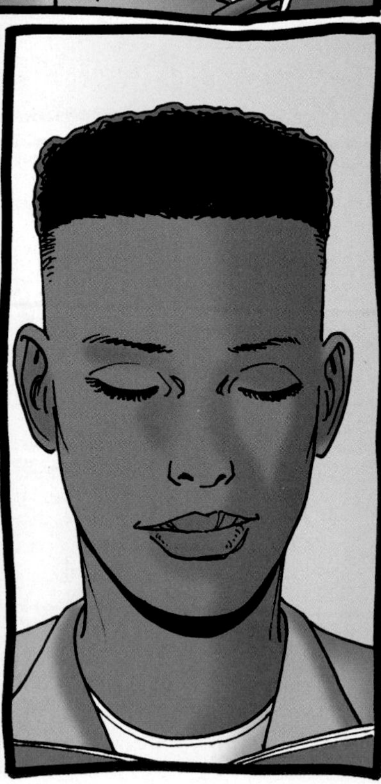

WUFF!
YOU LIKE HER, HUH?

NO GETTIN' AWAY FROM IT. SHE'S A PEACH.
SMART, TOO. GONNA TAKE SOME GETTIN' USED TO, BEIN' ON THIS SIDE'VE THE LAW.

WHICH I GUESS MEANS NO WORD OF GOD, AT LEAST FOR THE TIME BEIN'.
TRICKY ONE, SKEETER. DAMN THING'S LIKE A GUN: YOU PULL IT OUT WHEN YOU GOT NO CHOICE, FINE. YOU STICK IT IN SOME OL' RECEPTIONIST GAL'S FACE, WELL, THAT AIN'T SO GOOD.
THAT AIN'T MY STYLE.
?

NOW I WENT THROUGH SOME SHIT A WHILE BACK, BAD STUFF I CAN'T GET STRAIGHT IN MY HEAD. COULD BE IT'S MADE ME CARELESS.
AN' THE WORD... IT'S KINDA *OF* THAT TIME, AN' I AIN'T TOO SURE I'M READY TO GO BACK THERE JUST YET.

TRICKY.
JODIE'S

DID YOU COMB YOUR HAIR THIS MORNING?
JODIE'S

HUH? AW, MOM--!
JOKE.

HMH.
YOU LOOK REAL NICE.
THANK YOU. I FEEL NICE. I'VE BEEN ENJOYING MY FIRST WEEK OF BEING ME AGAIN.

Y'ALL EVER DO CROSSWORD PUZZLES?

NOT TOO OFTEN...
I THINK YOU TWO HAVE ALREADY MET. TOBY WORKS FOR ME.
SURE, DUDE. YOU SCARED THE CRAP OUTTA DAVY DREW.
SO I GOT NORTH AMERICAN BURROWIN' RODENT. SIX LETTERS.

G--
BUFFALO!

BEE-YOU-EFF-EYE-EL-OH...

HOW'S THAT GIRLFRIEND OF YOURS, TOBY?
OH MA'AM, WE HAD US A SCARE. TIRLENE THOUGHT SHE WAS PREGNANT.
BUT SHE WASN'T?
NO MA'AM. MISSED HER PERIOD. BUT THAT'S OKAY, IT HAPPENED ONCE BEFORE.
OH? WHEN?
LAST MONTH.
YOU MIGHT WANT TO HAVE TIRLENE DROP BY DOCTOR CHESNEY'S OFFICE, TOBY. JUST FOR A CHECK-UP.
FETCH UP A COUPLE MORE CASES OF LONE STAR THERE, COULD YOU?
YES, MA'AM.
JESUS--CHRIST--
THE WORST PART IS THAT THERE'S A GIRL OUT THERE WHO'D LET TOBY STICK IT IN HER.
AND THAT THEY BRED...
OH, HE'S A SWEET BOY. DOES WHAT HE'S TOLD, NEVER COMPLAINS. HAS THE I.Q. OF HANGING BEEF.
YOU KEEP THREATENING TO GET TO KNOW YOUR PEOPLE, SHERIFF. I THOUGHT TOBY WOULD MAKE A NICE START.
...YEAH.
BUT I THINK I KNOW A BETTER ONE.

I'VE BEEN EXPECTING YOU.

YEAH, WELL, I HEARD THERE WAS A NAZI SPY LIVIN' HERE. FIGURED IT MIGHT BE WORTH INVESTIGATIN'.
COME IN, SHERIFF.

NICE PLACE.
THANK YOU. FEEL FREE TO SMOKE.
SO...

SO, I CHECKED WITH THE RECORDS OFFICE IN THE TOWN HALL. ACCORDIN' TO THEM, THIS HOUSE BELONGS TO ONE MARK VAN DER POL.
HAS DONE FOR ALMOST FIFTY YEARS.

THAT NAME DON'T SOUND TOO GERMAN TO ME.
DUTCH. I STOPPED USING IT YEARS AGO. WHEN I BECAME AN AMERICAN CITIZEN I REVERTED TO MY OWN NAME, WHICH I'D BEEN USING SOCIALLY ALMOST SINCE I GOT HERE.
BUT VAN DER POL WAS THE NAME ON THE PASSPORT THAT GOT ME INTO SAN DIEGO, IN JUNE OF NINETEEN FORTY-THREE.

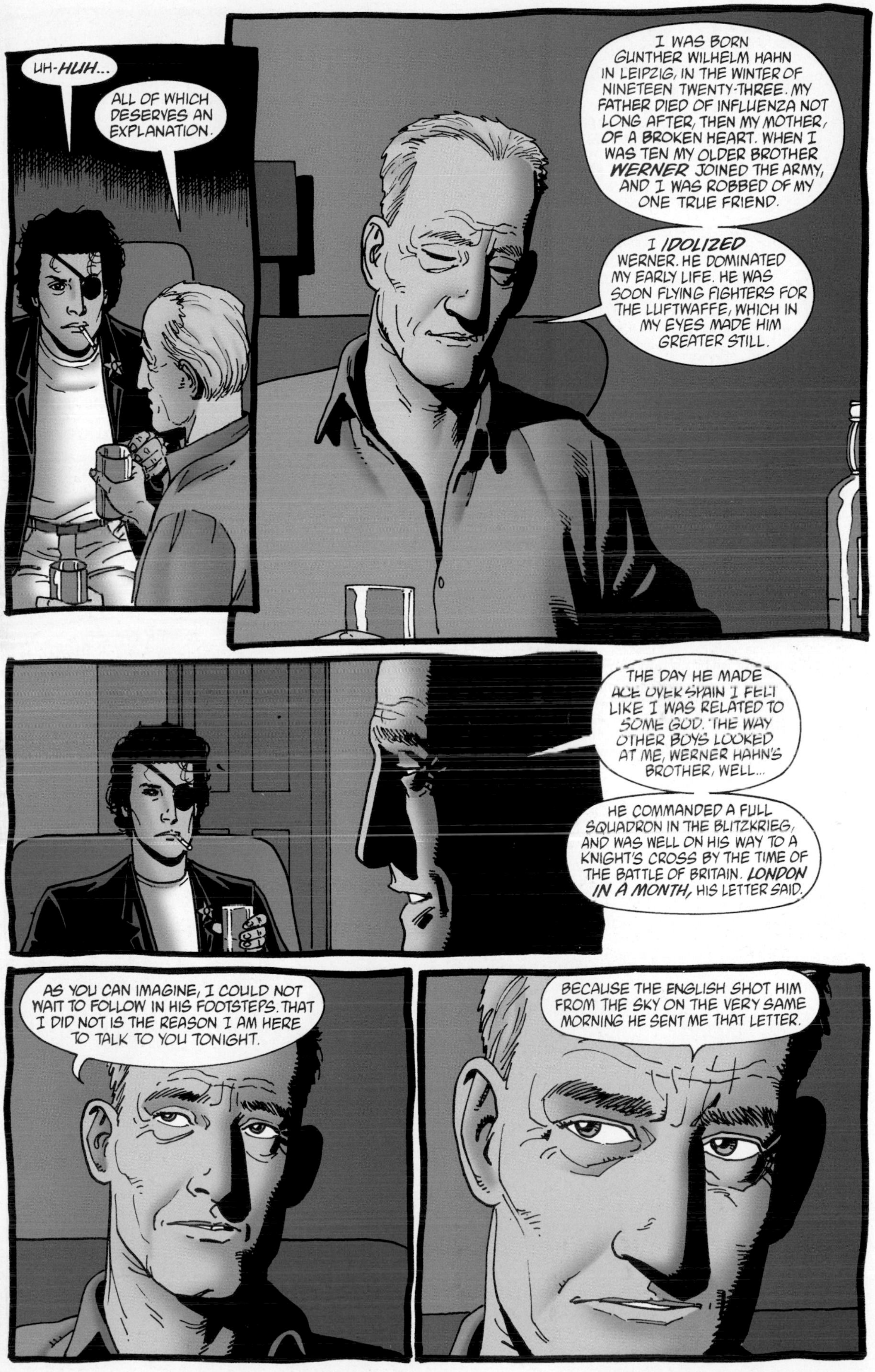

UH-*HUH*...

ALL OF WHICH DESERVES AN EXPLANATION.

I WAS BORN GUNTHER WILHELM HAHN IN LEIPZIG, IN THE WINTER OF NINETEEN TWENTY-THREE. MY FATHER DIED OF INFLUENZA NOT LONG AFTER, THEN MY MOTHER, OF A BROKEN HEART. WHEN I WAS TEN MY OLDER BROTHER ***WERNER*** JOINED THE ARMY, AND I WAS ROBBED OF MY ONE TRUE FRIEND.

I ***IDOLIZED*** WERNER. HE DOMINATED MY EARLY LIFE. HE WAS SOON FLYING FIGHTERS FOR THE LUFTWAFFE, WHICH IN MY EYES MADE HIM GREATER STILL.

THE DAY HE MADE ACE OVER SPAIN I FELT LIKE I WAS RELATED TO SOME GOD. THE WAY OTHER BOYS LOOKED AT ME, WERNER HAHN'S BROTHER, WELL...
HE COMMANDED A FULL SQUADRON IN THE BLITZKRIEG, AND WAS WELL ON HIS WAY TO A KNIGHT'S CROSS BY THE TIME OF THE BATTLE OF BRITAIN. ***LONDON IN A MONTH,*** HIS LETTER SAID.

AS YOU CAN IMAGINE, I COULD NOT WAIT TO FOLLOW IN HIS FOOTSTEPS. THAT I DID NOT IS THE REASON I AM HERE TO TALK TO YOU TONIGHT.

BECAUSE THE ENGLISH SHOT HIM FROM THE SKY ON THE VERY SAME MORNING HE SENT ME THAT LETTER.

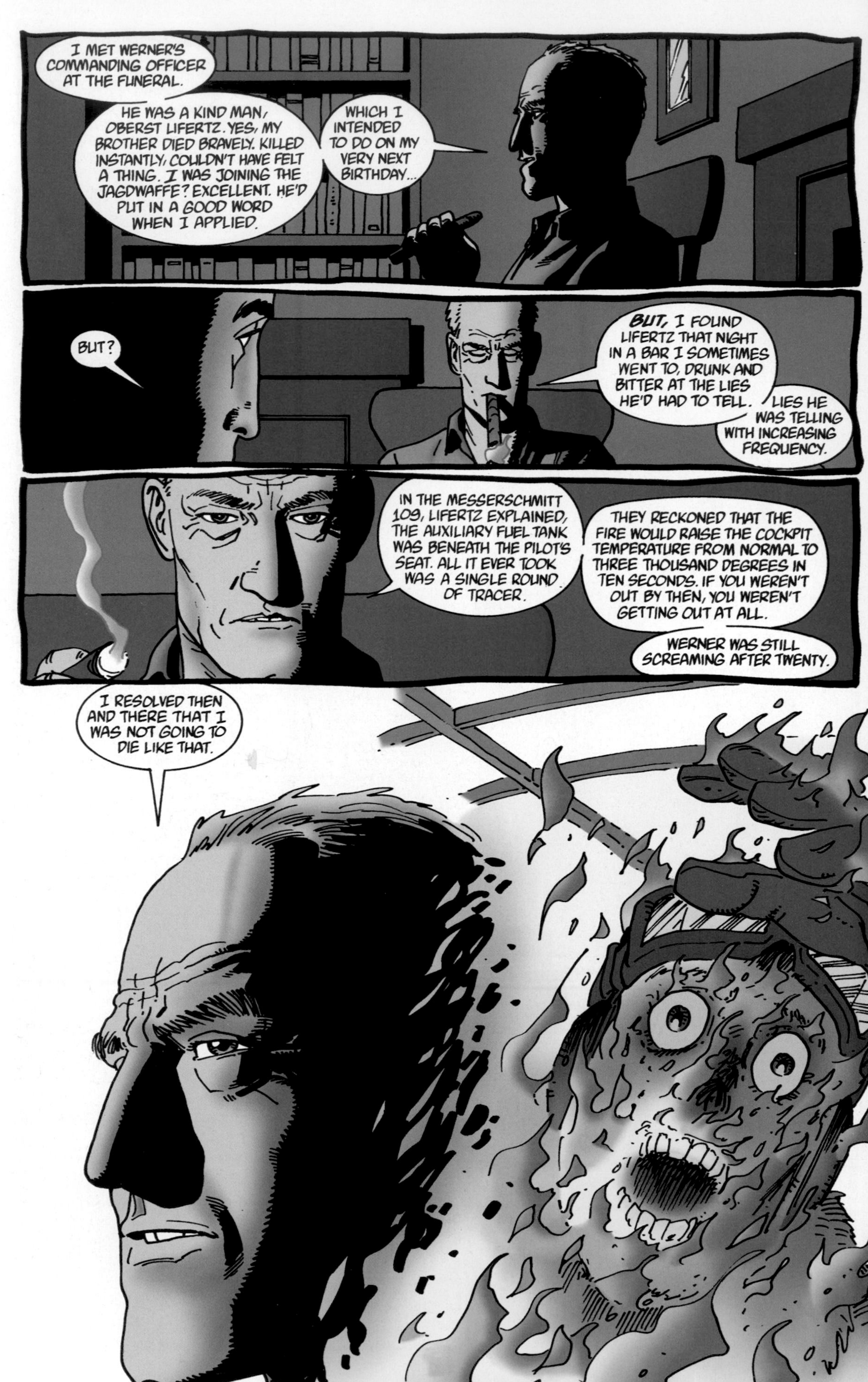
I MET WERNER'S COMMANDING OFFICER AT THE FUNERAL.
HE WAS A KIND MAN, OBERST LIFERTZ. YES, MY BROTHER DIED BRAVELY. KILLED INSTANTLY, COULDN'T HAVE FELT A THING. I WAS JOINING THE JAGDWAFFE? EXCELLENT. HE'D PUT IN A GOOD WORD WHEN I APPLIED.
WHICH I INTENDED TO DO ON MY VERY NEXT BIRTHDAY...
BUT?
BUT, I FOUND LIFERTZ THAT NIGHT IN A BAR I SOMETIMES WENT TO, DRUNK AND BITTER AT THE LIES HE'D HAD TO TELL.
LIES HE WAS TELLING WITH INCREASING FREQUENCY.
IN THE MESSERSCHMITT 109, LIFERTZ EXPLAINED, THE AUXILIARY FUEL TANK WAS BENEATH THE PILOT'S SEAT. ALL IT EVER TOOK WAS A SINGLE ROUND OF TRACER.
THEY RECKONED THAT THE FIRE WOULD RAISE THE COCKPIT TEMPERATURE FROM NORMAL TO THREE THOUSAND DEGREES IN TEN SECONDS. IF YOU WEREN'T OUT BY THEN, YOU WEREN'T GETTING OUT AT ALL.
WERNER WAS STILL SCREAMING AFTER TWENTY.
I RESOLVED THEN AND THERE THAT I WAS NOT GOING TO DIE LIKE THAT.

INSTEAD I JOINED THE LUFTWAFFE'S INTELLIGENCE DIVISION, TO WHICH I WAS MUCH BETTER SUITED.

I WAS NEVER A NATURAL WARRIOR, JESSE.

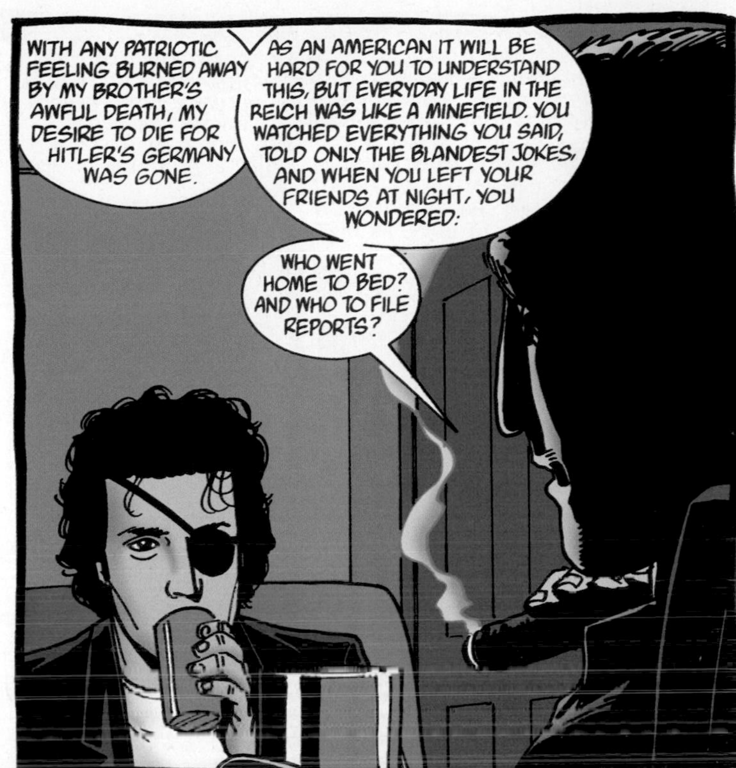
WITH ANY PATRIOTIC FEELING BURNED AWAY BY MY BROTHER'S AWFUL DEATH, MY DESIRE TO DIE FOR HITLER'S GERMANY WAS GONE.
AS AN AMERICAN IT WILL BE HARD FOR YOU TO UNDERSTAND THIS, BUT EVERYDAY LIFE IN THE REICH WAS LIKE A MINEFIELD. YOU WATCHED EVERYTHING YOU SAID, TOLD ONLY THE BLANDEST JOKES, AND WHEN YOU LEFT YOUR FRIENDS AT NIGHT, YOU WONDERED:
WHO WENT HOME TO BED? AND WHO TO FILE REPORTS?

IT WAS NO WAY TO LIVE.
I GREW *SICK* OF ENDLESSLY, FEARFULLY REVIEWING MY CONVERSATIONS FOR SEDITION, AND BY THE END OF FORTY-ONE I KNEW WE WOULD LOSE ANYWAY. RUSSIA WAS ONE THING, BUT ***AMERICA***...?

THINGS WOULD GET BAD, I WAS CERTAIN. I DOUBTED THERE WOULD EVEN *BE* A GERMANY ONCE THE DUST HAD SETTLED. HOW TO GET OUT, I WONDERED, HOW TO GET OUT...

GO BE A SPY IN THE STATES
IN ONE.

I VOLUNTEERED AND WAS ACCEPTED BY THE ABWEHR. TOP MARKS ALL THE WAY THROUGH TRAINING.

"HIGHLY MOTIVATED," MY INSTRUCTOR WROTE. "SHOULD GO FAR."

SO MARK VAN DER POL ARRIVED IN THE UNITED STATES, A REFUGEE FROM THE DUTCH EAST INDIES WITH FIVE HUNDRED DOLLARS SEWN IN HIS OVERCOAT.
I HAD A CONTACT ARRANGED IN LOS ANGELES. I HAD NO INTENTION OF GOING ANYWHERE NEAR IT.

FOR ALL I KNOW, "CODENAME EAGLE" IS STILL SITTING IN A BAR ON HOLLYWOOD BOULEVARD, WAITING FOR A TALL DUTCHMAN IN A BLUE HAT.
NO, I WENT EAST AND LOST MYSELF IN THE WIDE OPEN SPACES. NOBODY NOTICED ONE MORE DRIFTER. THE WAR WAS A WORLD AWAY.
I SETTLED... AND IT DIDN'T TAKE ME LONG TO REALIZE THAT I ENJOYED MY NEW LIFE VERY, VERY MUCH.

HOW SO?
BECAUSE IT WAS SO MUCH BETTER THAN WHAT I WAS USED TO.

I LIKE THIS COUNTRY, JESSE. I LIKE BASEBALL AND WHISKEY AND MOM'S APPLE PIE--NOT *MY* MOM'S APPLE PIE, BUT YOU KNOW WHAT I MEAN--AND THE STARS AND STRIPES, AND JOHN WAYNE, AND FIREWORKS ON THE FOURTH OF JULY...
AND I LIKE THE MYTH OF THE PLACE.

THE MYTH OF AMERICA: THAT SIMPLE, HONEST MEN, BORN OF HER GREAT PLAINS AND WOODS AND SKIES HAVE MADE A NATION OF HER, AND WILL PROVE WORTHY OF HER WHEN THE TIME IS RIGHT.

UNDER HARSH LIGHT IT IS FALSE.
BUT A GOOD MYTH TO LIVE UP TO, ALL THE SAME.

SO WHY TRUST ME WITH ALL OF THIS?
THIS IS YOUR TOWN NOW, JESSE. I FELT IT RIGHT THAT YOU SHOULD KNOW.
THIS IS HOW HONORABLE MEN DEAL WITH ONE ANOTHER, IS IT NOT?

AN' YOU RECKON THAT'S THE CASE HERE?
YOUR FIRST DAY IN TOWN YOU COULD HAVE SMASHED THAT BOY'S FACE, BUT INSTEAD YOU CHOSE TO LET HIM GO. THAT WAS THE KEY. AND TAKING ON THE TASK YOU HAVE...?
MEN LIKE YOU CANNOT DISGUISE WHAT THEY ARE.
WELL, NOW...

WAY I ALWAYS SEEN IT, GUNTHER, WHAT THIS COUNTRY'S ABOUT IS A SECOND CHANCE. FELLA COMES HERE, LEAVES THE OLD WORLD BEHIND, GETS ANOTHER SHOT AT MAKIN' IT.
YOU SEEM LIKE YOU MADE THE MOST'VE YOUR SHOT, SO WHO THE HELL AM I TO TAKE IT AWAY FROM YOU?

THERE... IS THE QUESTION OF MY ILLEGAL ENTRY TO THE STATES...
LAW'S ONLY ANY USE IF IT DOES SOME GOOD.

AND IS THAT HOW YOU INTEND TO APPLY IT, SHERIFF?

...
I GUESS IT IS.

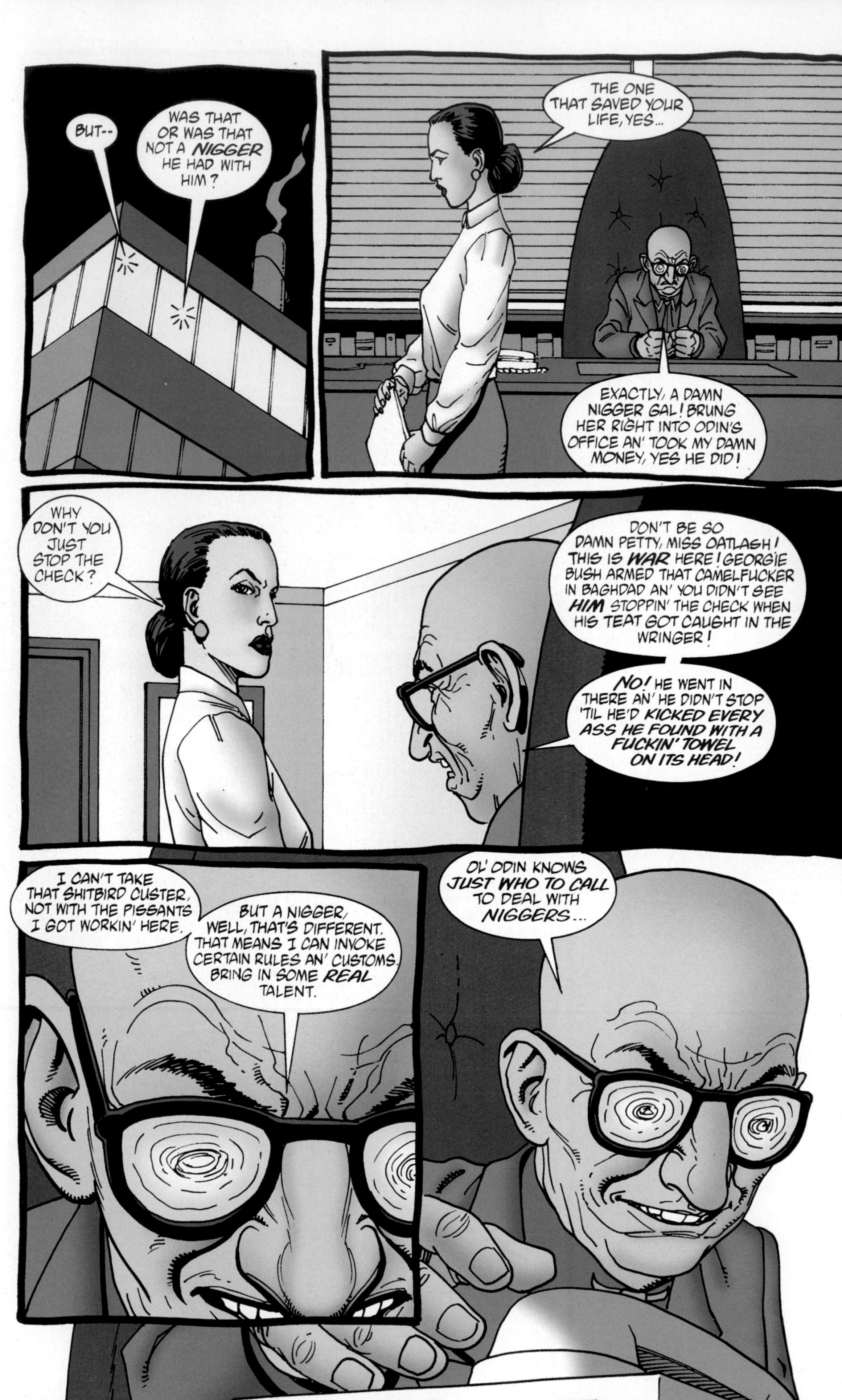
BUT--
WAS THAT OR WAS THAT NOT A NIGGER HE HAD WITH HIM?
THE ONE THAT SAVED YOUR LIFE, YES...
EXACTLY, A DAMN NIGGER GAL! BRUNG HER RIGHT INTO ODIN'S OFFICE AN' TOOK MY DAMN MONEY, YES HE DID!
WHY DON'T YOU JUST STOP THE CHECK?
DON'T BE SO DAMN PETTY, MISS OATLASH! THIS IS WAR HERE! GEORGIE BUSH ARMED THAT CAMELFUCKER IN BAGHDAD AN' YOU DIDN'T SEE HIM STOPPIN' THE CHECK WHEN HIS TEAT GOT CAUGHT IN THE WRINGER!
NO! HE WENT IN THERE AN' HE DIDN'T STOP 'TIL HE'D KICKED EVERY ASS HE FOUND WITH A FUCKIN' TOWEL ON ITS HEAD!
I CAN'T TAKE THAT SHITBIRD CUSTER, NOT WITH THE PISSANTS I GOT WORKIN' HERE.
BUT A NIGGER, WELL, THAT'S DIFFERENT. THAT MEANS I CAN INVOKE CERTAIN RULES AN' CUSTOMS. BRING IN SOME REAL TALENT.
OL' ODIN KNOWS JUST WHO TO CALL TO DEAL WITH NIGGERS...

GLENN
FABRY
99

"There is no direct evidence that the Führer held racist views."

SOUTHERN CROSS

GARTH ENNIS - Writer **STEVE DILLON - Artist**

PAMELA RAMBO - Colorist **CLEM ROBINS - Letterer** **AXEL ALONSO - Editor**

PREACHER created by GARTH ENNIS and STEVE DILLON

BRING OUT THE PRISONERS...
SHERIFF
QUINCANNON

WHAT ARE THE CHARGES?
MANY AN' VARIED. DISTURBIN' THE PEACE, PROPERTY DAMAGE, PUBLIC INDECENCY, ASSAULT, POSSESSION OF A OFFENSIVE WEAPON...

THEY SEEM A LITTLE THE WORSE FOR WEAR.
...RESISTIN' ARREST...

OH, AN' THIS'N FUCKED THAT'N IN THE CELLS. BUT I GUESS THAT'S THEIR BUSINESS.
RIGHT UP THE DAMN ASS...

I COME TO THIS TOWN TO GET LAID AN' BY GOD I WASN'T GOIN' HOME 'TIL I DID. YOU HADN'T OF LOCKED US UP, I WOULDN'T OF HAD TO SETTLE FOR BILLY...
UP THE ASS. SWEET JESUS.

AN' CELLS, WHO THE FUCK ARE YOU TRYNNA KID! THAT AIN'T NO CELL DOWN THERE, THAT AIN'T NOTHIN' BUT A GODDAMN STINKIN' OL' FRUIT CELLAR!
SHERIFF CUSTER, I NEED HARDLY REMIND YOU OF THE LAWS CONCERNING THE DETENTION OF PRISONERS IN HUMANE CONDITIONS...

I CAUGHT THIS DRUNK PIECE OF SHIT PISSIN' IN A FELLA'S MAILBOX. DON'T TALK TO ME 'BOUT HUMANE CONDITIONS.
NOW, YOU WANNA PUT UP THE BAIL FOR THESE FUCKS, YOU KNOW THE ROUTINE. SIGN THE FORM, LEAVE THE CHECK, GET 'EM OUTTA HERE AN' HAVE EVERY WORTHLESS ONE'VE 'EM IN FRONTA THE JUDGE MONDAY MORNIN'.

BOYS.

RIGHT, GET ON THE TRUCK...
THIRD TIME IN TWO WEEKS, MISS OATLASH. AIN'T YOU GOT TIREDA THIS YET?

MM?
COMIN' ALL THE WAY TO TOWN TO BAIL OUT THESE HERE PUKES? TAKIN' 'EM BACK TO YOUR RUNT OF A BOSS, ALL BUSTED UP SO THEY CAN'T WORK IN HIS STINKIN' FACTORY?
ALL YOU GOTTA DO IS KEEP 'EM OUTTA SALVATION ON THEIR DAYS OFF AN' WE AIN'T GONNA HAVE THIS PROBLEM...
I AM MR. QUINCANNON'S LEGAL ADVISOR. WORKER RECREATION POLICY HAS NOTHING TO DO WITH ME.
AND INCIDENTALLY, SHERIFF, DON'T THINK FOR A MINUTE THAT THE ILLEGALITY OF YOUR POSITION HAS PASSED ME BY. AS I UNDERSTAND IT, YOUR APPOINTMENT HAS YET TO BE RATIFIED BY ELECTION. YOUR POLICE BRUTALITY ISN'T EVEN THAT.
YEAH, WELL, CONSIDERIN' THE JUDGE THIS TRASH HAVE TO ANSWER TO IS IN QUINCANNON'S POCKET, I AIN'T TOO CONCERNED 'BOUT THE LEGAL STATUS OF ME KICKIN' THEIR ASSES.
SHIT, NEITHER'S ODIN. HE'S TAKEN THIS WHOLE THING PERSONAL. HE WIPES HIS ASS ON THE LAW'N A DAILY BASIS.
SILK, ACTUALLY. APPARENTLY.
UM...
DO YOU LIKE ITALIAN FOOD?

WHAT?
NOTHING!
...NOTHING.

'KAY. NOW, YOU GOT YOUR TRUCK-LOADA SCUM AN' YOUR RECEIPT, SO YOU'RE ALL THROUGH. TAKE THE PUNCHBAG TWINS AN' GO HOME.

Y'ALL STILL HERE?

AND THAT'S THE NEW SHERIFF'S DEPARTMENT OFFICIAL TRANSPORT, IS IT?

AW, I STILL HAD A CHUNKA CHANGE LEFT OVER AFTER I MAILED JOHNNY-LEE BACK HIS MONEY. AN' HELL, WAY I FIGURED, ONLY THING MORE QUINTESSENTIALLY AMERICAN THAN ONE'VE THESE'D BE A GODDAMN HORSE...
YOU ARE JUST LIKE YOUR FATHER, JESSE.

LIVING A WESTERN.

AM I REALLY LIKE HIM, MOM?
OH YES.

YOU HAVE A SENSE OF PURPOSE DRIVING YOU TO DO WHAT YOU FEEL YOU MUST. A STRONG ONE, LIKE A FIRE INSIDE YOU.
IN JOHN IT HAD ABATED. VIETNAM DID THAT. IT HADN'T BURNT OUT, BUT HE'D MADE HIS PEACE WITH IT.

I HOPE YOU CAN.

AFTER YOU, SIR.
WUFF.
GOOD MEN WITH ENGINES, TOO.

BUT THAT DIDN'T COME FROM HIM, DID IT?
I GUESS NOT.
THAT WAS JODY.

CREDIT WHERE CREDIT'S DUE, HE TAUGHT YOU WELL.
HE SURE DID. AN' MORE'N JUST ENGINES. HORSES. HUNTIN' AN' SHOOTIN'.
SHOWED ME HOW TO FIGHT LIKE A SON OF A BITCH, HELL, I DOUBT I COULDA HAD A BETTER TEACHER FOR THAT...

YOU STRANGLED HIM, RIGHT?

'TIL HIS GODDAMN EYES BUGGED OUT.
SEE YOU LATER, MOM.

BOYS, BOYS, I UNDERSTAND HOW YOU FEEL...
THEN HOW COME YOU AIN'T DONE NOTHIN' ABOUT IT?

THAT MOTHER-FUCKER CUSTER'S PUT SIX'VE OUR GUYS IN THE INFIRMARY SINCE HE STARTED, AN' THE DOC SAYS BIG JIM'S BALLS ARE RECEDED FOR GOOD!
NOW YOU *KNOW* THE ONLY REASON YOU GOT US TO MOVE TO THIS HERE SHIT-HOLE WAS YOU PROMISED US THE RUN OF THAT TOWN FOR LETTIN' OFF STEAM! AN' THAT MEANS DRINKIN' AN' WHORIN' AN' DOIN' AS WE PLEASE, NOT GETTIN' WHIPPED AN' JAILED AN' ENDIN' UP HAVIN' TO FUCK BILLY!
UP THE ASS, NO LESS.

BOYS, IF YOU'LL JUST LEAVE THINGS IN MY CAPABLE HANDS--
YOU AIN'T JERKIN' ME OFF. THAT'S WORSE'N FUCKIN' BILLY.
I SWEAR UP THE ASS.

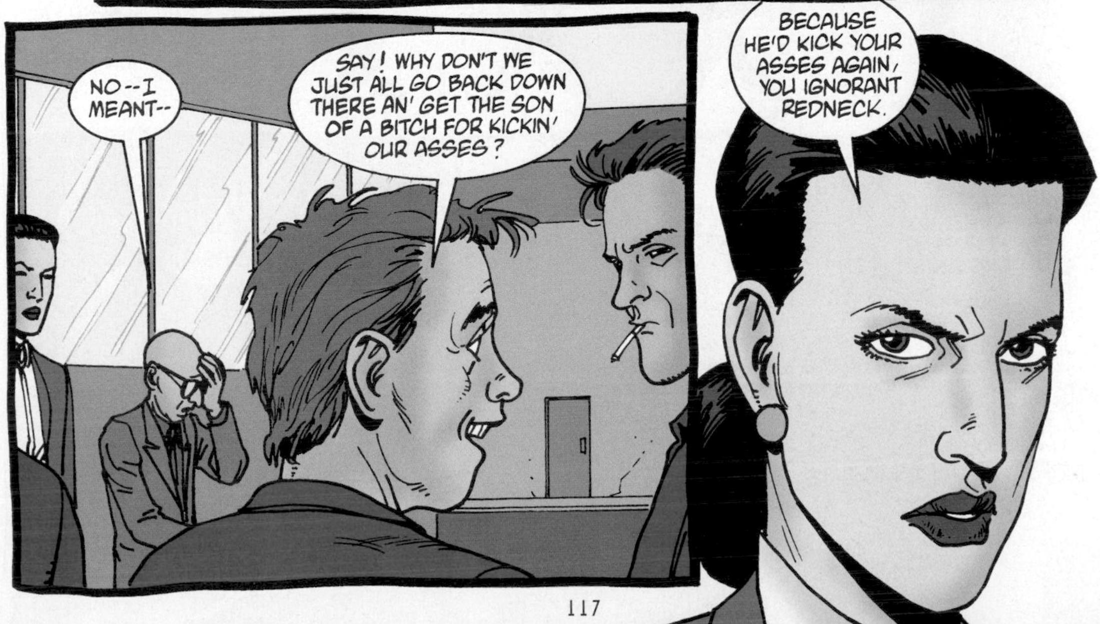
NO--I MEANT--
SAY! WHY DON'T WE JUST ALL GO BACK DOWN THERE AN' GET THE SON OF A BITCH FOR KICKIN' OUR ASSES?
BECAUSE HE'D KICK YOUR ASSES AGAIN, YOU IGNORANT REDNECK.

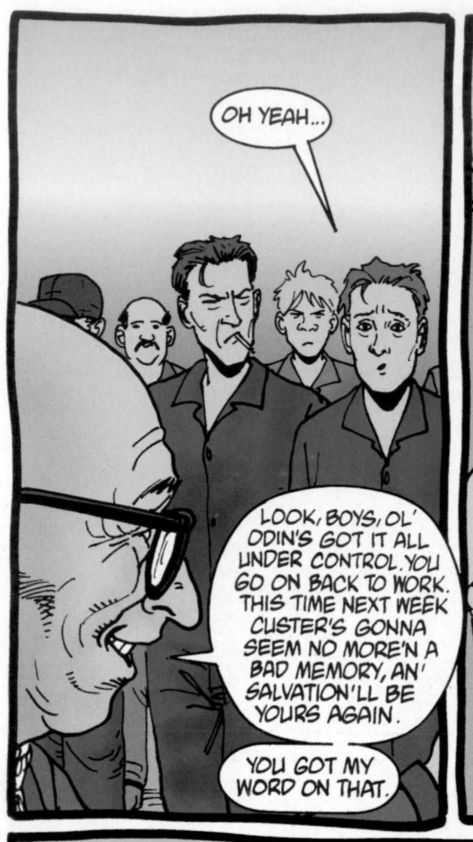
OH YEAH...
LOOK, BOYS, OL' ODIN'S GOT IT ALL UNDER CONTROL. YOU GO ON BACK TO WORK. THIS TIME NEXT WEEK CUSTER'S GONNA SEEM NO MORE'N A BAD MEMORY, AN' SALVATION'LL BE YOURS AGAIN.
YOU GOT MY WORD ON THAT.

I HOPE SO, QUINCANNON. 'CAUSE YOU DON'T FIX THIS THING, WE AIN'T STICKIN' ROUND HERE TO WADE IN BLOOD AN' COW-SHIT AN' SLICE UP THEM STINKIN' BEASTS OF YOURS. WE GONNA BE BACK IN HOUSTON FASTER'N A MINNOW SWIMMIN' A DIPPER.

YOU TWO ASSHOLES?

SIR?
THERE'S SOME BOYS ARRIVIN' AROUND FOUR THIS AFTERNOON. YOU SEE TO IT THEY AIN'T DELAYED BY SECURITY OR ANY'VE THAT BULLSHIT.
AND MISS OATLASH, YOU LET MY SECRETARY KNOW THEY AIN'T TO BE KEPT WAITIN'. SEND 'EM RIGHT IN.

TILL THEN ODIN AIN'T TO BE DISTURBED. NOT FOR ANYTHIN', UNDERSTAND?
YESSIR.

GOOD.

NOW LEMME SEE IF I GOT THIS STRAIGHT...

YOU, WALTER, BOUGHT A DOZEN NEW PINE BOARDS TO REPAIR YOUR FENCE AN' LEFT 'EM COVERED UP IN YOUR BACK YARD. YOU AN' YOUR FAMILY WENT TO FORT WORTH FOR THE WEEKEND, AN' WHEN YOU GOT BACK SUNDAY NIGHT THE LUMBER WAS GONE AN' BUCK'S SHED HAD SUDDENLY GOT A NEW ROOF.
YOU, BUCK, CLAIM ALL YOU DID WAS TO SAND AN' VARNISH THE OLD ROOF ON THE SATURDAY WALTER WAS GONE. THAT'S HOW COME IT LOOKS NEW AN' HAPPENS TO MATCH WALTER'S LUMBER. RIGHT?
YES SIR.
THAT'S ABOUT THE SIZE OF IT.
HE'S ALWAYS DOIN' THINGS LIKE THIS, SHERIFF. LONG AS I'VE LIVED HERE, BUCK ARLEN HAS TAKEN ADVANTAGE OF ME AN' POURED SCORN, I SAY *SCORN*, ON MY PROTESTS...
HELL, SHERIFF, LONG AS *I'VE* LIVED HERE OL' WALTER'S BEEN MAKIN' THESE DAMNFOOL PARANOID CLAIMS. I DON'T MIND THE BOY BEIN' CRAZY, BUT I SURE WOULD LIKE TO SEE HIM COME UP WITH SOME PROOF...
IT'S JUST LIKE *HIGH NOON*. I KNEW IT WOULD BE.
'KAY, HOW 'BOUT THIS:

BUCK, YOU AIN'T GOT NO OBJECTION, I'D LIKE TO TAKE A LOOK IN YOUR BACK YARD. I FIND ANY OL' ROTTED BOARDS LYIN' AROUND FROM, SAY, A RECENTLY REPLACED SHED ROOF, I KNOW YOU LIED TO ME. I DON'T, WELL...
HMMMM.
BE MY GUEST, SHERIFF, 'LONG AS YOU DON'T MIND WASTIN' HALF YOUR DAY. I GOT A LOTTA YARD BACK THERE.

HOW'D YOUR FENCE GET ALL SMASHED UP ANYHOW, WALTER?
THOSE DAMN QUINCANNON MEN, SHERIFF. START OF THE MONTH, SOME OF 'EM GOT DRUNK AN' KICKED MY FENCE DOWN IN A ACT OF WANTON, I SAY WANTON, VANDALISM...

AH, OL' WALTER'S RIGHT THERE, ACTUALLY. SAME BAD BOYS BURNED MY ROOF. CAME IN MY SHED TO SHIT ON MY LAWNMOWER AN' DROPPED A LIT CIGARETTE IN A CAN OF GASOLINE.
'COURSE, SINCE YOU STARTED, WE AIN'T HAD SO MUCH'VE THAT BULLSHIT...

YOU BOYS BOTH OWN BUSINESSES IN TOWN, DON'T YOU? QUINCANNON'S MEN QUIT COMIN' HERE, Y'ALL'RE GONNA LOSE A LOTTA INCOME.
YES SIR, THEY DO HAVE MONEY TO SPEND. BUT IT BARELY COVERS THE COST OF REPAIRING THE DAMAGE THEY CAUSE.
THAT'S A FACT.

uh-huh. WELL, LET'S SEE WHAT WE GOT HERE--

BE MY GUEST, SHERIFF, 'LONG AS YOU DON'T MIND STICKIN' YOUR HANDS IN A LOTTA SOILED TAMPONS AN' SANITARY TOWELS AN' ALL KINDSA AWFUL FEMALE MENSTRUAL BYPRODUCTS. MY OL' LADY JUST CAME OFF THE RAG.

I TELL A LIE.
IT AIN'T A BIT LIKE HIGH NOON.
YOU BLACK, I SAY BLACK, LIAR...
BUCK?
UH...
TWO WAYS WE CAN SETTLE THIS THING, FELLAS.
ONE IS OFFICIALLY, WHERE I FILL OUT ENOUGH FORMS TO PAPER A GOOD-SIZE BARN AN' AFTER A LONG, LONG TIME WAITIN' FOR THAT SHITHEEL OF A JUDGE TO GET OFF HIS ASS, BUCK PAYS WALTER BACK FOR THE LUMBER AN' MAYBE ENOUGH EXTRA TO COVER 'BOUT HALF HIS COURT COSTS...
OTHER IS UNOFFICIALLY, WHERE BUCK PAYS WALTER BACK FOR THE LUMBER AN' LETS HIM HAVE A FREE SHOT IN THE MOUTH, AN' WE CALL IT QUITS HERE AN' NOW.
OH BOY... OH BOY...
YOU'RE SAYIN' YOU'RE GONNA STAND THERE AN' LET HIM BUST ME ONE IN THE FACE?
IF YOU'RE AGREEABLE.

...
HELL, WHY NOT?
ALL YOURS, WALT.
AFTER ALL THIS TIME--

WELL, I SURE DO FEEL A WHOLE LOT BETTER FOR HAVIN' TOOK MY PUNISHMENT LIKE A MAN. YES SIR, THIS IS WHERE I BECOME A RESPONSIBLE CITIZEN...
WORD OF ADVICE, WALTER?

DON'T DROP YOUR SHOULDER LIKE THAT 'FORE YOU SWING. HE'LL SEE WHAT'S COMIN', HAVE TIME TO GET READY.
HUH?

LIKE THAT.
BUCK WAKES UP, TELL HIM I'M HAVIN' A LITTLE MEETIN' TONIGHT TO TALK OVER THE QUINCANNON THING. SEVEN-THIRTY AT JODIE'S BAR AN' GRILL.
SEE YOU THERE.

I CAN'T BELIEVE YOU'RE INVOLVING AN ORGANIZATION LIKE THAT. NOT ONLY IS IT HIGHLY DANGEROUS, ON A PURELY MORAL LEVEL IT MAKES ME FEEL DEEPLY UNCOMFORTABLE...

MORAL LEVEL MY ASS, ODIN QUINCANNON'S BEEN A FULLY PAID-UP MEMBER SINCE NINETEEN FORTY-ONE. THEM FELLAS ARE HEROES AN' PATRIOTS AN' THAT'S ALL THERE IS TO IT.
ANYHOW, WHAT THE HELL'S GOT UP YOUR ASS? THOUGHT YOU'DA BEEN RIGHT BEHIND US, WITH ALL YOUR BIG HERO ADOLF HAD TO SAY 'BOUT NIGGERS AN' SUCH...
THERE IS *NO DIRECT EVIDENCE* THAT THE FÜHRER HELD RACIST VIEWS.

THERE *AIN'T*?
A VILE SMEAR ON THE PART OF HIS DETRACTORS. THAT ASPECT OF THE THIRD REICH HAS BEEN **BLOWN OUT OF ALL PROPORTION**.
BUT THEY GOT HIS SPEECHES ON TAPE! I FUCKIN' HEARD 'EM!
SPEECHES CAN BE *DUBBED*.

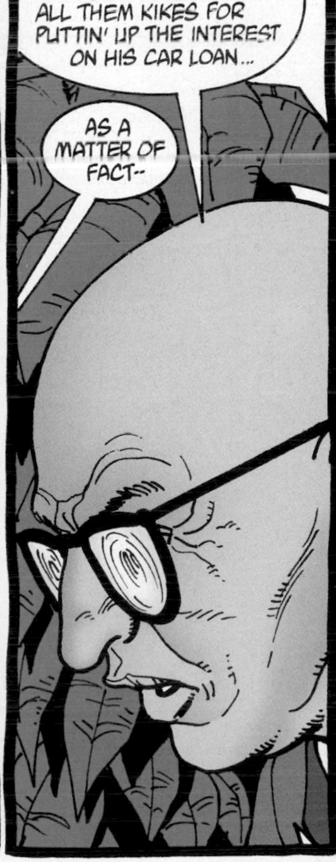
RIGHT, AN' I GUESS *MEIN KAMPF* WAS FORGED AN' HE GASSED ALL THEM KIKES FOR PUTTIN' UP THE INTEREST ON HIS CAR LOAN...
AS A MATTER OF FACT--

WE'RE GETTIN' OFF THE POINT, MISS OATLASH. NOW, THESE BOYS SAY THEY'RE GONNA TAKE A LOOK AT CUSTER--MAYBE TEST HIM A LITTLE BIT, SEE WHICH WAY HE JUMPS. I SAID I'D GO ALONG.
I GOT A FEELIN' IT'S GONNA BE WORTH IT...

I STOP QUINCANNON'S MEN FROM COMIN' INTO TOWN MUCH LONGER AN' THE SON OF A BITCH IS GONNA CUT UP ROUGH. AN' WHEN HE DOES THAT, I CAN'T AFFORD NO CRYIN' OR BACKIN' DOWN.
YOU FOLKS LIVE HERE. IT'S THE HOMES AN' BUSINESSES YOU OWN THAT MAKE SALVATION A COMMUNITY. I NEED TO BE CERTAIN 'FORE I TAKE ONE MORE STEP THAT THIS IS WHAT YOU WANT FROM ME, OR ELSE Y'ALL MAY AS WELL ELECT ANOTHER YES-MAN.
CLOSED

'KAY, SPEECH OVER. ANY QUESTIONS?

CORA?
HOW COME YOU INVITED THEM PEOPLE OVER THERE?

GREAT WHITE WHALE'S SORTA GOT HERSELF A POINT. WHEN THE LAW 'ROUND HERE EVER GIVE A DAMN 'BOUT FOLKS IN JOHN'S HOLLOW, ANYHOW?
YOU RECALL JIM BEWLEY ARRESTIN' A QUINCANNON MAN FOR TRESPASSIN' ON YOUR PROPERTY, MARVIN? 'CAUSE LAST WEEK ME AN' JESSE DID IT TWICE.
"JESSE", HUH?
er--
MAY I SAY SOME-THING?
THANK YOU.
PERHAPS MY VIEWS WILL LACK LEGITIMACY FOR SOME OF YOU. I WAS NOT BORN OR RAISED HERE. BUT IT SEEMS TO ME A VITAL POINT IS BEING OVER-LOOKED.
JUST BECAUSE SALVATION IS A TINY TOWN DOES NOT MEAN ITS PROBLEMS CAN BE IGNORED AS INSURMOUNT-ABLE. TO QUIT IN THE FACE OF DAUNTING ODDS--TO DISIN-TEGRATE IN OUR OWN APATHY AND PETTY DIFFERENCES BECAUSE WE CAN NO LONGER EVEN HOPE FOR VICTORY--WOULD BE A TERRIBLE MISTAKE.
AND, IF I MAY BE SO BOLD, COMPLETELY CONTRARY TO THE SPIRIT OF THE LAND IN WHICH WE LIVE.

WHAT'S HE SAYIN'?

HE'S SAYIN' Y'ALL ARE TEXANS.

AN' IT'S UP TO YOU TO DECIDE WHAT THAT'S GONNA MEAN HERE.
IS IT A BUNCHA FAT, BIGOTED REDNECKS GIVIN' IN TO CROOKS AN' CORPORATIONS, 'CAUSE THEY'RE TOO BIG TO FIGHT AN' WE KINDA LIKE 'EM IN CHARGE OF US ANYHOW? WAY THE YANKEES SEE US?
CLOSED

OR IS IT DRAWIN' A LINE IN THE DUST AN' SAYIN' *NO FURTHER*.

I'LL FIGHT THE SON OF A BITCH.
YOU JUST SAY YES OR NO.

THANKS FOR SPEAKIN' UP LIKE YOU DID.
IT WAS MY PLEASURE.

THE PEOPLE HERE HAVE BEEN DESERTED. THEY HAVE SEEN LOCAL GOVERNMENT, AND UP 'TIL NOW THE LAW, BOUGHT AND TAKEN FROM THEM. TO WHOM DO THEY PROTEST? TO WHOM DO THEY GO FOR PROTECTION?
BUT YOU SPOKE OF COMMUNITY. AND THAT IS THE KEY. A COMMON PURPOSE FORGED WITHIN, NOT SOUGHT WITHOUT.
ALL I DID WAS REMIND THEM OF THAT.

THERE IS A CERTAIN VIEW THAT AMERICANS ARE LAZY, SELFISH PEOPLE. THAT THEY TAKE THE EASY OPTION, AND IF THAT OPTION IS TO KNUCKLE UNDER, SO BE IT.
BUT I DO NOT CHOOSE TO SUBSCRIBE TO THAT VIEW.

NOT THAT I AM IMBUING THE GOOD FOLK OF SALVATION WITH THE SPIRIT OF THE FRONTIER, OR ANYTHING SO GRAND. ALL THEY HAD TO DO WAS SEND THEIR HERO OUT TO FIGHT ON THEIR BEHALF.

SHERIFF'S JOB, AIN'T IT?
'SIDES.

I AIN'T NO HERO, GUNTHER.

SHERIFF...
SHERIFF
TRIED IT ONCE.
BUT IT DIDN'T TAKE.

SHERIFF
LOOK!

SHERIFF
IT'S THAT DAMN NIGGER GAL, JUST LIKE I TOLD YOU! HE'S PROBABLY PUTTIN' IT TO HER! THERE'S YOUR GODDAMN MISCEGENATION RIGHT THERE!
CALM DOWN, ODIN. LET'S SEE WHAT HAPPENS.
OFF YOU GO, BOYS...

THE LIGHT WAS ON.
...
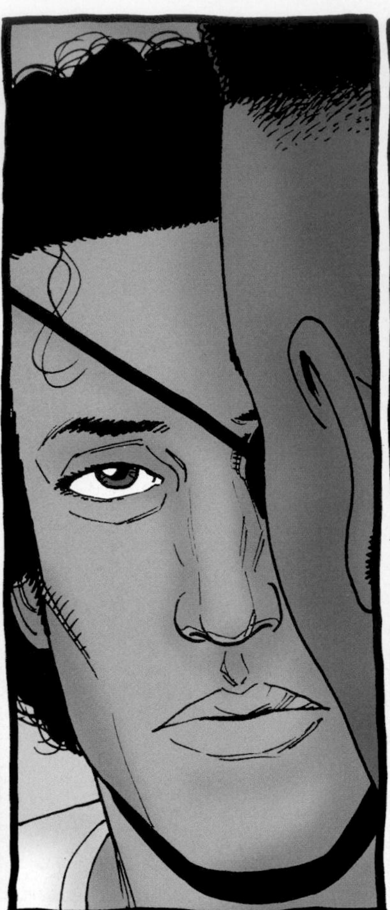

YOU'RE DRUNK.
IT'S BEEN KNOWN.

WHAT WAS THAT?

SOMEONE OUTSIDE...?
I DON'T--

SHIT!

ASSHOLES...

THAT'S HIM! WATCH HIM NOW! WATCH HIM!

...

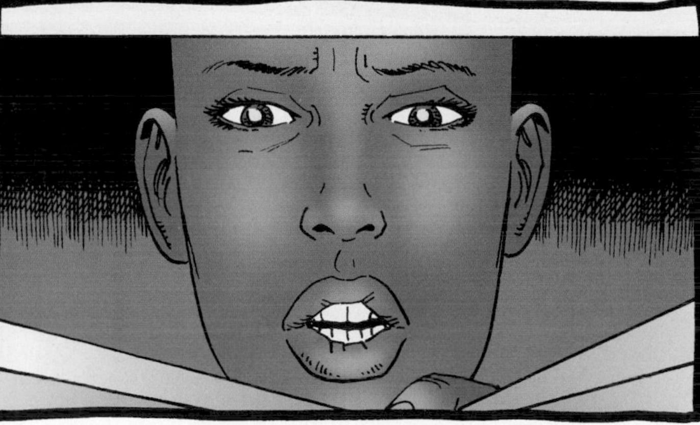

THINK WE GOT KLAN TROUBLE.

THINK SO?

OKAY, ODIN.

WE'LL
KILL HIM.

GLENN
FABRY
·90·

"Just the other day me an' Luke had a real good conversation about tractor pulls."

ABOUT LAST NIGHT...
KRAK

UH, YEAH. WELL I JUST APOLOGIZE LIKE HELL, CINDY. I AIN'T NEVER DONE NOTHIN' AS, UH, AS CRUDE AS THAT IN FRONT OF A LADY BEFORE.
I AIN'T GONNA GET SO DAMN DRUNK AGAIN, I PROMISE.

ACTUALLY... I MEANT BEFORE THAT. IN THE OFFICE.

OH.

WUFF-WUFF-WUFF.

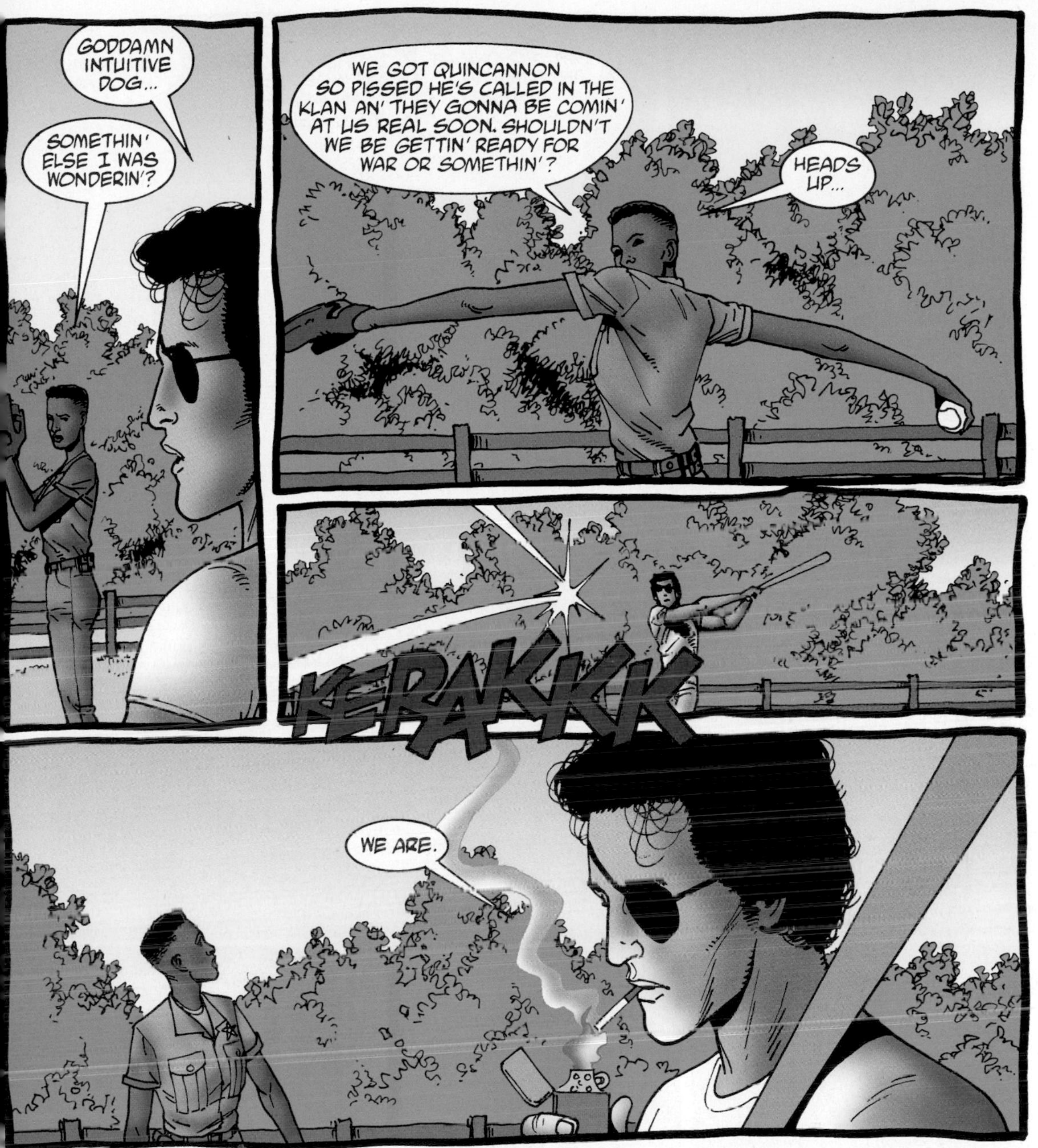

WHITE MISCHIEF

GARTH ENNIS - Writer **STEVE DILLON - Artist**

PAMELA RAMBO - Colorist **CLEM ROBINS - Letterer** **AXEL ALONSO - Editor**

PREACHER created by GARTH ENNIS and STEVE DILLON

PROBE THE ROOT...
UH, SORRY, MA'AM. MR. QUINCANNON AIN'T TO BE DISTURBED.

MA'AM, NO! HE SAID NO ONE AT ANY TIME! NOT IN HERE!
I'M HIS LAWYER, YOU IMBECILES. I CAN SEE HIM WHENEVER I WANT.
MA'AM, HE SAID ON PAIN OF DEATH--
OH, GET OUT OF THE WAY!

MR. QUIN-CANNON?
PROBE THE ROOT...

SIR...?

NIBBLE THE VEINS...

NIBBLE THE VEINS...

AND--

SAY THE NAME...

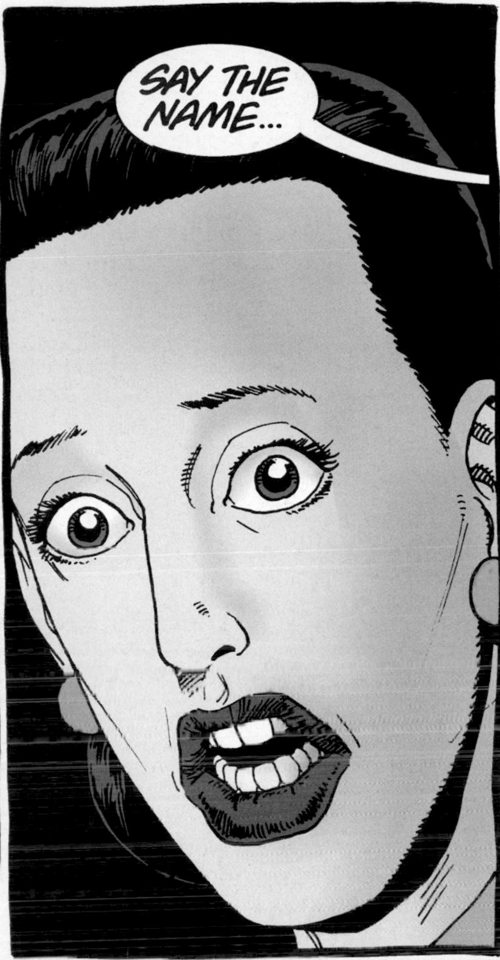
SAY THE NAME...

SAY THE NAME

AN' HAVE THE DAMN CAR CLEANED, TOO.
HELL'S WRONG WITH YOU, MISS OATLASH? YOU PREGNANT?
MUST'VE BEEN--SOME-THING I--ATE--

YEAH, PROBABLY PREGNANT. GODDAMN SPLIT-TAILS.

MR. QUINCANNON, REALLY, IF YOU INVOLVE THE KLAN IN THE MURDER OF A TOWN SHERIFF--HOWEVER DUBIOUS HIS POSITION--THERE'S NOTHING I CAN DO TO PROTECT YOU. I'M ASKING YOU FOR THE LAST TIME TO GIVE IT UP...
LIKE HELL!
IN THAT CASE YOU LEAVE ME NO CHOICE. I'M OFFICIALLY TENDERING MY RESIGNATION AS YOUR--
YEAH, SURE! THAT'LL BE THE DAY!
WHERE THE HELL YOU GONNA FIND ANOTHER OPPORTUNITY LIKE THIS, MISS OATLASH?
WHERE YOU GONNA FIND SOMEONE'LL HIRE A WOMAN TO PRACTICE CORPORATE LAW AT A LEVEL THIS HIGH? SOMEONE WITH THE KINDA MONEY CAN BUY A SENATOR? SOMEONE WILLIN' TO INDULGE YOUR GODDAMN HEATHEN NAZI PERVERSIONS, WITH A WORKFORCE DUMB ENOUGH TO VOLUNTEER FOR 'EM?
WHERE YOU GONNA FIND ANOTHER BOSS LIKE ODIN...?
CUSTER DIES TONIGHT, SO YOU BETTER JUST GET USED TO IT! YOU BE READY WITH THAT GODDAMN LEGAL MAGIC OF YOURS IN CASE THERE'S ANY SLIP-UPS, AN' LEAVE THE REST TO ME!

THIS IS SO COOL...!
LOOKS LIKE IT COULD SHOOT THE TITS OFF A MARTIAN. ONE YOU WANTED, RIGHT?
EXACTLY THE ONE I WANTED.
SO WHAT'S THE PLAN?
PLAN IS YOU, ME AN' YOUR NEW TOY GO OUT AN' TAKE IT TO 'EM, 'STEADA SITTIN' HERE WAITIN' TO GET HIT. YOU MAKE THAT CALL?
CALLED HOUSTON P.D., OL' GUY I KNOW UP THERE. SAID HE'D FAX US WHAT THEY HAD.
HERE WE GO...
SHERIFF
?

IT'S A TRAP.
BONE TREE
MIDNIGHT
A FRIEND
YEAH?
C'MON, REALLY, WHO'S GONNA WARN US? WE AIN'T GOT NO FRIENDS WOULD KNOW ABOUT THIS...
MAYBE NOT.
'CEPT I CAN THINK OF A DOZEN WAYS TO DRAW US IN BETTER'N THIS. WE'RE THE SHERIFF'S DEPARTMENT; ALL IT TAKES IS A CALL TO REPORT A INTRUDER OR SOMETHIN' AN' WE GO WHEREVER THEY WANT US.
...WHAT THE HELL'S A BONE TREE?
IT'S ON SAWYER ROAD ON THE WAY OUTTA TOWN. OL' BLASTED, DRIED-UP OAK STANDS APART FROM THE PINES.
I THINK I SEEN IT THE DAY I ARRIVED...
IT DIDN'T ALWAYS LOOK LIKE THAT. BACK IN THE FIFTIES IT WAS FIVE TIMES AS HIGH, HAD GREAT LONG BRANCHES AN' GREEN LEAVES ALL OVER IT.
HAD LYNCH ROPES HANGIN' FROM IT, TOO.

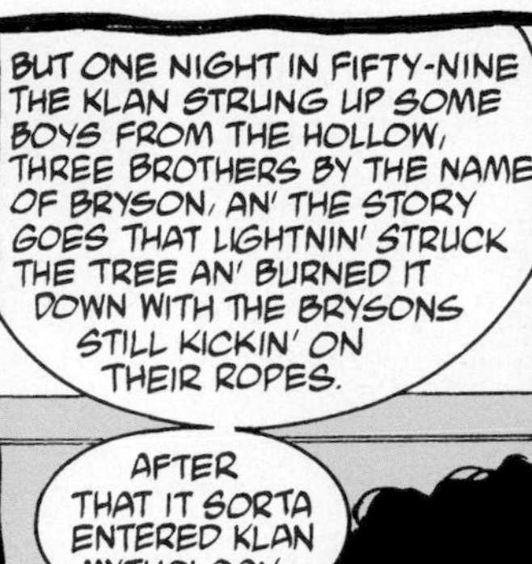
BUT ONE NIGHT IN FIFTY-NINE THE KLAN STRUNG UP SOME BOYS FROM THE HOLLOW, THREE BROTHERS BY THE NAME OF BRYSON, AN' THE STORY GOES THAT LIGHTNIN' STRUCK THE TREE AN' BURNED IT DOWN WITH THE BRYSONS STILL KICKIN' ON THEIR ROPES.

AFTER THAT IT SORTA ENTERED KLAN MYTHOLOGY.

"AS PROOF GOD HATED NIGGERS."

WHAT I KNOW OF THE LORD, I GUESS IT WOULDN'T SURPRISE ME.
IT'S SHITTY, CINDY.

IT'S THE SOUTH.

HAVE YOU SEEN THOSE TWO?
MM?

GUNSLINGERS, SHARING ONE LAST DRINK BEFORE DOING WHAT THEY'VE GOT TO DO. THAT'S WHAT THEY REMIND ME OF.
I WONDER WHAT THEY'RE UP TO...

ME TOO.
YOU THINK THERE'S SOMETHING BETWEEN THEM, GUNTHER?
I WOULD BE VERY SURPRISED IF THERE WAS NOT. BUT I IMAGINE JESSE IS CURRENTLY PREOCCUPIED WITH HIS FIRST LOVE.

WHICH IS?
HIS DUTY. I'VE KNOWN MEN LIKE HIM BEFORE.
MOSTLY SOLDIERS.

AND MOSTLY DEAD?
SOME OF THEM. OTHERS GROW OLD, FATHER A BROOD OF YOUNG, SPEND THEIR TIME WONDERING WHY THEY MADE IT HOME AND NOT THE BOYS WHO DIED BESIDE THEM.
THEY WONDER WHAT DIFFERENCE THEIR DUTY HAS MADE, BUT NEVER ONCE BETRAY IT.

THEIR MOTHERS ARE ALWAYS BEAUTIFUL, OF COURSE.

THOSE TWO'RE GETTIN' KINDA COZY, AIN'T THEY?
SO THEY ARE.
THAT BOTHER YOU?
I AIN'T SURE.
GUNTHER'S A SWELL GUY. BUT IT'S MY MOM, YOU KNOW?
GUNTHER'S A REAL NICE GUY...
DAMN, WHAT IS IT ABOUT TOUGH GUYS AN' THEIR MOTHERS? SHE'S THE ONE S'POSED TO WORRY ABOUT YOU.
HEY, IF SHE WAS MRS. HAHN, I GUESS THAT'D SORTA MAKE HIM YOUR DADDY, WOULDN'T IT?
NO IT WOULDN'T.

THERE'S MY LITTLE *HECTOR*...! I WON'T LET THE NASTY MEN TELL NO MORE MEXICAN JOKES!

'LESS THEY'RE FUNNY ONES, THAT IS! *HAAAAWW!*
ELEVEN-TWENTY. TIME TO VENTURE FORTH AN' DO BATTLE ON BEHALF OF THE GOOD FOLK OF SALVATION...

THEY MAY BE REDNECKS, BUT THEY'RE *OUR* REDNECKS.
YOU GOT THE PLAN STRAIGHT?
AYE-FIRMATIVE.

FIVE DOWN IS *ALAMO,* TOBY.
"REMEMBERED IN TEXAS"? REALLY?
YOU TWO LEAVING ALREADY?
YES MA'AM.

WELL...BE CAREFUL, WILL YOU? WHAT ARE YOU DOING OUT THIS LATE, ANYWAY?

WHAT WE GOTTA.
NIGHT, MOM.

WHERE'S ODIN?
GONE FOR A SHIT.

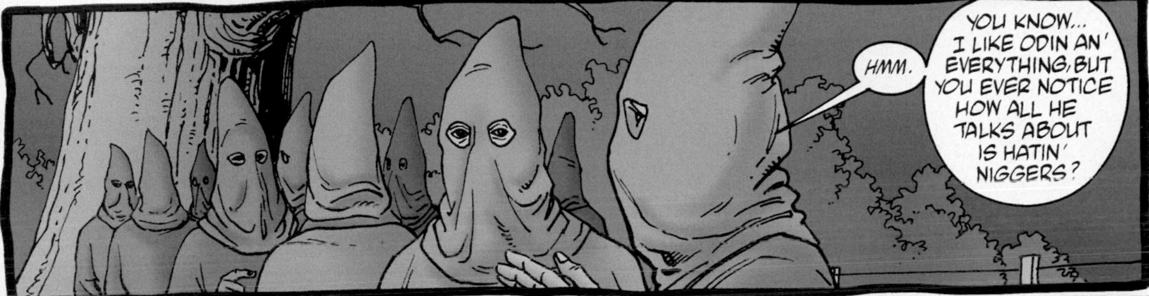
HMM.
YOU KNOW... I LIKE ODIN AN' EVERYTHING, BUT YOU EVER NOTICE HOW ALL HE TALKS ABOUT IS HATIN' NIGGERS?

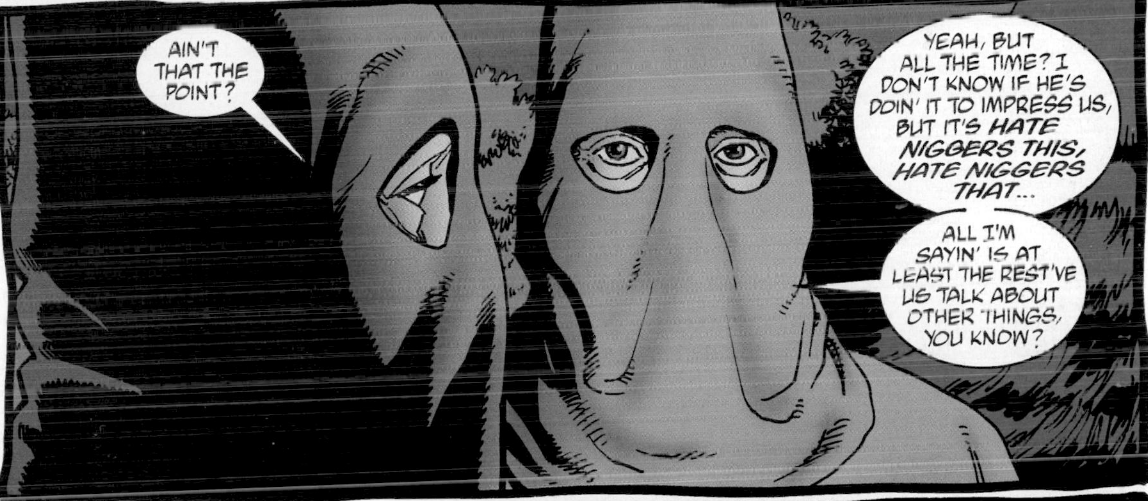
AIN'T THAT THE POINT?
YEAH, BUT ALL THE TIME? I DON'T KNOW IF HE'S DOIN' IT TO IMPRESS US, BUT IT'S *HATE NIGGERS THIS, HATE NIGGERS THAT...*
ALL I'M SAYIN' IS AT LEAST THE REST'VE US TALK ABOUT OTHER THINGS, YOU KNOW?

YEAH?
SURE. JUST THE OTHER DAY ME AN' LUKE HAD A REAL GOOD CONVERSATION ABOUT TRACTOR PULLS.
HEY, FELLAS!

BOY, I SURE DO HATE NIGGERS--
ENOUGHA THIS HORSESHIT.

MAN, I DON'T KNOW ABOUT THIS...
ALL WE GOTTA DO IS WATCH THE CAR.
YEAH, BUT THE KLAN, YOU KNOW? I KNEW A LOTTA BLACK BOYS IN THE NAVY AN' SOME OF THEM WEREN'T BAD GUYS...
NO SIR, DON'T LIKE THIS A BIT...
WHAT'RE YOU, SOME KINDA COMMUNIST?
WELL--
OH NO.
WE KNIGHTS OF THE WHITE DAWN ARE GATHERED HERE IN OUR PLACE OF POWER, TO DISCUSS THE KILLIN' OF THIS NIGGER-LOVIN' SHERIFF'S BEEN CAUSIN' BROTHER ODIN ALL THE TROUBLE...

...GUT THE SON OF A BITCH LIKE A GOD-DAMN CATFISH AN' MAKE THAT COON BITCH OF HIS LAP UP THE MESS...

NOW ODIN TELLS US THIS FELLA AIN'T EVEN BEEN PROPERLY APPOINTED --SO WE DO HIM AN' THE FEDS OR THE RANGERS LOOK INTO IT, THEY GONNA FIND SO MUCH SHIT WE GONNA BE LONG GONE BY THE TIME THEY FINISH.
'KAY, ANY QUESTIONS?

I GOT ONE.

YOU LADIES MAKE THEM DRESSES YOUR-SELVES OR YOU BUY 'EM FROM CRACKERS-R-US?

IT'S HIM!
MISTER--

YOU ARE FUCKIN' DEAD.

THREATENIN' AN OFFICER OF THE LAW. OH MY.

WE ABOUT TO DO A LOT MORE THAN THREATEN, ASSHOLE!

FUCK!

FIRST OFF, I THINK WE'LL HAVE THEM DUMB-LOOKIN' MASKS OFF...
FUCK YOU--

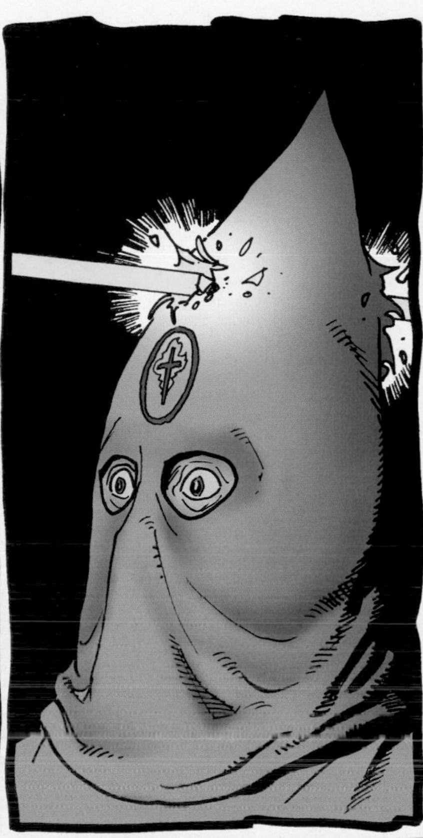

HOODS OFF, BOYS! NOW!

JESUS CHRIST.

WHY IS IT THE GREATEST CHAMPIONS OF THE WHITE RACE ALWAYS TURN OUT TO BE THE WORST EXAMPLES OF IT? YOU!
WH-WH-WH--?
WHERE THE FUCK IS YOUR CHIN?

I SWEAR.
ANYHOW... I COULD HAVE YOU TRASH SHOT DOWN HERE AN' NOW, SAVE US ALL A LOTTA TROUBLE. OR HELL, YOU KNOW WHAT I COULD DO? I COULD **TELL YOU** TO GET THE HELL OUTTA HERE AN' GO BE BETTER PEOPLE, AN' **YOU WOULD...**
YEAH, **RIGHT--!**

SHIT YOURSELF.

BUT I AIN'T GONNA DO EITHER'VE THEM THINGS, 'CAUSE THAT AIN'T WHERE MY AUTHORITY COMES FROM IN THIS INSTANCE.

SO WHERE DOES IT COME FROM, EXACTLY?

WHY, FROM MY BEIN' A LAW OFFICER OF THE GREAT STATE OF TEXAS. WHICH MEANS I CAN KICK YOUR REDNECK ASSES HALF TO DEATH AN' ALL YOU CAN DO IS ASK FOR MORE.

SO YOU CAN KICK OUR ASSES, HUH?
ONE AT A TIME OR ALL TOGETHER, TURD-BREATH.

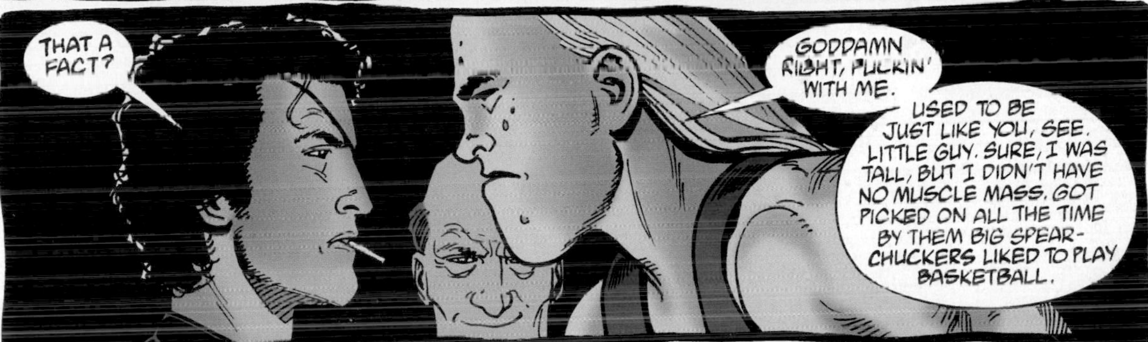

THEN I SAW A ADVERT IN *BEEFCAKE MAGAZINE*, SHOWIN' THIS BOOK 'BOUT BUILDIN' MUSCLE MASS. WROTE OFF AN' GOT THE FREE STEROID COURSE CAME WITH THE HARDBACK EDITION. LEARNED SOME KINDA CHINK ZEN THING, 'BOUT FOCUSIN' YORE WILL ON YORE BODY WHEN YOU WORK OUT.

BUILT MYSELF THIGHS OF IRON.

ARMS OF STEEL.

PECS OF *ROCK*.

BALLS OF MUSH.

WAAAAAHH!!

I COULD KILL A THOUSAND OF YOU ASSHOLES, OR ORDER YOU TO GO TO HELL, AN' A THOUSAND MORE'D GROW FROM THE SAME OL' SHIT. SO I'M GONNA DO LIKE YOU DO: I'M GONNA MAKE *FEAR* MY WEAPON. EVERYBODY READY?
NOW FEAR THIS:

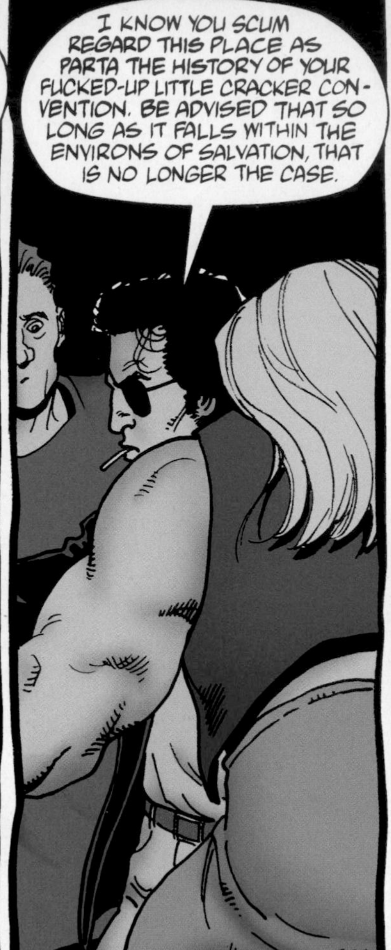
I KNOW YOU SCUM REGARD THIS PLACE AS PARTA THE HISTORY OF YOUR FUCKED-UP LITTLE CRACKER CONVENTION. BE ADVISED THAT SO LONG AS IT FALLS WITHIN THE ENVIRONS OF SALVATION, THAT IS NO LONGER THE CASE.

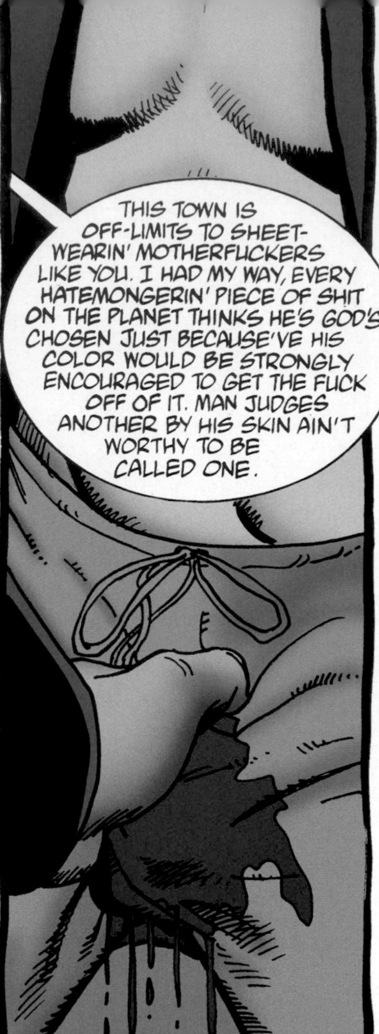
THIS TOWN IS OFF-LIMITS TO SHEET-WEARIN' MOTHERFUCKERS LIKE YOU. I HAD MY WAY, EVERY HATEMONGERIN' PIECE OF SHIT ON THE PLANET THINKS HE'S GOD'S CHOSEN JUST BECAUSE'VE HIS COLOR WOULD BE STRONGLY ENCOURAGED TO GET THE FUCK OFF OF IT. MAN JUDGES ANOTHER BY HIS SKIN AIN'T WORTHY TO BE CALLED ONE.

NOW YOU GATHER UP YOUR GARBAGE--INCLUDIN' BRAINS OF SHIT HERE--AN' YOU GO ON HOME TO YOUR FAT OL' KLAN SOWS. AN' THE NEXT TIME YOU'RE PLANNIN' SOMETHIN' STUPID YOU PRAY TO FUCKIN' JESUS SOMEONE LIKE ME DON'T TAKE A INTEREST. WE *ARE* OUT THERE.
MESSAGE ENDS.

HEY, FUCK YOU, CUSTER! YOU DON'T TELL US HOW TO LIVE, NOT 'TIL YOU SEEN YOUR WAY OF LIFE GETTIN' SWALLOWED UP BY GODDAMN ALIEN CULTURES!

HUH?
OH YEAH, I HEARD THAT'N BEFORE. "YOU AIN'T BEEN WHERE WE HAVE, SO HOW CAN YOU GIVE US SHIT FOR ACTIN' LIKE SAVAGES?" FUCK YOU...
YOU COME ALONG WITH ME, BOSS MAN. WE STILL GOT SOME MATTERS TO DISCUSS.

AAAAAOWW...!

WELL FUCK HIM, HUH, FELLAS? WE AIN'T LETTIN' HIM GET AWAY WITH THAT, RIGHT?
LET'S KICK HIS NIGGER-LOVIN' ASS!

FELLAS?
FELLAS...!

FELLAAAAAAHHS!!

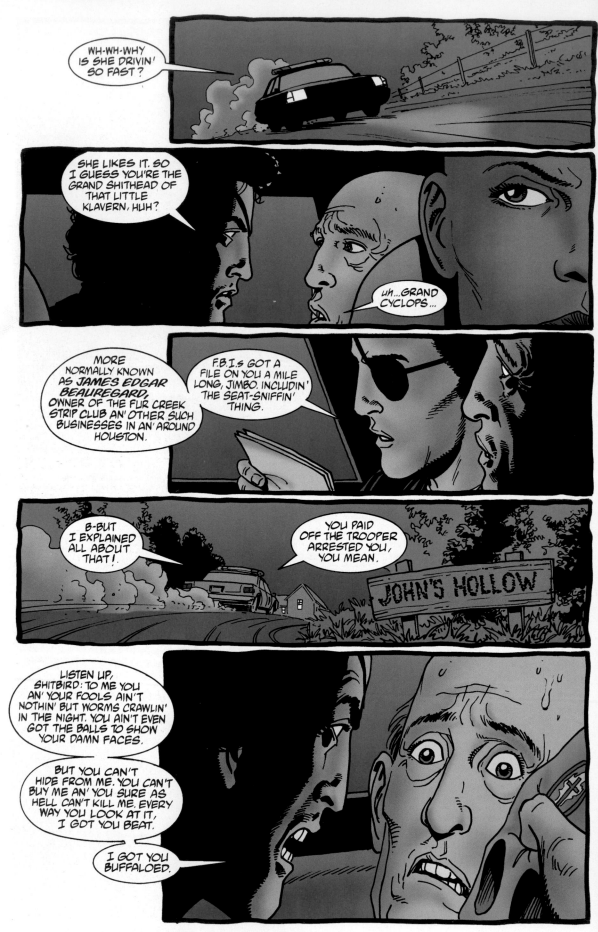

WH-WH-WHY IS SHE DRIVIN' SO FAST?

SHE LIKES IT. SO I GUESS YOU'RE THE GRAND SHITHEAD OF THAT LITTLE KLAVERN, HUH?
uh...GRAND CYCLOPS...

MORE NORMALLY KNOWN AS **JAMES EDGAR BEAUREGARD,** OWNER OF THE FUR CREEK STRIP CLUB AN' OTHER SUCH BUSINESSES IN AN' AROUND HOUSTON.
F.B.I.s GOT A FILE ON YOU A MILE LONG, JIMBO. INCLUDIN' THE SEAT-SNIFFIN' THING.

B-BUT I EXPLAINED ALL ABOUT THAT!
YOU PAID OFF THE TROOPER ARRESTED YOU, YOU MEAN.
JOHN'S HOLLOW

LISTEN UP, SHITBIRD: TO ME YOU AN' YOUR FOOLS AIN'T NOTHIN' BUT WORMS CRAWLIN' IN THE NIGHT. YOU AIN'T EVEN GOT THE BALLS TO SHOW YOUR DAMN FACES.

BUT YOU CAN'T HIDE FROM ME. YOU CAN'T BUY ME AN' YOU SURE AS HELL CAN'T KILL ME. EVERY WAY YOU LOOK AT IT, I GOT YOU BEAT.

I GOT YOU BUFFALOED.

NOW GET THE FUCK OUT!!
WHA-- NO--

AAAAAAHHH!!

AAAAH! AWHH! AAAHH!

LAWSY ME AN' OTHER SUCH UTTERANCES. A FELLA ATTIRED IN THE MANNER OF A WELL-KNOWN RACIST ORGANIZATION.

"PECKERWOOD WALKS TO HOUSTON NAKED."
NOW SPORTS.

SO WHAT--
HNNNHH--
YOU GONNA DO--
GUHHH--
NOW, MR. QUINCANNON--?

THROW A BARBECUE.

I'M GONNA BURN THAT FUCKIN' TOWN CLEAR DOWN TO THE GROUND.

GLENN FABRY 98

"Here's everythin' you fought to protect gone in a fuckin' instant! Here it comes!"

YOU GOT A TWO-GALLON KEG OF NAPALM BEHIND EACH BUILDIN'. DETONATORS'RE STUCK ON WITH STRIPS OF C4.
THAT I LIKE THE SOUND OF...

TRANSMITTER. PRESS THE TOP BUTTON ONCE AN' THE FIRST CHARGE GOES UP, THE ONE AT THE SHERIFF'S OFFICE LIKE YOU SAID. EACH SUCCESSIVE PUSH OF THAT BUTTON WILL SET OFF ANOTHER ONE, UP TO A TOTAL OF TWENTY-THREE.
AN' YOU'RE IN A HURRY, THE SECOND BUTTON'LL DO 'EM ALL AT ONCE.

AN' YOU COVERED EVERY PLACE ON THE MAIN STREET? DIDN'T NOBODY SEE YOU?
TIME OF NIGHT I DID IT, LOCAL FUCKS'RE EITHER SNORIN' OR RUTTIN'. WEREN'T NO BIG THING.

SO YOU'RE SURE THIS IS ALL WIRED UP OKAY? 'CAUSE THE LAST BOY OL' ODIN BROUGHT IN, THE JOB HE DID WASN'T WORTH A HANDFULLA ASSFLAKES...

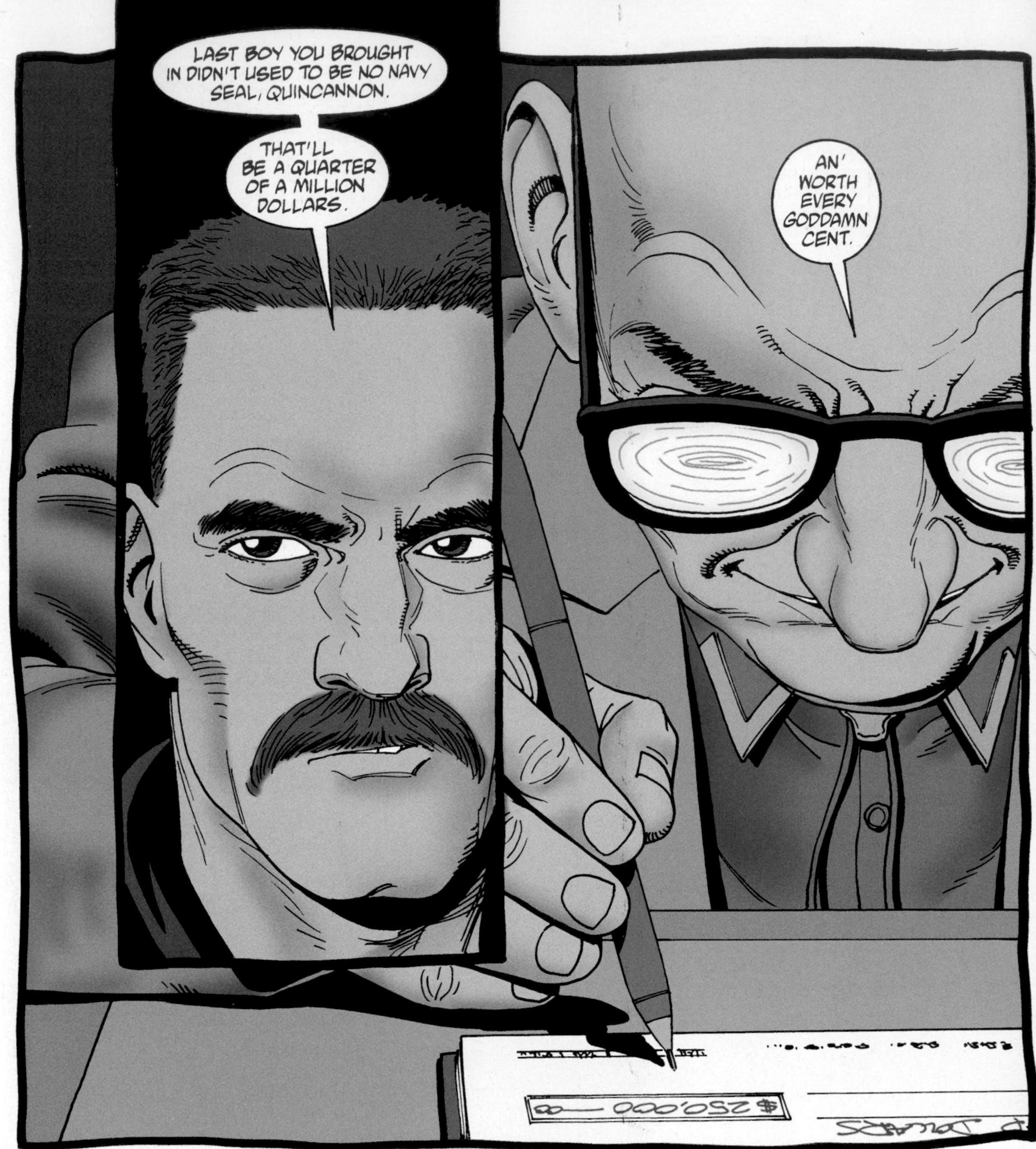

JESSE GET YOUR GUN

GARTH ENNIS - Writer **STEVE DILLON - Artist**

PAMELA RAMBO - Colorist **CLEM ROBINS - Letterer** **AXEL ALONSO - Editor**

PREACHER created by GARTH ENNIS and STEVE DILLON

DAYS TURN INTO WEEKS AN' THE WEEKS TURN INTO MONTHS, HUH, SKEET?
WUFF...
THE MOST PEACEFUL MONTHS IN THE RECENT HISTORY OF SALVATION, IN FACT. I TRUST THE GOOD SHERIFF WILL ALLOW ME TO BUY HIM A BEER?
JUST THE ONE. I GOT ALL THIS WHISKEY TO DRINK 'FORE I START WORK.

HERE'S TO YOU, GUNTHER.
AND TO YOU. THE JOB IS AS DEMANDING AS EVER, THEN?

HELL, EVER SINCE QUINCANNON BACKED OFF AN' HIS BOYS LEFT FOR HOUSTON, WORST WE GOTTA HANDLE IS CORA TINES AN' HER FOOLS.
SAY, TOBY? YOU GOT CORN IN YOUR NOSE AGAIN.

OH THANKS, DUDE.
AIN'T NOTHIN'.
CORA'S HARMLESS. 'CEPT I DO HEAR IT SAID MEN HAVE NEVER BEEN SEEN AGAIN...

CORN IN HIS NOSE?
EVERY COUPLE HOURS OL' TOBE REMEMBERS HE'S GONNA BE A DADDY COME DECEMBER. HAS TO DROP EVERYTHIN' AN' RUN OUTSIDE AN' THROW UP.

MM.
I DON'T THINK QUINCANNON IS FINISHED WITH US YET.

NOPE.
AND THAT'S WHY YOU'RE STILL WITH US, ISN'T IT?

YOU DIDN'T TAKE THIS JOB TO DRINK WHISKEY AND LISTEN TO THE CRICKETS ON PLEASANT SUMMER EVENINGS. IF OUR TROUBLE HERE WERE REALLY OVER, YOU'D HAVE GONE A LONG TIME AGO.
YOU SIGNED UP TO BEAT THE BAD GUY.

COULD BE. BUT HE AIN'T DONE YET, NOT BY A LONG WAY. I SEEN FELLAS LIKE HIM BEFORE; HE'S OUT AT THAT PLANTA HIS AN' US BEATIN' HIM AS BAD AS WE DID IS EATIN' AT HIS GUT LIKE A *CANCER*.
NO, ONLY ONE WAY THIS IS GONNA END.

THESE ARE ON THE HOUSE.
WAY *WHAT'S* GOING TO END?
OH, MAN. WAY THIS IS GOIN', CRIME IN SALVATION'S GONNA RUN RAMPANT...
NOTHIN', MOM.
I'LL BET. YOU BE CAREFUL, JESSE. I DON'T WANT YOU GOING AROUND THINKING YOU'RE THE LONE RANGER.

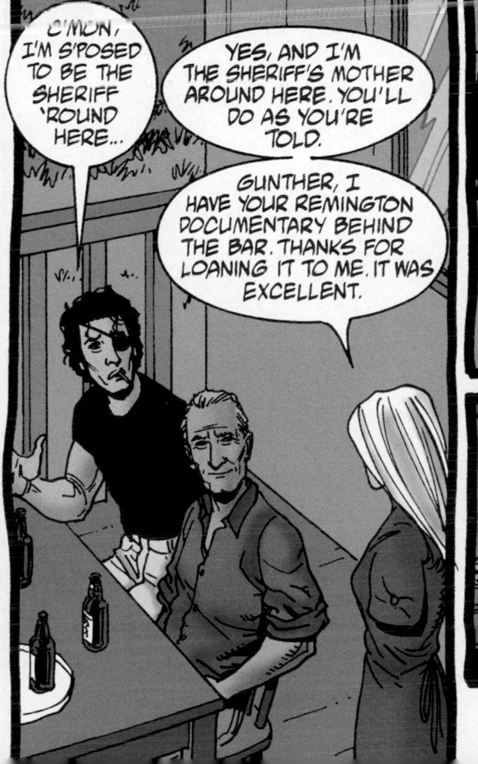
C'MON, I'M S'POSED TO BE THE SHERIFF 'ROUND HERE...
YES, AND I'M THE SHERIFF'S MOTHER AROUND HERE. YOU'LL DO AS YOU'RE TOLD.
GUNTHER, I HAVE YOUR REMINGTON DOCUMENTARY BEHIND THE BAR. THANKS FOR LOANING IT TO ME. IT WAS EXCELLENT.

JESUS...
MY PLEASURE. REMIND ME TO SHOW YOU MY SET OF HIS PRINTS ON THURSDAY NIGHT.
YES, WHAT ARE YOU COOKING FOR ME?

EVENIN', BOSS!
HEY, CINDY. ALL QUIET ON THE WESTERN FRONT?

YOU KNOW IT. WAY THINGS ARE AROUND HERE, TWO OF US'LL HAVE TO DO SOMETHIN' OURSELVES TO SPICE THINGS UP.
I'M GOIN' OVER TO KILKANE FOR CHINESE FOOD. YOU WANT SOME?

THAT'D BE REAL GOOD. 'LONG AS YOU DON'T START SHOWIN' OFF WITH THEM DAMN CHOPSTICKS AGAIN, 'KAY?
THEN IT'S A DATE. SEE YOU IN THE OFFICE IN A HOUR OR TWO.

WHAT?

GODDAMMIT...!
JUST GOOD FRIENDS, OKAY?
MORE FOOL YOU, THEN. SHE LIKES YOU MORE THAN FRIENDS, AND YOU KNOW IT.
DON'T YOU LIKE GIRLS?

HEH! GUNTHER, I GET DOWN ON MY KNEES EVERY MORNIN' AN' GIVE ETERNAL THANKS FOR THE EXISTENCE OF GIRLS IN A OTHERWISE POINTLESS UNIVERSE...
OF COURSE.

SO WHAT'S STOPPING YOU?

MONEY ALWAYS WINS, MISS OATLASH.

THAT'S WHAT BOYS LIKE THAT CUSTER FELLA NEVER DO GET. I OFFERED TO PAY HIM AN' PAY HIM WELL, BUT HE CHOSE TO FIGHT ME. TOOK ONE LOOK AT OL' ODIN AN' FIGURED HE COULD WIN, YES SIR.
BUT IT AIN'T WHAT YOU LOOK LIKE, OR HOW TOUGH YOU ARE, OR ANY-THIN' ELSE 'CEPT WHAT YOU CAN *AFFORD*...

AIN'T GOT WHAT IT TAKES TO WIN? NO BIGGIE. JUST GO ON OUT AN' BUY IT.
HELL, I RECALL ME AN' SOME FRIENDS SAVED UP AN' BOUGHT OURSELVES A PRESIDENT ONCE.

REALLY?
YEAH, 'CEPT THE DUMB BASTARD MADE A MESS OF IT. ROYALLY SCREWED THE POOCH.
WAY THIS COUNTRY WORKS, MISS OATLASH. MONEY GREASIN' THE WHEELS. DON'T LET NOBODY TELL YOU DIFFERENT.

YOU'D BETTER HOPE SO, MR. QUINCANNON. PRODUCTIVITY AT THE PLANT HAS DROPPED AWAY TO ALMOST NOTHING. ANOTHER DOZEN MEN LEFT THIS AFTERNOON.
BIG FUCKIN' DEAL, SO WE LOST A FEW MONTHS' TURNOVER. THEY'LL COME BACK WHEN CUSTER'S GONE, YOU JUST SEE IF THEY--

THERE'S STILL A GUARD ON SHED NUMBER FOUR, AIN'T THERE? THE COLDSTORE?

THE COLDSTORE... OH, YES. AS PER YOUR SPECIFIC INSTRUCTIONS.
GODDAMN RIGHT. AIN'T NOBODY GOES IN THERE 'CEPT ODIN.

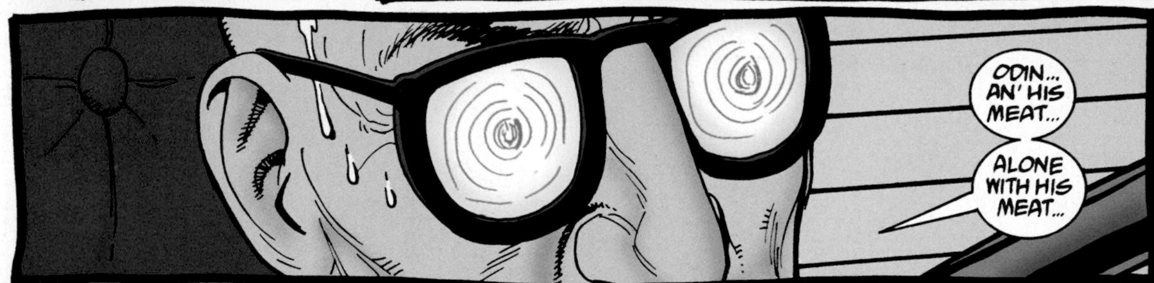
ODIN... AN' HIS MEAT...
ALONE WITH HIS MEAT...

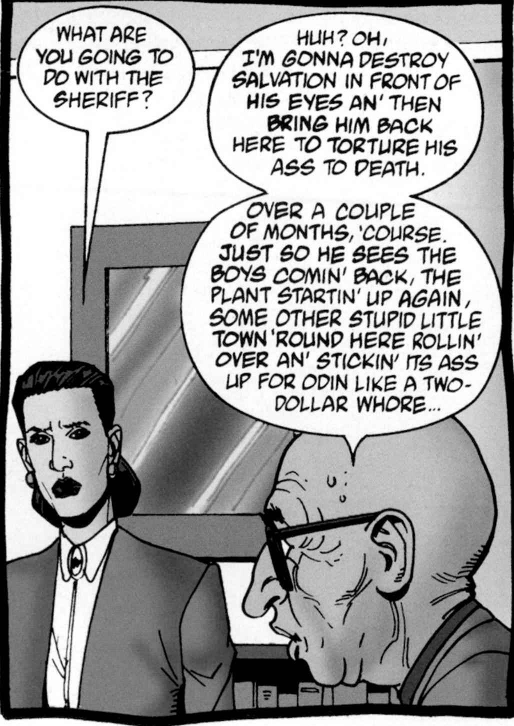
WHAT ARE YOU GOING TO DO WITH THE SHERIFF?
HUH? OH, I'M GONNA DESTROY SALVATION IN FRONT OF HIS EYES AN' THEN BRING HIM BACK HERE TO TORTURE HIS ASS TO DEATH.
OVER A COUPLE OF MONTHS, 'COURSE. JUST SO HE SEES THE BOYS COMIN' BACK, THE PLANT STARTIN' UP AGAIN, SOME OTHER STUPID LITTLE TOWN 'ROUND HERE ROLLIN' OVER AN' STICKIN' ITS ASS UP FOR ODIN LIKE A TWO-DOLLAR WHORE...

JUST SO HE KNOWS HE NEVER MADE NO DIFFERENCE AFTER ALL.
AND YOU EXPECT JE-- SHERIFF CUSTER TO SIT STILL FOR THIS?

MISS OATLASH, I 'SPECT THE SON OF A BITCH TO COME ALONG IN HERE MEEK AS A LAMB.
EVEN AS WE SPEAK, STEPS ARE BEIN' TAKEN TO ENSURE IT.

Y'ALL NEED ANY HELP?
DOH--

BUDD YUH DUH, BIDTH.
GUB YUH HUNDTH UHN THUD UN GUD UHDA THUH KUHH. THLUHLY.
WHAT?

HE, HE SAID KEEP YOUR HANDS IN SIGHT AND GET OUT OF THE--
NAD FUGGIG THYERIFF DUD THUZZA MUH!

HUH?
THUDDUB! HUNDTH UHNA UHNUH UHH! GUDD UHNUH TRUNG!
uh... MAYBE IF I DID THE TALKING...

YEAH, OR GOT THIS MOTHERFUCKER SOME SUBTITLES--
THUDDUB!

A FELLA COULD GO CRAZY WAITIN' FOR YA TA LIGHT THAT THING. **HERE!**

AN' YA **KNOW** WHAT'S STOPPIN' YA. IT AIN'T GOT NOTHIN' TA **DO** WITH HER.

IT'S THE **OTHER** LITTLE GAL, **AIN'T IT?**

THAT... AIN'T SOMETHIN' I'M REAL KEEN ON THINKIN' 'BOUT RIGHT NOW...
PILGRIM, THERE'S THINGS A MAN'S JUST GOTTA...CHOKE DOWN WHETHER THEY STICK IN HIS CRAW OR NOT. THINGS YA CAN'T HIDE FROM NOR PUT BEHIND YA. I THOUGHT YA KNEW THAT.
BUT LATELY, YA...HELL, YA GOT YERSELF A COZY LITTLE PLACE WITH YER MOM AN' ALL THESE NEW FOLKS, AN' YA BEEN DOIN' JUST WHAT YA GOTTA AN' NOT ONE INCH MORE. YA BIN TREADIN' WATER. AN' THAT AIN'T WHAT I EXPECT FROM YA!
THAT LOONY FELLA IN THE DESERT--YA AIN'T TAKEN WHAT HE SAID TA HEART, HAVE YA?
"FUCK YOU TO THE WORLD"?
AH, THAT KINDA GODDAMN PROFANITY NEVER DID NO ONE NO GOOD...
WELL, THERE WAS A SHORT WHILE WHEN JOHNNY LEE WOMBAT MADE A KINDA SENSE. BE LYIN' IF I SAID OTHERWISE.
BUT I THOUGHT I PUT THAT BEHIND ME. I'M DOIN' WHAT I CAN TO HELP THESE FOLKS AN' STOP THAT LITTLE GOBLIN MESSIN' UP THEIR TOWN...
THAT'S EXACTLY WHAT I'M TALKIN' ABOUT, GODDAMMIT! YA SHOULDA PUT THE RUNT IN THE GROUND A LONG TIME AGO AN' GONE BACK TA THE JOB YA TOOK ON IN THE BEGINNIN'!
YER TREADIN' WATER!!
WELL, THAT SURE IS A HARSH JUDGMENT.

HELL, PILGRIM.
YA KNOW ANY OTHER KIND WORTH A DAMN?

NO.
NO I DON'T.

SEE... BEFORE THE VALLEY, THE BOMB AN' ALL, I KNEW IT'D GET BAD. I JUST NEVER IMAGINED HOW BAD.
THAT'S WHY I DON'T FEEL RIGHT 'BOUT GOIN' BACK TO ALLA THAT. 'CAUSE THEY'RE A PARTA IT. CASSIDY... AN'...

OH SHIT, THE THOUGHTA HER WITH ANYONE ELSE AT ALL-- AFTER EVERYTHING WE DID AN' SAID AN' SWORE, THAT JUST 'BOUT CUTS THE GODDAMN HEART OUTTA ME.
THAT RIGHT THERE IS WHAT'S STICKIN' IN MY CRAW. THE THOUGHTA THEM TOGETHER LIKE THAT, NOT A MONTH AFTER WHAT HAPPENED.

'CAUSE TULIP'S...
IF I'M TO FINISH THIS THING I GOTTA BE AT MY BEST. AN' WITHOUT HER I'M NO MORE'N A DAMN SHADOW.
WITHOUT THAT GIRL I'M NOTHIN'.

THEN I GUESS YA KNOW WHAT YA GOTTA DO, DON'T YA?

I GUESS SO.

WUFF! WARRF! WARRFFF!
YEAH, I KNOW. STORM'S COMIN' IN.
CINDY, WHERE ARE YOU, GIRL? ME AN' YOU GOTTA HAVE OURSELVES A TALK...
FOR YOU.
NO... IT ACTUALLY SOUNDS LIKE--
CINDY?
DAMN!!
SHERIFF
Heh, heh, heh, heh, heh...
QUINCANNON?!
YOU LITTLE FUCKIN' COCKSUCKER, WHAT THE HELL ARE YOU DOIN'?
WHY, I'M THROWIN' A PARTY, SHERIFF. AN' YOU DON'T WANT THE RESTA SALVATION NAPALMED AN' YORE NIGGER WHORE FUCKED AN' BUTCHERED, YOU BETTER GET YORE ASS ALONG TO IT.
HERE'S WHAT YOU DO:

WE'RE MEANT TO KILL HER AFTERWARDS? SINCE WHEN?
BOHZ THED THO.
BOHZ HADETH NIGGERTH.
IT'S MUTUAL--
FUCK!
THYID!
DYETHUTH CHRYTH! GEDDUB, YUH UHZHULL!
NA BOHZ UTH GUHNUH KUHL UHTH!

WARRROOOOWW! RRROOOWWW!

SKEETER, DUDE, YOU GOTTA CHILL, MAN! HE SAID YOU HAD TO STAY, YOU MIGHT GET HURT OUT THERE!

SHERIFF SAYS THE WHOLE PLACE IS WIRED...

THAT FUCKIN' QUINCANNON, SWEAR TO GOD...

SAID IF WE TRY RUNNIN' HE'LL SEND UP THE ENTIRE DAMN TOWN...

CHRISTINA, WHAT ARE YOU DOING?

GOOD GOD, CHRISTINA! HE SAID HE'D HANDLE IT! WE'RE NOT SUPPOSED TO FOLLOW HIM!

THE HELL WITH THAT. I LOST HIM ONCE AND I'M NEVER LOSING HIM AGAIN.

HE'S MY SON! HE'S OUR SHERIFF!

WHO'S WITH ME?!

COMES A PISSANT...

HOWDY!

I KNEW THIS DAY WOULD COME.

MINUTE YOU FLUNG ODIN THROUGH THAT WINDOW, I KNEW THE TIME'D COME I'D HAVE YOU WHERE I WANTED YOU. WHERE I COULD *CRUSH YOU*.
THAT'S WHAT ALWAYS HAPPENS, SEE. FELLA FUCKS WITH ODIN QUINCANNON, SOONER OR LATER HE LEARNS TO REGRET IT.
USUALLY 'ROUND 'BOUT THE TIME HE GETS HIT SO HARD HE DISAPPEARS UP HIS OWN FORESKIN, YES SIR...

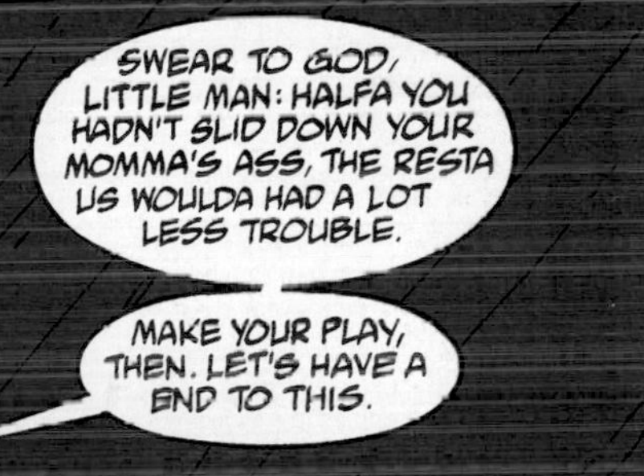
SWEAR TO GOD, LITTLE MAN: HALFA YOU HADN'T SLID DOWN YOUR MOMMA'S ASS, THE RESTA US WOULDA HAD A LOT LESS TROUBLE.
MAKE YOUR PLAY, THEN. LET'S HAVE A END TO THIS.

WATCH YORE MOUTH! YOU WATCH YORE MOUTH, HEAR?
I'M CALLIN' THE SHOTS HERE, BOY--I'M THE ONE WITH HIS FINGER ON THE GODDAMN BUTTON! AN' DON'T YOU TRY THAT FUCKIN' MOJO SHIT I SEEN YOU DO, 'CAUSE SOON AS I SEE THEM EYES GO RED I WILL BY GOD PUSH IT!
AN' DON'T FORGET THE NIGGER. ANYTHING HAPPENS TO ME SO I AIN'T AROUND TO GIVE THE WORD, WELL...
HOW DO I KNOW YOU GOT MY DEPUTY, EXACTLY?
Heh! ONE SECOND--

IT'S ME. YOU TWO ASSHOLES GOT THAT BLACK BITCH THERE?

UH--YESSIR, WE GOT HER... SHE JUST CAN'T COME TO THE PHONE RIGHT NOW, IS ALL...
AN' WHY NOT, GODDAMMIT?
WELL WE--UH--WE HIT HER KINDA HARD WHEN WE GOT HER, SEE, AN' SHE AIN'T QUITE WOKE UP YET...

WELL, SOON'S SHE DOES YOU CALL ME--
BA-DAM
FUCK!
WHAT THE HELL WAS THAT?
THAT-- THAT WAS THUNDER, SIR--

I AIN'T SO SURE YOU GOT SHIT, QUINCANNON.
OH YEAH?

I GOT THIS, MOTHERFUCKER! MATTER OF FACT, YOU TAKE A REAL GOOD LOOK AT YOUR PRECIOUS LITTLE TOWN DOWN THERE! 'CAUSE I TELL YOU, IT'S GONNA BE YORE LAST!

SON OF A BITCH--
KEEP YORE DISTANCE! REMEMBER THE NIGGER!
NO, SALVATION'S GONNA BURN, IT'S GONNA FRY LIKE FUCKIN' BACON IN FRONTA YORE EYES AN' AIN'T NOTHIN' YOU CAN DO TO STOP IT! AN' THEN YOU, ME AN' THE JUNGLE BUNNY'RE GONNA HAVE OURSELVES A PARTY YOU'LL NEVER FORGET!

SO HERE IT COMES! WATCH AN' LEARN, YOU FUCK! HERE'S EVERYTHIN' YOU FOUGHT TO PROTECT GONE IN A FUCKIN' INSTANT!
HERE IT COMES!!

WHAT... THE HELL...?

WELL, THAT WAS PRETTY FUCKIN' LUCKY...!

NUHHHHHH
JESUS!!

GEDDAWAY! DON FUGGIN TUDGE ME!
SHIT, YOU GOT IT--
GEDDAWAY!!
HECTOR!!
OH, FUCK--!
?
NO! NOT MY POOR LITTLE HECTOR! BABY, HECTOR, DON'T YOU DIE ON ME!
GUNTHER, YOU HOLD THIS JACKET HERE, KEEP PRESSURE ON IT!
THE NEAREST HOSPITAL'S IN KILKANE--

OH HECTOR, I'M SORRY I CALLED YOU A DUMB BEANER...
WE GOTTA GET HIM OVER THERE NOW--
HEY, WHERE'S THE EVIL DUDE?
HUH? SHIT!
ASSHOLE MIGHT STILL HAVE CINDY. I'M GONNA HAVE TO GO GET HIM.
ALONE?
YEAH, ALONE!
I TOLD YOU FOLKS TO STAY OUTTA THIS AN' I MEANT IT, GODDAMMIT! NOW Y'ALL GET THIS BOY OUTTA HERE AN' LEAVE THAT PIGFUCKER TO ME, AN' BY GOD I WILL FINISH THIS ONCE AN' FOR ALL!
WUFF!
JESUS! 'KAY, YOU COME IF YOU FUCKIN' WANT...

WUFF!
MM.

FAR AS YOU GO, BUDDY. THIS ASSHOLE'S GONE CRAZIER'N A LIZARD WITH A SUNSTROKE AN' I DON'T WANT YOU STOPPIN' A BULLET...

GUHH--!

UHN

NOW, MY DARLING. MY SUPERMAN.
YOU ARE MY ARYAN DREAM, JESSE CUSTER. MY ULTIMATE PHYSICAL IDEAL. OUR JOINING WILL BE A TRIUMPH OF NATIONAL SOCIALIST PURITY.
YOU ARE ALMOST PERFECT, DARLING...

ALMOST.

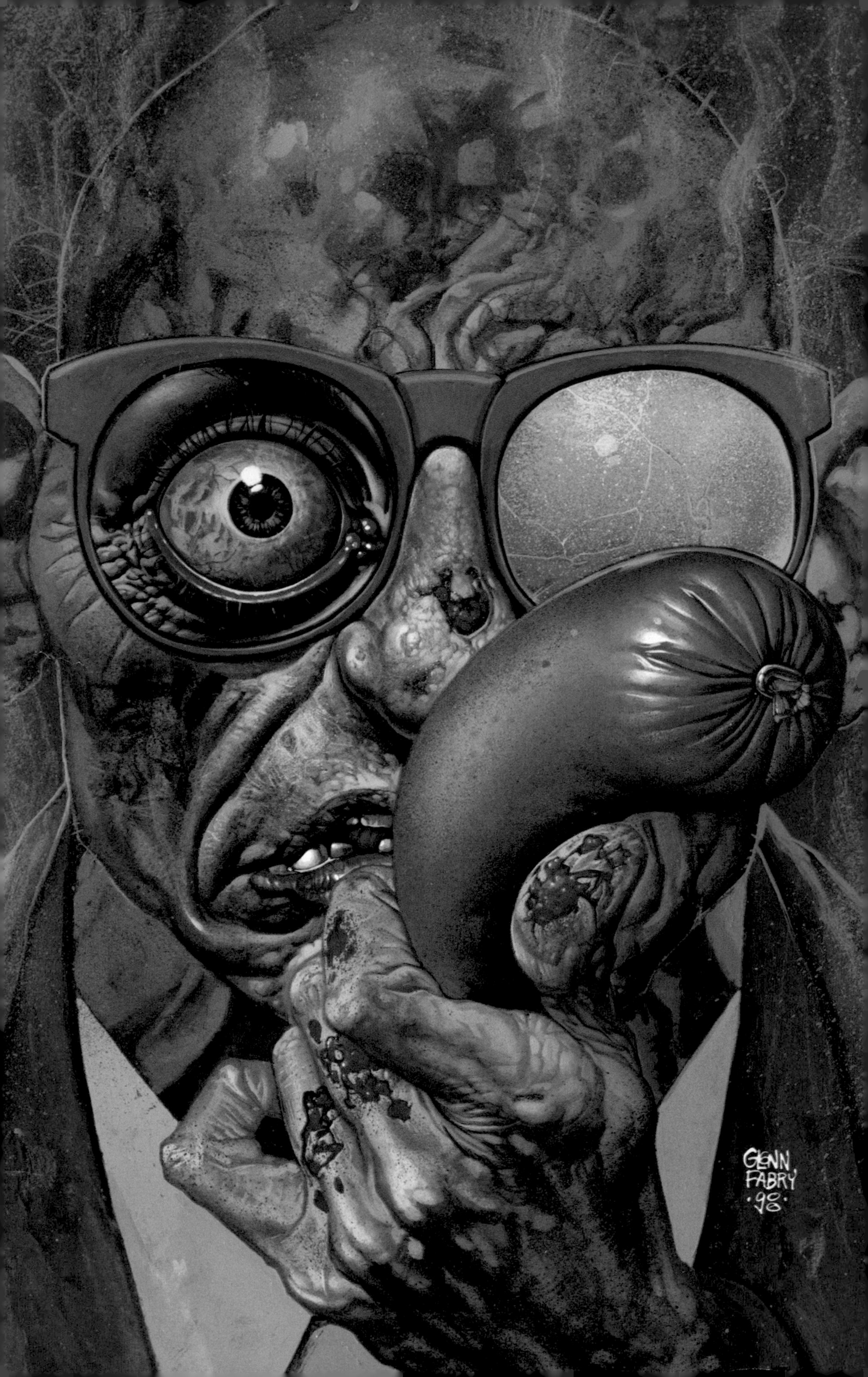
GLENN FABRY

"Can you see past unimaginable horror to find forgiveness in your heart?"

UNNHH...?
UNNHH!!
WHAHH EH HUGGK EH IHH?!!
PATIENCE, DARLING...
I'M GETTING ALL... READY FOR YOU.
DON'T START WITHOUT ME.

WUFF!
HEEHRR!

HEEHR, OO AWBY HYHEHD! HEHL HEAH!

RRRR-- GRRRRRR--
ANBY, HEEHRR! HHD UHG! HHD UHG!

MY DARLING...
HID!
WRR--!

...MY FÜHRER OF LOVE.

SINCE THE MOMENT I SAW YOU I HAVE WANTED YOU...
THIS WILL BE THE LOVE OF GODS, DARLING. OF VALKYRIE AND NIBELUNG.
YOUR ENTRY WILL BE LIKE LIGHTNING. YOU WILL INVADE ME, OCCUPY ME--AND JUST WHEN I CAN TAKE NO MORE YOU WILL OPEN UP A SECOND FRONT...
THIS WILL BE...
BLITZKRIEG...
IN YOUR NAME!
RRRAARRGGH, FUCK ME!
FUCK ME HARD AND CALL ME EVA!

YOU--

ARE A VERY SICK WOMAN.
I LIKE IT LIKE THIS.

JESUS...
YOU CAN'T ESCAPE THIS, JESSE CUSTER! IT IS DESTINY!
DIVINE RIGHT!

ONE I OWE YOU, SKEETER. ALL I GOTTA DO NOW'S GET OUTTA HERE 'FORE ANYONE SEES ME WEARIN' THIS--
LIFE IN HITLER'S REICH
THE U-BOAT BOYS
STALINGRAD

...SHIT.
JESSE?

uh... ANY-THIN' YOU WANNA TELL ME ABOUT...?
LONG, LONG STORY. WHAT YOU DOIN' WITH THIS SORRY SON OF A BITCH?
THAT'S KIND OF A LONG STORY TOO.
THOUGHT THERE WERE USUALLY TWO OF THESE ASSHOLES...
IN BACK.
OH.
GUESS THAT JUST LEAVES QUINCANNON.
LOOKS LIKE HE AIN'T GONNA BE TOO HARD TO FIND...
NO!
YOU SAY SOMETHIN', DICKCHEESE?
DON'T GO IN THERE! HE'S GOT SOMETHIN' IN THERE!
HE MADE US STAND GUARD WHILE HE WENT IN, HE WOULDN'T LET NO ONE SEE IT! BUT I...I HEARD NOISES! TERRIBLE NOISES!
I SWEAR TO GOD, THERE'S SOMETHIN' GOD-AWFUL IN THERE!
CINDY...
WOULD YOU PLEASE WAIT OUT HERE?

SMEAR THE CHEESE...
SMEAR THE CHEESE...
PLUCK THE HAIRS...
PLUCK THE HAIRS...
NOW...
SAY THE NAME...
SAY THE NAME

YYEEEEESSSSS...

I SEEN SOME FUCKED-UP THINGS IN MY TIME.
BUT THAT ABOUT TAKES THE FUCKED-UP COOKIE.

UH

THIS AIN'T A MERCY KILLIN', I'D SURE LIKE TO KNOW WHAT IS.
KRAKK

DO THE HONORS?
MY PLEASURE.
WHOA...
WOULDA BEEN A SHAME TO WASTE ALL THAT NAPALM.

AAH--!
CHRIST, YOU SCARED ME! HOW DID YOU GET IN?
AIN'T NO ONE LOCKS THEIR DOORS 'ROUND HERE, GUNTHER. YOU OUGHTTA KNOW THAT, BEIN' SUCH A CHAMPION OF SMALL-TOWN TEXAS.
JESSE, IT IS NEARLY FOUR A.M.... WHAT IS THIS ABOUT?
'BOUT A BOOK I FOUND IN MISS OATLASH'S PLACE THIS MORNIN', 'FORE I SENT HER THINGS ON TO THE BIN. GAL'S GOT SHIT YOU WOULDN'T BELIEVE.
JAGERS: FIGHTER ACES OF THE LUFTWAFFE
BUT--
SO I SAW THIS AN' I THOUGHT HEY, MAYBE THEY GOT SOMETHIN' IN HERE 'BOUT GUNTHER'S BROTHER. AN' THEY DO.
AN' RIGHT AFTER IT THEY GOT "MAJOR HAHN'S YOUNGER BROTHER GUNTHER ALSO JOINED J.G. FIFTY-THREE, BUT WAS SHOT DOWN AND KILLED BY HURRICANES OF FIVE-OH-ONE SQUADRON ON OCTOBER EIGHTEENTH, WITHOUT HAVING OPENED HIS SCORE."
"HIS BODY WAS WASHED ASHORE AT WISSANT THREE DAYS LATER."
WHO THE HELL ARE YOU?

I--
LOOK--
WAIT--
I CALLED THE IMMIGRATION PEOPLE. THEY GOT YOU COMIN' INTO SAN DIEGO--UNDER THE VAN DER POL NAME--IN JUNE *FORTY-SIX,* WHICH IS THREE YEARS LATER'N YOU SAID BEFORE.
THE TRUTH.
PLEASE, GIVE ME A CHANCE--

THE *TRUTH*.

MY NAME IS SIEGFRIED VECHTEL--!

HOW DID YOU... HOW...
I FOUND HAHN'S NAME IN THE RECORDS... HE WASN'T EVEN A *FOOTNOTE* IN HISTORY, I NEVER THOUGHT I'D BE CAUGHT OUT...

WHY NOT JUST INVENT A NAME?
I NEEDED... I WANTED THERE TO BE A KIND OF TRUTH TO IT. FOR ME AS MUCH AS ANY-BODY ELSE.

Uh-huh. PILOT LOSES HIS BROTHER, SHARP KINDA FELLA, FOOLS HIS BOSSES INTO SENDIN' HIM TO SPY IN AMERICA. REAL ROGUE.
NICE *SAFE* SORTA EX-NAZI.

DO YOU KNOW WHAT A POLICE BATTALION WAS?

...I THINK I DO.
THEY THE BOYS WENT IN AFTER THE FIGHTIN' WAS OVER? WEHRMACHT OCCUPIED TERRITORY, THEN THE POLICE BATTALIONS CAME AN' TURNED FOLKS INTO SLAVES?
OR JUST PLAIN FUCKIN' *KILLED 'EM*?

WHOLE VILLAGES. REGIONS. ACROSS POLAND, THE BALKANS, THE CRIMEA...
ON AND ON IT WENT, NEVERENDING. DIG A PIT OUTSIDE OF TOWN, LINE THEM UP, A COUPLE OF MACHINE-GUNNERS...
AND LATER, CHRIST, LATER-- IN THE CAMPS--

I HAD TO, THEY GAVE ME ORDERS AND I *HAD TO*... YOU DON'T UNDERSTAND WHAT IT WAS *LIKE*, THEN...
SHIT, DON'T EVEN FUCKIN' *TRY* THAT'N.

HMH.
SAID ALL THE RIGHT GODDAMN THINGS, DIDN'T YOU?

WHAT...?
YOU SEE THIS NEW FELLA IN TOWN, THIS REDNECK SHERIFF STIRRIN' SHIT UP, YOU THINK HEY, WHY DON'T I FUCK WITH THIS ASSHOLE A LITTLE BIT...

YOU TELL YOUR DAMN STORY AN' IT SOUNDS REAL GOOD; IT'S KINDA FUNNY AN' CHARMIN' AN' IT'S EVEN PARTLY TRUE, 'CEPT IT HAPPENED TO SOMEBODY ELSE. THAT SURE THROWS HIM OFF THE SCENT.
AN' THEN, HELL, YOU REALLY GO TO TOWN. ALL THAT MEN OF HONOR STUFF, ALL THAT DOWN-HOME BULLSHIT. *THE MYTH OF AMERICA,* WASN'T THAT WHAT YOU SAID?
GOTTA HAND IT TO YOU, GUNTHER. ONE LOOK AT ME AN' YOU KNEW JUST WHICH BUTTONS TO PUSH.

THAT-- OH MY GOD-- THAT WASN'T IT *AT ALL*...!

IT WAS *TRUE,* JESSE! ALL OF IT, I MEANT EVERY WORD OF IT!
I *DO* LOVE THIS COUNTRY! I ALWAYS HAVE, WITH ALL MY HEART! DON'T YOU SEE AMERICA IS MY *SECOND CHANCE*...?

I HAVE DONE TERRIBLE THINGS. I HAVE COMMITTED *NIGHTMARES* AGAINST HUMANITY. BUT I ESCAPED FROM THAT TIME AND CAME HERE, AND I LOVED THIS PLACE BECAUSE IN IT I SAW HOW I COULD REDEEM MY SINS: HOW I COULD CAST THE OLD WORLD ASIDE AND REJOICE IN THE NEW ONE, WHICH IS THE GOD-GIVEN RIGHT OF ALL AMERICANS.
I HAVE LIVED A GOOD LIFE IN THE TIME THAT I'VE HAD HERE. I BELIEVED THAT IF I DID, AMERICA WOULD REACH OUT AND POINT THE WAY TO MY REDEMPTION.

AND AFTER ALL THIS TIME, YOU CAME.

DON'T YOU SEE...?
DON'T YOU REALIZE WHAT IT MEANS, YOU BEING HERE?

YOU COME FROM--YOU ARE OF AMERICA. YOU CAME HERE TO DO WHAT WAS RIGHT. AND YOU WOULD NOT COMPROMISE OR SELL OUT TO THE DEVIL, AND I KNEW THAT YOUR FRIENDSHIP--YOUR ACCEPTANCE--WOULD MEAN THAT I HAD BEEN REDEEMED...
CAN YOU SEE PAST UNIMAGINABLE HORROR TO FIND FORGIVENESS IN YOUR HEART? PLEASE, JESSE? CAN YOU DO IT?

CAN YOU REACH OUT A HAND TO A FRIEND?

THERE'S THINGS CAN'T EVER BE PUT RIGHT.
YOU KNOW IT.

BUT...I...
GO TO HELL.

I'M REAL SORRY YOUR BROTHEL BURNED DOWN, JESSE.

DON'T YOU WORRY NONE, LORIE. IT WASN'T MUCH OF A, *uh*, A BROTHEL TO BEGIN WITH.
YOU'RE GOING TO LEAVE US SOON, AREN'T YOU? I SAW A BAG PACKED ON THE FRONT SEAT OF YOUR ELEPHANT.
SHERIFF

YEAH, ALL MY WORLDLY GOODS... SHIT, LOOK AT THIS. LITTLE BASTARD DIDN'T EVEN LEAVE ME A POT TO PISS IN.

I'LL MISS YOU. I THINK A LOT OF PEOPLE WILL.
WELL HELL, I'LL MISS YOU TOO, LORIE ...*uh*...

JODIE'S BA
FIVE ACROSS-- "JOHN WAYNE," DEE SOMETHIN', KAY SOMETHIN'... DAMN, WHAT COULD THAT BE?
TOBY?
YEAH, DUDE?

...NOTHIN'.
SURE, DUDE.
SO.

YOU'RE LEAVING TONIGHT, THEN? HAVEN'T YOU TOLD ANYONE?
JUST THE FOLKS I'M CLOSE TO.

WHICH IS LESS'N YOU MIGHT THINK...

IT'S--
I KNOW, I KNOW.
IT'S THE SOUTH.

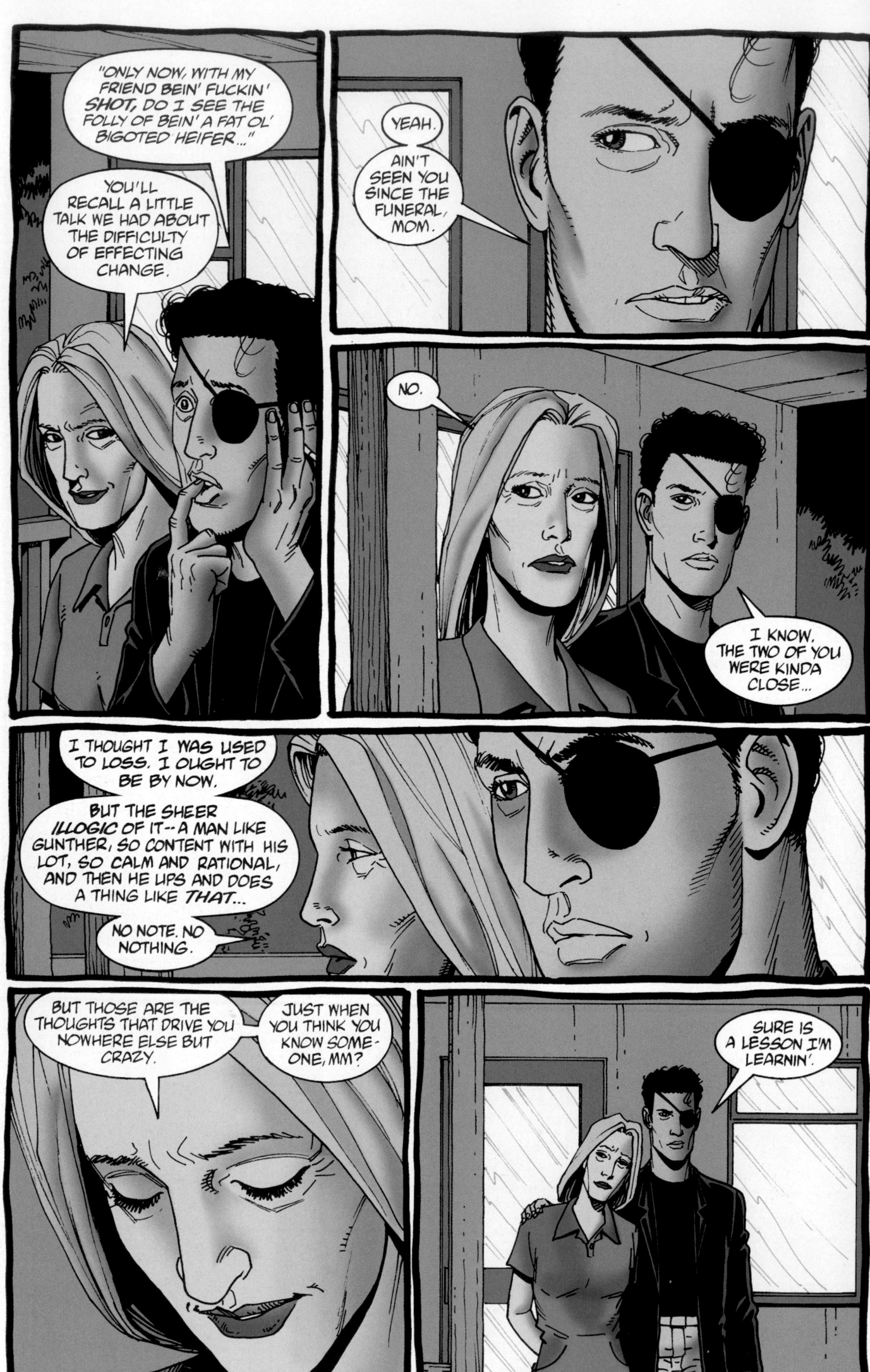
"ONLY NOW, WITH MY FRIEND BEIN' FUCKIN' SHOT, DO I SEE THE FOLLY OF BEIN' A FAT OL' BIGOTED HEIFER..."
YOU'LL RECALL A LITTLE TALK WE HAD ABOUT THE DIFFICULTY OF EFFECTING CHANGE.
YEAH.
AIN'T SEEN YOU SINCE THE FUNERAL, MOM.
NO.
I KNOW. THE TWO OF YOU WERE KINDA CLOSE...
I THOUGHT I WAS USED TO LOSS. I OUGHT TO BE BY NOW.
BUT THE SHEER ILLOGIC OF IT-- A MAN LIKE GUNTHER, SO CONTENT WITH HIS LOT, SO CALM AND RATIONAL, AND THEN HE UPS AND DOES A THING LIKE THAT...
NO NOTE. NO NOTHING.
BUT THOSE ARE THE THOUGHTS THAT DRIVE YOU NOWHERE ELSE BUT CRAZY.
JUST WHEN YOU THINK YOU KNOW SOME-ONE, MM?
SURE IS A LESSON I'M LEARNIN'.

WHAT ARE YOU GOING TO DO?
WELL, I BEEN THINKIN' ABOUT THAT.
I'M GONNA GO FIND OUT SOME THINGS I NEED TO KNOW, AN' THEN I'M GONNA FINISH THIS JOB I GOTTA DO.
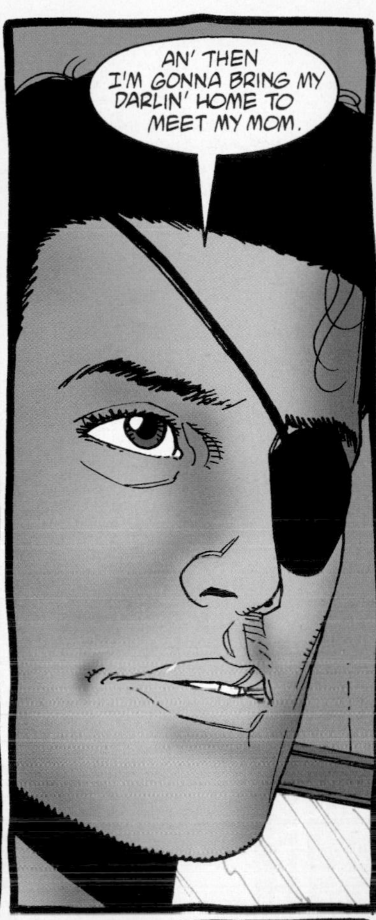
AN' THEN I'M GONNA BRING MY DARLIN' HOME TO MEET MY MOM.

BA

WELL, IT'S A COLD, HARD WORLD OUT THERE, JESSE CUSTER. YOU TAKE CARE IN IT, D'YOU HEAR ME?
OH MOM, IT AIN'T THAT HARSH A WORLD, TRULY IT AIN'T...

I AIN'T CRIED SINCE THAT MORNIN' IN THE CORN, I TELL YOU THAT?

BUT SOMETIMES I SURELY DO COME CLOSE.

THERE'S ONE LAST THING.

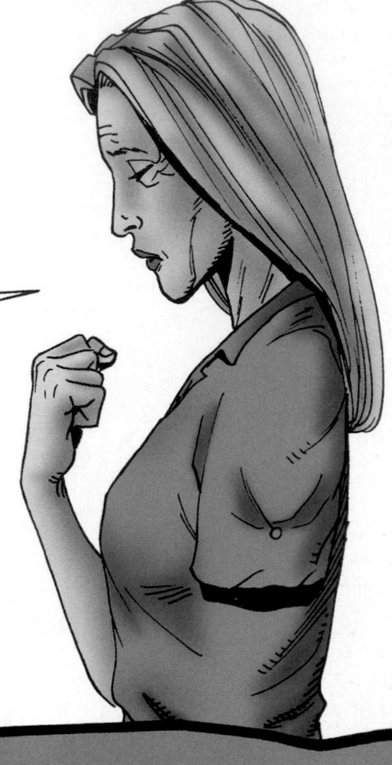
I KEPT THIS WITH ME ALWAYS. IT WAS WITH ME WHEN I WENT INTO THE SWAMP, AND ALL THROUGH THE ASYLUM, ALTHOUGH BY THEN I HAD NO IDEA WHY.
WHEN I CAME HERE I PUT IT IN A DRAWER AND FOR-GOT ABOUT IT. AND THEN YOU ARRIVED.

YOUR FATHER GAVE ME THIS FOR YOU THE NIGHT BEFORE HE DIED. JUST IN CASE, HE TOLD ME.
FOR WHEN YOU WERE A MAN.

MOM...

THIS HERE'S THE MEDAL OF HONOR.

JESSE.
CINDY.

SO I WAS GONNA STOP BY AN' SEE YOU TOMORROW, 'FORE I LEFT.
YEAH, YEAH.

I KNOW YOUR KIND. GONE LIKE A THIEF IN THE NIGHT IS MORE LIKE IT.
heh.
LOOK, uh...IF I CAUSED YOU TO THINK SOMETHIN' WAS GONNA HAPPEN HERE...I MEAN I KNOW WE GOT KINDA CLOSE...

OH JESSE, IF FLIRTIN'S A CRIME THEN YOU BETTER DEPUTIZE YOUR MOM AN' HAVE HER LOCK US BOTH UP...!
I KNEW YOUR PROBLEM RIGHT AFTER THAT NIGHT IN YOUR OFFICE. NEXT MORNIN', I BROUGHT IT UP, YOU CHANGED THE SUBJECT JUST AS QUICK AS YOU COULD.

MY PROBLEM...?

YOU'RE *IN LOVE WITH SOMEBODY ELSE*, JESSE.

YOU CAN TELL THAT?
uh-huh.

DAMN.

SO WHY WERE YOU GONNA STOP BY, ANYHOW?
JUST SOME-THIN' I GOT FOR YOU. AN' SOMETHIN' I WANTED TO SAY.
AN' WHAT MIGHT THAT BE?
THAT YOU ARE PRETTY AS THE STARS AT EVENIN'.

GOODNIGHT AND GOD BLESS

GARTH ENNIS - Writer **STEVE DILLON - Artist**

PAMELA RAMBO - Colorist **CLEM ROBINS - Letterer** **AXEL ALONSO - Editor**

PREACHER created by GARTH ENNIS and STEVE DILLON

GLENN
FABRY 98

"Yore gal here, she's with me now.
Reckon she prefers the taste of evil dick."

FIRST CONTACT

GARTH ENNIS - Writer **STEVE DILLON - Artist**

PAMELA RAMBO - Colorist CLEM ROBINS - Letterer AXEL ALONSO - Editor

PREACHER created by GARTH ENNIS and STEVE DILLON

SKEETER, WHY DON'T YOU JUST RUN ALONG AN' HIDE IN THE TRUCK, HUH? I'M JUST 'BOUT TO SWALLOW A BIG DOSE OF HALLUCINOGENS AN' THINGS'RE APT TO GET A LITTLE STRANGE AROUND HERE...

MM?
NO?
YOUR FUNERAL, BUDDY.

THERE'S THINGS I GOTTA KNOW, SEE. EVERYTHING FROM FALLIN' OUTTA THAT DAMN PLANE TO WAKIN' UP IN THE DESERT, ALL THAT IS LOST TO ME.
AN' THEN THERE'S THE REASON I GOT THIS HERE PEYOTE IN THE FIRST PLACE, WHICH IS GENESIS. GODDAMN SPOOK'S BEEN IN MY HEAD THE BEST PART'VE A YEAR, AN' I STILL AIN'T NO NEARER USIN' IT TO TRACK DOWN THE LORD...

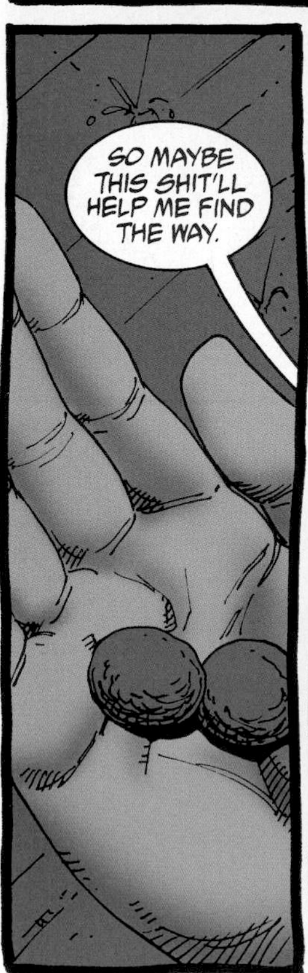
SO MAYBE THIS SHIT'LL HELP ME FIND THE WAY.

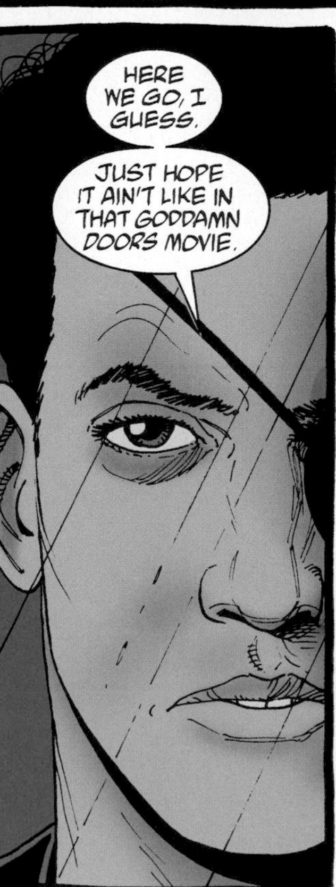
HERE WE GO, I GUESS.
JUST HOPE IT AIN'T LIKE IN THAT GODDAMN DOORS MOVIE.

BOY DID IT SUCK.
WUFF.

WUFF! WUFF! WUFF!
YEAH, BUT... AIN'T NO ONE GONNA BOTHER US, ALL THE WAY OUT HERE...
DAMN...

IS IT S'POSED TO MAKE YORE FINGERS SEE-THROUGH?
OR IS IT?
NOT?

I MEAN... HEY...!

GODDAMN, WHAT'S-- SHIT--
WHAT THE FUCK IS--

HOW'RE YEH!

CASS...?
SORT OF. MORE THE WAY YEH SEE ME, TO BE HONEST WITH YEH.

THIS IS YER BRAIN SHOWIN' YEH WHAT YEH EXPECT TO SEE, RIGHT? SO IT'S GOT ME SET UP AS A NASTY, SLIMY, GIRLFRIEND-STEALIN', BLOODSUCKIN', HORRIBLE WEE LEECH...
THAT AIN'T HOW I SEE YOU!

ISN'T IT?
WELL-- NO--I MEAN--
JESUS, THIS IS FUCKED-UP...

COURSE IT'S FUCKED-UP, YEH EEJIT! YEH'VE THE BASTARD OFFSPRING OF A DEMON AN' AN ANGEL LIVIN' IN YER MIND AS A SPIRITUAL ENTITY--YEH DIDN'T THINK THIS WAS GONNA BE A NORMAL PEYOTE TRIP, DID YEH?
WHAT-EVER THE FUCK THAT IS...

GODDAMMIT, CASS... KNOCK IT OFF...
ULK-- ULK-- ULK--

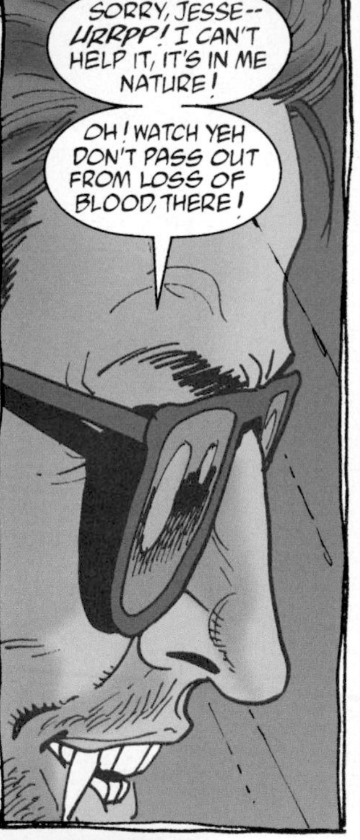
SORRY, JESSE-- URRPP! I CAN'T HELP IT, IT'S IN ME NATURE!
OH! WATCH YEH DON'T PASS OUT FROM LOSS OF BLOOD, THERE!

THERE HE IS...
UH...?
PASSED OUT, HUH? HE STILL BREATHIN'?
HE PROBABLY NEEDS A LITTLE MOUTH-TO-MOUTH...
YEEEAAGGHH!!
HOWDY THERE, LITTLE JESSE!
YOU'RE HOME.

THE FUCK I AM--
JESSE? IS THAT YOU?
LOOK WHAT THEY *DONE TO ME*, JESSE...!

BILLY-BOB?
THEY USED THE POKER, JESSE! HEATED IT IN THE COALS! OH LORD ABOVE US, LORIE'LL NEVER TAKE ME NOW!

YOU COME ON WITH ME, FUCKHOLE. GOT ME A SWEET LITTLE IDEA FOR THAT THERE SOCKET OF YORES.
SOMEONE ELSE YOU MIGHT WANT TO SAY HOWDY TO, BOY.

YOU CALLED, JODY HONEY?
NO!!
YORE GAL HERE, SHE'S WITH ME NOW. RECKON SHE PREFERS THE TASTE OF EVIL DICK.

SHE WOULDN'T! NOT HER! NOT TULIP, NOT WITH A PIECE'VE FUCKIN' SHIT LIKE YOU!

BUT ISN'T THAT HOW YOU SEE ME NOW, JESSE? DOWN AMONGST THE SHIT? A FILTHY LITTLE SLUT WHO'D GIVE HERSELF TO ANYONE?
YOU HATE ME FOR WHAT I'VE DONE, THE VERY THOUGHT OF ME DISGUSTS YOU...

NO! NEVER! NOT IN A GODDAMNED LIFE-TIME! FUCK ALLA THAT SHIT, AN' IF THERE IS A PARTA ME WOULD EVER THINK THAT-- FUCK IT TOO!
YOU COCKSUCKER, JODY! I'LL KICK YOUR ASS A THOUSAND TIMES!!

IT'S A VISION, DUMBASS. AIN'T YOU GOT THAT YET?

EVERYONE HOLDS DARKNESS IN THEIR HEART, JESSE CUSTER. DON'T EVER FORGET THAT WE ARE THE DARKNESS IN YOURS.
JODY?

GIT ON ABOUT YORE DAMN VISION, BOY.

OH JESUS-- THIS IS IT--
THIS IS IT--

!

FOR THE GREAT HEREAFTER--

THIS LOOKS A HELL OF A LOT LIKE UTAH.

I GUESS YOU'D BE THE LORD.

REJOICE.
FOR YOU WHO WERE LOST ARE FOUND AGAIN. YOU WHO STOOD AT THE GATES OF DEATH ARE SAVED BY MY MOST MERCIFUL HAND.
YOU, MY SON.

I AIN'T YOUR GODDAMN SON.

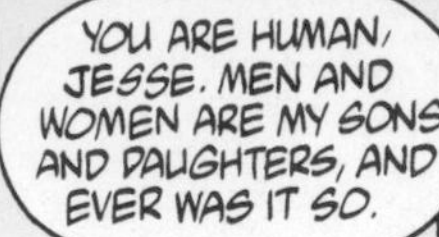
YOU ARE HUMAN, JESSE. MEN AND WOMEN ARE MY SONS AND DAUGHTERS, AND EVER WAS IT SO.
REJOICE IN THIS. REJOICE THAT I HAVE SAVED YOU FROM YOUR FATAL FALL. AND YET REJOICE STILL FURTHER.

FOR I DO LOVE YOU STILL.

TWICE BEFORE I HAVE WARNED YOU. TWICE BEFORE I HAVE COME TO YOUR COMPANIONS, ENTRUSTED THEM WITH MESSAGES.
"TELL HIM TO TURN BACK, TO END HIS SEARCH." "TELL HIM TO LEAVE ME BE, OR THE THIRD TIME OUR PATHS CROSS I SHALL DESTROY HIM."
AND SEE, THEY HAVE CROSSED ONCE MORE. AND BECAUSE I AM A JUST GOD, AND A MERCIFUL GOD, AND MOST OF ALL A LOVING GOD--

YOU ARE FORGIVEN.

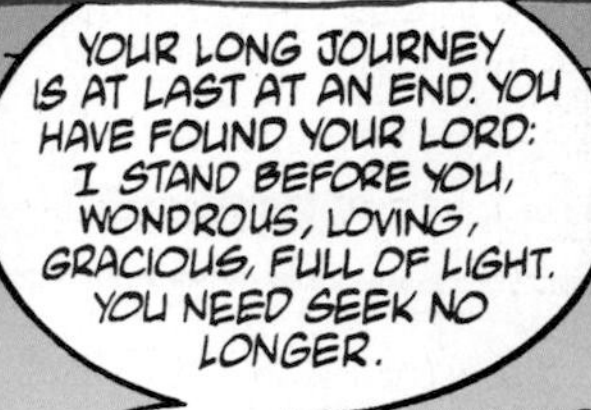
YOUR LONG JOURNEY IS AT LAST AT AN END. YOU HAVE FOUND YOUR LORD: I STAND BEFORE YOU, WONDROUS, LOVING, GRACIOUS, FULL OF LIGHT. YOU NEED SEEK NO LONGER.

GO NOW AND LIVE IN PEACE.

THE FUCK I WILL, MISTER.

YOU WILL NOT ACCEPT MY BLESSING...?
I AIN'T ACCEPTIN' SHIT FROM YOU.

THERE'S QUESTIONS YOU GOTTA ANSWER. NOT JUST WHY CREATION'S FULLA PAIN AN' MISERY, OR WHY YOU'D MAKE A WORLD THIS COLD.
NO, YOU TELL ME WHY YOU'RE RUNNIN' FROM ME, BOY. TELL ME WHAT GIVES YOU THE RIGHT TO DESERT YOUR PLACE IN HEAVEN, TO RUN OUT ON FOLKS YOU MEAN SO MUCH TO.

AN' TELL ME WHY I SHOULDN'T ***SEND YOUR ASS RIGHT BACK THERE***.

THE CREATION CANNOT MAKE DEMANDS OF ITS CREATOR...!

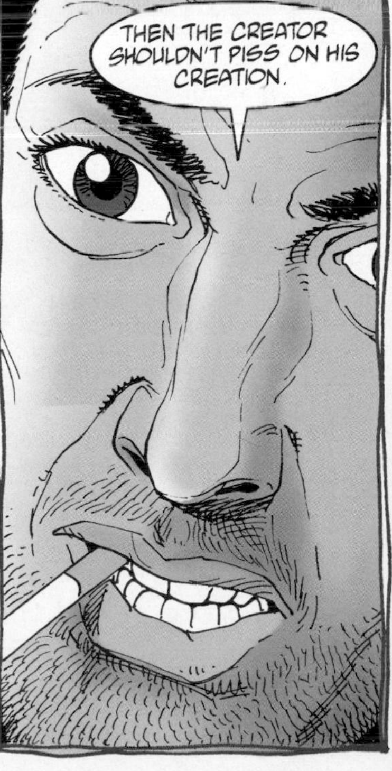
THEN THE CREATOR SHOULDN'T PISS ON HIS CREATION.

JESSE, JESSE... SEE SENSE...
LOOK UPON THE CARNAGE THIS QUEST OF YOURS HAS WROUGHT. THINK ABOUT THE PAIN.
AND MORE THAN THAT, YOU SIMPLY CANNOT DO THIS. YOU CANNOT STAND BEFORE THE LORD YOUR GOD AND THEN DEFY MY WILL...
SO HOW COME YOU AIN'T SMITIN' ME FOR MY SACRILEGE, EXACTLY?
OH WILLFUL MAN, HOW OFTEN MUST YOU HEAR IT SAID?
BECAUSE I AM A LOVING GOD...!
THINK ABOUT THE CHANCES I HAVE GIVEN YOU. REMEMBER HOW I TOOK AWAY THE POWER YOU HOLD, AND RETURNED IT WHEN YOU WERE AT THE MERCY OF YOUR ENEMIES...
OH, I REMEMBER THAT'N, ALL RIGHT. I REMEMBER HOW TULIP GOT SHOT.
HOW YOU BROUGHT HER BACK JUST TO SEND ME A WARNIN', JESUS, WHAT THE HELL KINDA LOVIN' GOD COULD TREAT A LIFE SO CHEAP--!
SEE, I'M WONDERIN' WHY IT TOOK YOU SO LONG TO FIND THE BALLS TO FACE ME, INSTEADA USIN' HER AN' CASS. YOU REALLY SUCH HOT SHIT, OR COULD IT BE YOU AIN'T AS STRONG AWAY FROM HOME AS YOU'D LIKE FOR ME TO THINK?
THIS POWER I GOT... DID YOU RETURN IT, THAT TIME?
OR DID IT MAYBE JUST COME ON BACK BY ITSELF?

IT'S TIME YOU--

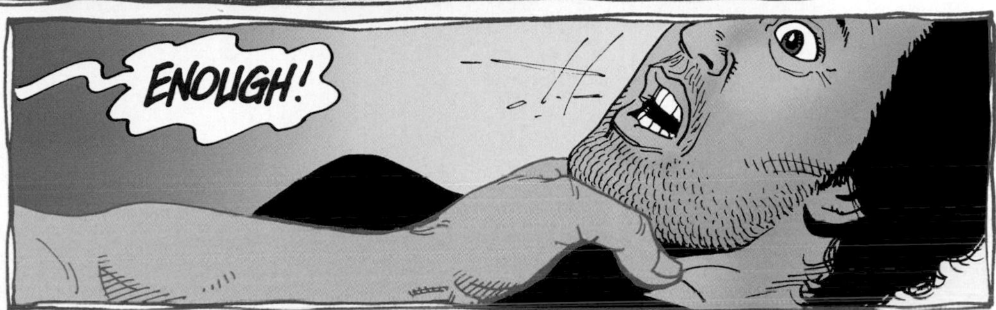
ENOUGH!

YOU WOULD COMMAND YOUR GOD, OH MAN? YOU WOULD STAIN HIS HOLY BEING WITH SUCH ULTIMATE BLASPHEMY?!
REPENT, O SINNER! FALL DOWN BEFORE YOUR MASTER! BEG FORGIVENESS!
BEG!

RRRAAAHH!
HHHH--!

SSSHHSSS

HHSS--!

RRAAARR!!
EEEEAAGGHH!

BELIEVE IN THE LOVING GOD! REPENT YOUR SIN BEFORE THE LOVING GOD! TREMBLE AT THE MIGHT OF THE LOVING GOD!
ACCEPT ME AS YOUR SAVIOR OR BE DAMNED!!

ANSWER OR BE--
YOU
WANT IT QUICK?
MAY AS WELL, PREACHER.
YOU'RE DYIN' ANY-HOW.

DYIN'...?

AIN'T MANY SURVIVE THE TOUCH OF GOD, BOY. SAINTS, MOSTLY. MAYBE A PROPHET OR TWO.
YOU DID LIVE YOU'D GO CRAZY. AIN'T NO WAY YOU'D REMEMBER ANY OF THIS.

BUT YOU DON'T LOOK TO ME LIKE YOU'RE GONNA LIVE THROUGH IT...
OH-- YEAH--?

I AIN'T DYIN'. AIN'T GOIN' CRAZY. AN' I BY GOD **WILL** REMEMBER, ONE WAY OR THE OTHER.
I DON'T NEED NO QUICK WAY OUT FROM YOU.

'CAUSE YOU AN' ME--
GONNA TAKE THAT BASTARD--
DOWN...

I AIN'T HELPIN' YOU WITH NOTHIN', PREACHER.

SO LONG.

YOU JUST DID... BIG MAN...

YOU... JUST... DID...

JOHN, NO! I KNOW THEM! THEY'RE KILLERS!
THEY'RE TRASH WITH GUNS, IS ALL THEY ARE.
YOU HOLD THIS FOR ME, T.C.?
DAD!

BAMM
SPLATCH!
SPLITCH
BAMM
SPLATCH!
SPLITCH
WHAT'S DADDY DOING? WHAT'S DADDY DOING?
WELL, THOSE MEN HAVE BEEN VERY BAD, AND DADDY'S--ah-- SPANKING THEM...
THAT IS FAR ENOUGH, YOU UNGRATEFUL LITTLE HARLOT!
NO!!
HONEY, WHAT'S THE-- DAMN!
THAT BOY IS MINE.

MINE FOREVER, TO RAISE AS I SEE FIT! TO SET TOWARDS THE DESTINY I DECIDE FOR HIM!
AND WE ALL KNOW WHAT THAT WILL BE, DON'T WE?!
YOU'RE GOING TO BE A PREACHER, JESSE CUSTER...!
YOU'RE GOING TO BE A PREACHER! FOREVER AND EVER! AND EVER AND EVER!
NO ESCAPE, OH NO, NOT FROM GRAN'MA! YOU'RE GOING TO BE A PREACHER! YOU'RE GOING TO BE A PREACHER!
YOU'RE GOING TO BE A PREACHER, JESSE CUSTER!!

WELL GODDAMN! MUCH OBLIGED, SIR!
HELL, IT WAS A PLEASURE.
GOT A... MESSAGE FOR THE LITTLE PILGRIM, THERE. FRIENDA HIS IS KINDA SCARED FOR HIM AN'...WANTED ME TO PASS IT ALONG.
YA READY, SON?
WHEEEE!
WUFF. WUFF-WUFF-WUFF-WUFF... WUFF-WUFF.

WHOA--!
WUFF!

OH, YOU GOOD DOG, YOU! YOU GOOD LITTLE GUY!
I SWEAR...
WUFF-WUFF-WUFF!

SAW IT IN HIS EYES, SKEET.

ALL THEM THINGS WERE LOST TO ME THAT I KNOW NOW, AN' THAT'S WHAT STANDS OUT MOST.
THE LOOK IN HIS GODDAMN EYES.

IT AIN'T HOW I USE GENESIS TO FIND HIM; IT'S THE OTHER WAY AROUND.
WHY'D HE GIVE ME ALL THEM CHANCES TO QUIT, ONLY TO COME OUT AN' CONFRONT ME HIM-SELF? WHY COULDN'T HE STAY AWAY?
HELL, MAY AS WELL ASK WHY GOD WOULD CREATE THE DAMN WORLD IN THE FIRST PLACE...

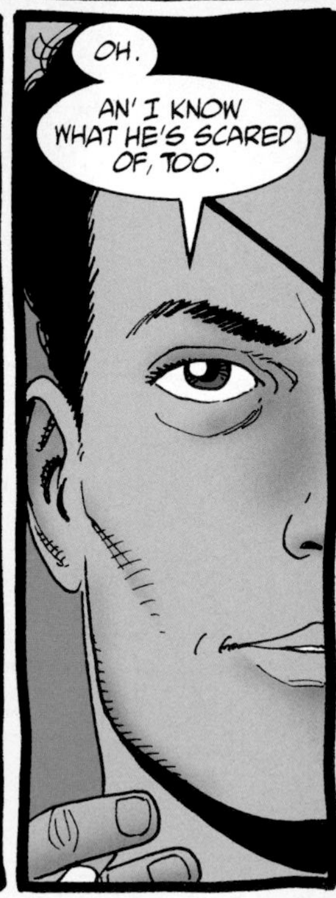
OH.
AN' I KNOW WHAT HE'S SCARED OF, TOO.

AN' HELL IS RIDIN' WITH ME.

ROCHHI • PETER
OBINSON • SALVAT
EINHAMP • DAVI
MENECH • JAMES
RDIFFI • GARETH
RRIDGE • MIKE T
BURNSON • ALAN
ZZARD • JUAN L

"How come you shitheads never write?"

THE LAND OF BAD THINGS

GARTH ENNIS - Writer **STEVE DILLON - Artist**

PAMELA RAMBO - Colorist **CLEM ROBINS - Letterer** **AXEL ALONSO - Editor**

PREACHER created by GARTH ENNIS and STEVE DILLON

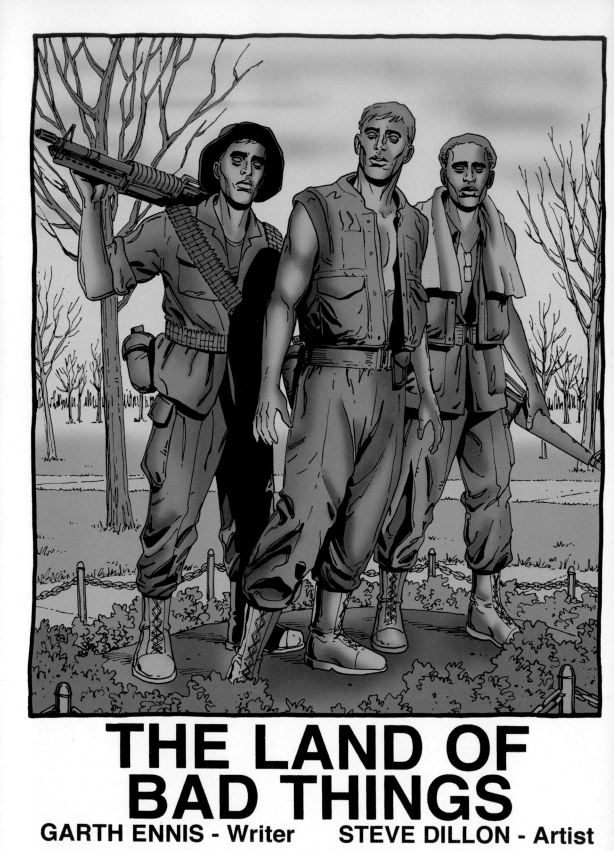

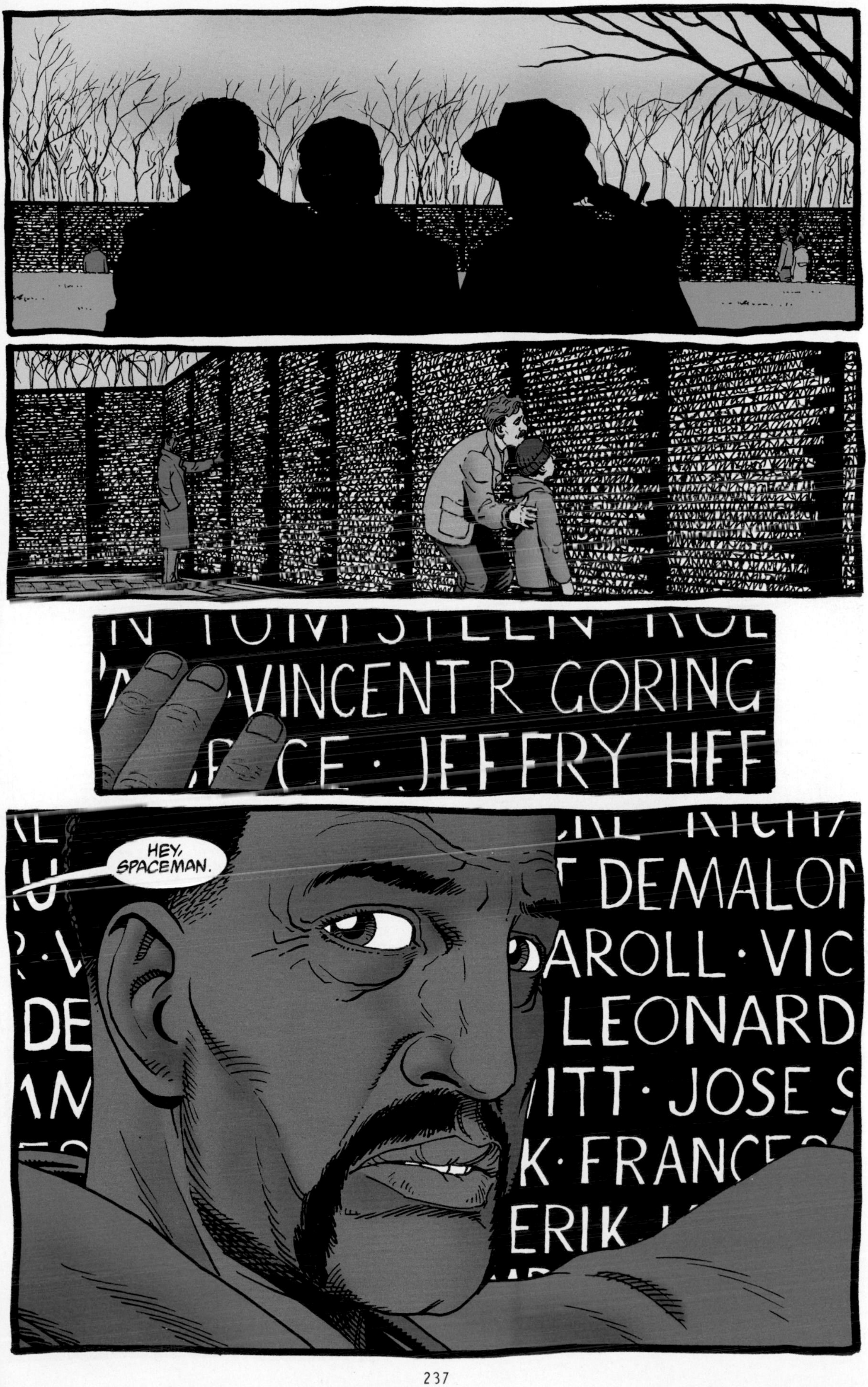

VINCENT R GORING
JEFFRY HEF

HEY, SPACEMAN.

DEMALON
AROLL · VIC
LEONARD
JOSE
FRANC
ERIK

...HELLO, JESSE.
GODDAMN, YOU LOOKIN' MORE LIKE HIM THAN EVER. 'CEPT FOR THE EYE.
'CEPT FOR THAT.
IT SURE IS GOOD TO SEE YOU.

YOU TOO. STILL A PREACHER, HUH?
AIN'T THE KINDA JOB YOU WALK AWAY FROM, I GUESS. HOW 'BOUT YOU, HOW YOU DOIN'?

OKAY. MY LITTLE GIRL JOANIE, SHE EXPECTIN' AGAIN. MY YOUNGEST, WILLIAM JUNIOR, HE JUST QUIT HIGH SCHOOL. SAYS HE GONNA BE EAST COAST HANDBALL CHAMPION AN' HE GOTTA WORK ON HIS GAME.

DIDN'T EVEN KNOW THEY HAD A CHAMPION...
JUST ABOUT. WILLIAM AN' HIS FOOL FRIENDS BUSTIN' THEY ASSES ALL DAY ON THEM COURTS AT CONEY ISLAND, WAITIN' FOR A GODDAMN HANDBALL LEAGUE AIN'T NEVER GONNA AMOUNT TO SHIT.
SHIT, NO MUTHAFUCKA EVER MADE A CENT OFFA THAT STOOPID GAME...

NEVER CAN TELL WHEN IT COMES TO MONEY, SPACE.
NO, BUT YOU CAN MAKE A EDUCATED GUESS. THAT'S WHY FOLKS INVEST IN GOLD FUTURES, 'STEADA IN POWDERED BUFFALO SHIT.
STILL, I GUESS IT BEATS THE BOY SMOKIN' CRACK OR JOININ' SOME GODDAMN GANGSTA SET.

OR WORSE...

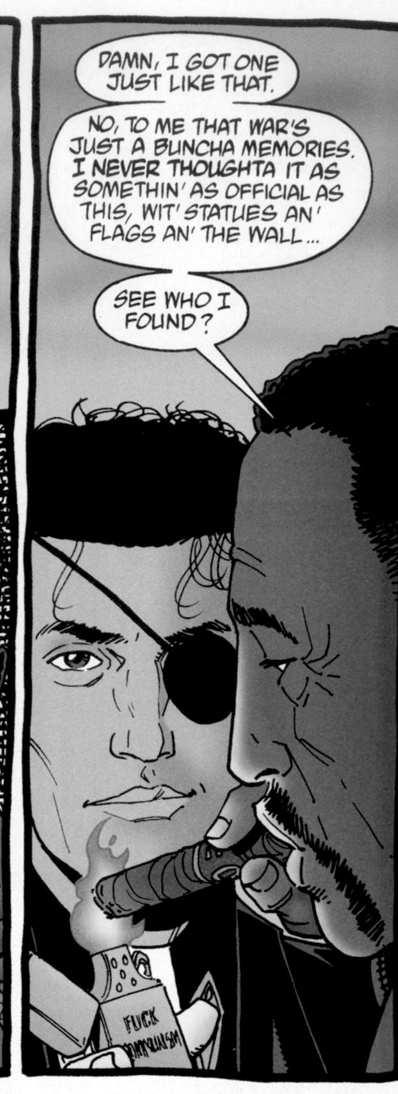

VINCENT A. GORING... IS THAT GONNY?
HOW 'BOUT THAT, HUH? CRAZY LITTLE FUCKER'S IMMORTAL.
LET'S YOU AN' ME TAKE US A WALK.

SO HOW YOU LOSE A DAMN EYE, ANYHOW?
PREACHIN'.
I BET. SOME CHURCH YOU GOT GOIN' THERE, REVEREND.

IT HAS ITS MOMENTS.
FOUND MY MOM, THOUGH, WHICH WAS GOOD 'CAUSE I NEVER EXPECTED TO SEE HER AGAIN. SHE HAD SOMETHIN' FOR ME FROM MY DADDY.
I WAS HOPIN' YOU COULD TELL ME A LITTLE ABOUT IT.

WELL...THEY PROBABLY GOT THE CITATION IN CONGRESSIONAL RECORDS...

THEY PROBABLY DO, BUT IT'S THE HIGHEST AWARD THIS COUNTRY CAN GIVE YOU. I GUESS I'D LIKE TO KNOW HOW HE GOT IT.
FROM SOMEONE WAS ACTUALLY THERE.

OH, I BET YOU DO. BUT YOU DUNNO WHAT YOU ASKIN'. YOU DUNNO HOW THAT MUTHAFUCKA YOU GOT IN YOUR HAND ALMOST KILLED US BOTH.
AN' THE SHIT THAT GOES ALONG WIT' IT, I DON'T THINK I'M TOO PROUDA SOME A' THAT...
FUCK.
YOU SWEAR YOU'LL DO ANYTHIN' FOR SOME DUDE, ALL YOU EXPECT IS TO HAVE TO SAVE HIS ASS. MAYBE TAKE A GOOK BAYONET IN THE CHEST FOR HIM, SOMETHIN' EASY LIKE THAT...
THE LAST GODDAMN THING YOU THINK IT MEANS IS TELLIN' HIS BOY THE TRUTH THIRTY FUCKIN' YEARS LATER.
THE WORST PARTA IT IS WE WAS BOTH NEARLY OUTTA THAT SHITHOLE. ONE AN' GODDAMN DAYS.
TEXAS AN' THE SPACEMAN, SO SHORT THEY COULDN'T EVEN HOLD A LONG CONVERSATION...

RUN FOR YOUR FUCKIN' LIVES!!

WHOLE FUCKIN' N.V.A. BATTALION--
FALL BACK! C'MON, GET THE FUCK OUT--
CAP'N, SARGE, FUCK, HEEELLP..
AAAAAHHH
THEY LEAVIN'! THEY DUSTIN' OFF, I FUCKIN' HEAR 'EM!

ONLY TWO! THIRD SLICK'S STILL WAITIN' FOR US!
JESUS CHRIST--!
WE'RE GONNA MAKE IT!

WELL, SHIT.

THEY STOPPED SHOOTIN'...
MUSTA DONE ALL THE WOUNDED.

FUCKIN' SLOPE COCK-SUCKERS--!
WHOA, OL' HOSS. YOU WANNA TAKE ALLA THEM ON, YOU MAY AS WELL RUN OUT THERE WAVIN' YOUR PECKER.
HOW'S THAT?

KINDA NUMB JESUS!!

YOU FELT THAT, I GUESS I AIN'T GONNA HAVE TO AMPUTATE JUST YET...
MUTHA-FUCK--!
I THOUGHT IT WAS CLEAN, IT WENT RIGHT FUCKIN' THROUGH...

IT WAS 'TIL WE RAN THROUGH THAT SWAMP FULLA DEAD HOGS AN' MONKEY SHIT AN' ALL KINDSA AWFUL BUGS. YOU PROBABLY GOT A GODDAMN PLAGUE FACTORY SET UP IN THERE RIGHT NOW.
GOOD NEWS IS, I AIN'T EVEN GOT A SCRATCH.

YOU ONE ETERNAL RAY OF HOPE, TEXAS. ANY MUTHAFUCKA EVER TELL YOU THAT?
WELL, LET'S THINK 'BOUT WHAT WE *DO* GOT GOIN' FOR US: WE GOT NEARLY ALLA OUR SHIT, AN' YOU GRABBED YOUR PACK WHEN THEY HIT US SO WE GOT C-RATS FOR MAYBE THREE OR FOUR DAYS...

AN' WE GOT THIS HERE MAP I TOOK OFFA CAP'N LINDSAY, WHICH IS GONNA COME IN REAL USEFUL ON THE WALK HOME.

WHAT?

HE'S DEAD, SPACE. HE AIN'T GONNA NEED IT.

NO, I MEAN ***WALK HOME?*** YOU GONE FUCKIN' CRAZY? GOTTA BE TWO HUNDRED KLICKS FROM HERE TO KHE SAN, AT LEAST!

YEAH, BUT IT AIN'T EVEN HALFA THAT TO VAHN LO, HERE, WHERE IT LOOKS LIKE THE ARMY GOT SOME KINDA FORWARD OUTPOST. LAST PARTA IT ISN'T EVEN JUNGLE.

SHIT, MAN, IT'S STILL A FUCKIN' LONG WAY...! AN' I GOT THIS FUCKED-UP LEG, TOO!

WELL THE ALTERNATIVE IS TO SURRENDER, AN' THAT MEANS LETTIN' THESE SONSA-BITCHES TAKE US BACK UP NORTH TO GIVE UNCLE HO BLOW JOBS FOR THE RESTA OUR LIVES.

THAT AIN'T FOR US.

WE'RE DOWN TO FORTY DAYS AN' A WAKE-UP.

WE'RE GOIN' HOME.

WE AIN'T HERE TO WIN NO FUCKIN' WAR, WE AIN'T HERE TO BEAT NO ONE...

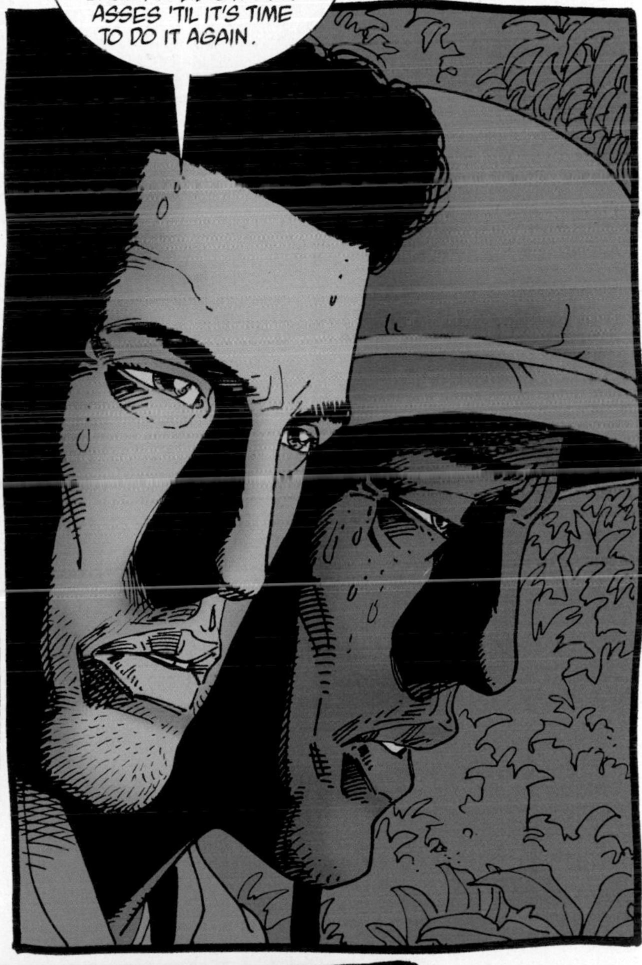
THAT AIN'T HOW YOU WIN; YOU'RE S'POSED TO TAKE AN' HOLD TERRITORY AN' THEN TAKE SOME MORE...
WHAT DO WE DO, WE BUILD A BUNCHA GODDAMN FIREBASES OUT IN THE BUSH AN' THE HUEYS FLY US IN AN' OUT, AN' ONCE WE GET A COUPLE K.I.A. CONFIRMED WE GO BACK AN' LIE ON OUR ASSES 'TIL IT'S TIME TO DO IT AGAIN.

AN' POLICE ACTION MY ASS, NOBODY'S TELLIN' ME WE'RE PRO-TECTIN' SHIT OUT HERE. HALF THE VILLES WE WALK INTO WE BURN TO THE FUCKIN' GROUND.

I BEEN TRYNNA THINK OF IT LIKE A BAD DREAM, I GUESS.
HOW SO?

WELL, WAY IT'S S'POSED TO WORK IS, YOU WORK REAL HARD AN' YOU'RE REWARDED WITH A GOOD LIFE AN' THE FREEDOM TO ENJOY IT. THAT'S AMERICA, OKAY? THAT'S HOW I ALWAYS UNDER-STOOD IT.
AN' MY DADDY, WHO WAS A MARINE BACK IN WORLD WAR TWO AN' FOUGHT ON GUADAL-CANAL AN' OKINAWA AN' ALL KINDSA TERRIBLE PLACES, HE TOLD ME SOMETIMES YOUR COUNTRY DEMANDS A PRICE FOR THEM THINGS. SOMETIMES YOU GOTTA GO OFF AN' FIGHT.
BUT THAT WAS OKAY WITH ME, 'CAUSE TO ME MY COUNTRY WAS WORTH IT.

BUT ***THIS***... BEIN' FED INTO THIS GODDAMN MEAT-GRINDER, ANY FOOL CAN SEE THIS DON'T DO AMERICA NO GOOD AT ALL. AN' I DON'T KNOW WHO THE HELL WOULD WANT US HERE, WHO'D BE HAPPY AT SO MANY BOYS BEIN' SENT OUT HERE TO DIE, BUT I DO KNOW IT'S NOBODY GOOD...

SO I TRY TO BELIEVE IT'S LIKE THIS OVER HERE IN 'NAM--BUT THEN YOU GO HOME AN' WAKE UP AN' IT'S BACK TO THE WAY THINGS ***WERE***. THE GOOD WAY, IN THE COUNTRY PLAYS FAIR BY YOU IF YOU PLAY FAIR BY IT.
THE NIGHTMARE'S OVER, I SAY TO MYSELF.

EXCEPT IT'S JUST BEGINNIN', AN' THERE AIN'T NO WAKIN' UP FROM IT.
'CAUSE IT WAS OUR COUNTRY THAT SENT US HERE.

SO I LOOKED AT THIS KID FROM WEST TEXAS, FEELIN' ALL CUT UP AN' BETRAYED 'CAUSE HE SUDDENLY REALIZED THE LAND OF THE FREE BEEN FUCKIN' HIM IN THE ASS ALL HIS LIFE--

AN' I TOLD MYSELF, SHIT, SO THAT'S WHAT IT'S LIKE TO BE THE WHITE BOY.

ANY NIGGA YOU ASK CAN TELL YOU THAT'S HOW AMERICA WORKS.

SO WHAT YOU GONNA DO NOW YOU THINK EVERYTHING'S SO SHITTY?
HELL, I'M GONNA ROTATE HOME FROM THE LAND OF BAD THINGS AN' FIND ME A SWEET LITTLE GAL WITH BIG BROWN EYES, AN' WE GONNA FUCK LIKE JACKRABBITS FOR THE RESTA OUR NATURAL LIVES.
WE GONNA RAISE A WHOLE LOTTA KIDS, STARTIN' WITH A BOY, I RECKON...

AN' ANY TIME I HAVE TO, I'LL FIGHT LIKE HELL FOR *THEM*.

SO I LOOKED AT THIS KID FROM WEST TEXAS AGAIN, DRAGGIN' MY CRIPPLED ASS THROUGH THE BOONIES, NEVER EVEN HEARDA QUITTIN'--
AN' I TOLD MYSELF TO SHUT THE FUCK UP.

I AIN'T GONNA MAKE IT...
BULLSHIT.

LEG'S FUCKED. CAN'T WALK NO MORE. YOU GOTTA LEAVE ME.
BULLSHIT.
TEXAS, YOU... YOU GONNA GET YOURSELF KILLED OUT HERE FOR NUTHIN'. I'M DEAD ANYWAYS.

BULLSHIT.

FUCK YOU.

WHAT THE FUCK'RE YOU DOIN'?

...
WHAT THE FUCK'RE YOU DOIN'?

DROP THE FUCKIN' GUN! QUIT IT!
YOU OUTTA YOUR FUCKIN' MIND? YOU GONNA KILL ME TO STOP ME FROM SHOOTIN' MYSELF?
PUT IT THE FUCK DOWN!

FUCK YOU! YOU CRAZY, MAN! I'M TRYNNA SAVE YOUR DUMBASS FROM DYIN' IN THIS MUTHA-FUCKIN' JUNGLE AN' NOW YOU PULLIN' THIS SHIT! WHAT THE FUCK!
FUCK YOU, BOY! I AIN'T HAULED YOU HALFWAY ACROSS HELL'S CREATION JUST SO YOU CAN PUSSY OUT ON ME NOW! YOU CAN'T JUST THROW IT ALL AWAY LIKE THIS, THIS IS FUCKED!

NO, YOU! YOU FUCKED! YOU STOOPID FUCKIN' REDNECK, I NEVER ASKED YOU FOR SHIT AN' I AIN'T FUCKIN' ASKIN' NOW!!

WHY YOU BLACK SON OF A BITCH, I DON'T BELIEVE YOU FUCKIN' SAID THAT! YOU PULL THIS SHIT ON *ME*, *NOW*, AFTER EVERYTHING WE FUCKIN' BEEN THROUGH!
MUTHAFUCKA, I'M FUCKIN' TELLIN' YOU TO FUCKIN' LEAVE ME!
YOU IGNORANT PIGFUCKIN' WHITE TRASH COCKSUCKER, I DON'T NEED YOUR MUTHA-FUCKIN' CRACKER ASS HELPIN' ME! YOU GO AN' FUCK YOURSELF, WHITE BOY! FUCK YOU AN' ALL YOUR FUCKIN' KIND!
THE HELL WITH YOU, NIGGER! YOU FUCKIN' JUNGLE BUNNY! I WOULDN'T HELP YOU IF YOU WERE THE RICHEST COON IN HARLEM AN' YOUR EVERY FUCKIN' TOOTH WAS SOLID GOLD!

THEY AIN'T.
YOUR DADDY'DA STOOD BETWEEN ME AN' THE REAPER.

ACROSS THAT OPEN GROUND?

AFTER DARK.

WELL.

THAT IS A PROBLEM.

YEAH, BUT...TEXAS, MAN, THIS FUCKIN' LEG GONNA DROP OFF ANYTIME! CHARLIE DON'T SMELL US COMIN', HE SURE AS FUCK GONNA SEE US WHEN THE SUN COMES UP AN' WE ONLY GONE TWENNY FUCKIN' YARDS!

I COULD GET USED TO THIS...
SHUT THE FUCK UP!

YES SIR, ONLY MUTHA-FUCKIN' WAY TO TRAVEL...
JESUS!

ANYTHING OUT THERE, SERGEANT?

NO SIR.
WELL, STAY ON IT. YOU KNOW CHARLIE.

YES SIR, CAPTAIN HOLDEN.

SHHH...
YOU SHHH, GODDAMMIT!
AAAAHHH!
JESUS CHRIST, MAN, WHAT THE MUTHAFUCK!
I DON'T KNOW, I FUCKIN' STOOD ON SOMEONE! WHO THE FUCK'S THERE?
STARSHELL! STARSHELL!
FIRE!!

AN' THIS NEXT PART I'LL NEVER BELIEVE 'TIL MY DYIN' FUCKIN' DAY, BUT IT'S HOW YOU WIN' THE MEDAL OF HONOR.

NOT AT US! HOLD YOUR FIRE!
JESUS CHRIST, WE'RE FUCKIN' AMERICANS!!

OH FUCK, NO--
SHIT, SIR, I THINK THEY WERE--
DRIVER, START HER UP! COVERING FIRE!

THEY'RE WHO?

I SAID I THINK THEY'RE MARINES, SIR!

WELL THAT FIGURES--

WHO ELSE'D BE DUMB ENOUGH TO TRY WALKING IN THROUGH A GODDAMNED MINEFIELD?

OKAY, GET 'EM OUT OF HERE! GO!

THAT TANK CAP'N, HE WAS THE ONE WROTE UP JOHN'S CITATION, AFTER HE TALKED TO ME LATER ON.
FUCKIN' UP A COMPANY-STRENGTH V.C. ATTACK, HELPIN' A WOUNDED COMRADE ACROSS A HUNDRED KLICKS OF ENEMY TERRITORY, AND BRINGIN' HIM IN UNDER FIRE--THAT WAS MORE'N ENOUGH.

THEY WAS TAKIN' US INTO VAHN LO TO WAIT FOR A MEDEVAC, BOTH OF US SHOT FULLA MORPHINE, AN' ALL OF A SUDDEN I COULD HEAR SOMEONE SAYIN' MY NAME...

THIS AIN'T OUR TIME TO DIE.

THEN I PASSED OUT AN' NEVER SAW HIM AGAIN.

I WAS SHOT UP WORSE'N HE WAS, AN' IT TOOK A COUPLE OPERATIONS BY A SPECIALIST 'FORE THEY WAS SURE I COULD KEEP THE LEG.
BY THEN TEXAS WAS OUTTA THE HOSPITAL AN' POSTED DOWN TO DA NANG, FINISHIN' HIS TOUR ON SOME KINDA BULLSHIT MILK RUN. AN' BY THE TIME I WAS DOIN' THE SAME THING HE GOT SENT HOME.

BUT YOU KNOW SOMETHIN'? HE SAW IT. IN THEM SIX LITTLE WORDS HE SAW THROUGH TO THE CLEAR, PURE-D TRUTH THAT SHOULDA MATTERED MORE TO ME THAN ANYTHING.
ALL THIS TIME I BEEN FUCKED UP AN' MAD ABOUT THE SHIT WENT DOWN OVER THERE, WONDERIN' WHY ALL THEM DUDES GOT WASTED AN' I MADE IT, CURSIN' THE GOVERNMENT FOR FUCKIN' US LIKE THAT... AN' IT'S ONLY NOW I CAN SEE LIKE HE DID.

WE MADE IT.
WE DIDN'T END UP ON NO WALL.

I'M GLAD YOU GOT WHAT'S YOURS, JESSE. JOHN BE PROUD AS HELL TO SEE YOU WITH IT.
YEAH.
I AIN'T EARNED THIS, SPACE.
HUH?
THIS AIN'T NO TRINKET. YOU BUY THIS WITH YOUR BLOOD AN' YOUR PAIN, AN' I AIN'T DONE THAT.
BUT YOU SAID HE GAVE IT TO YOUR MOMMA TO GIVE TO YOU. HELL, HE'DA GIVEN IT TO YOU HIMSELF IF HE COULDA...
YEAH. BUT HE'DA WAITED 'TIL HE FIGURED I DESERVED IT, AN' THAT SURE AS HELL AIN'T FOR ME TO JUDGE. AN' HE AIN'T HERE NO MORE, SO HE CAN'T JUDGE IT EITHER.
ONE THING I KNOW FOR SURE IS HE'DA WANTED ME TO DO WHAT WAS RIGHT WITH IT...
SO HOW 'BOUT WE LEAVE IT HERE WITH ALL THESE OTHER BOYS?

I WANNA THANK YOU, SPACE.

YEAH?
YEAH.
SEE, I GOT A JOB TO DO...

AN' FOR THE FIRST TIME EVER I KNOW WHAT I GOTTA DO TO FINISH IT.
BUT I SWEAR, KNOWIN' MY DADDY WON THAT THING, I COULDN'TA TAKEN ANOTHER STEP UNTIL I FOUND OUT HOW.

IT HELPS TO KNOW THE KINDA MAN YOU GOTTA MEASURE UP TO.
IT GIVES YOU HOPE.

YOU GONNA STAY A WHILE?
YEAH, I...

I KINDA LIKE IT HERE.

I LIKE HOW THEY GOT THE GRUNTS' NAMES UP, ALL OF 'EM, STEADA JUST THE DATESA THE WAR OR SOME SHIT. AN' I LIKE HOW IT'S QUIET HERE.
AN' I 'SPECIALLY LIKE HOW THEY GOT THEM THREE DUDES IN THE TREES OVER THERE, LIKE THEY COMIN' OUTTA THE BOONIES AFTER SOME PATROL, AN' THEY ONLY JUST SEEN ALLA THIS--
AN' THEY LIKE, "MUTHA*FUCKA*..."
"SOMEONE REMEMBERED."

1 · VINCENT R GORINC

SO TELL ME SOMETHIN'.

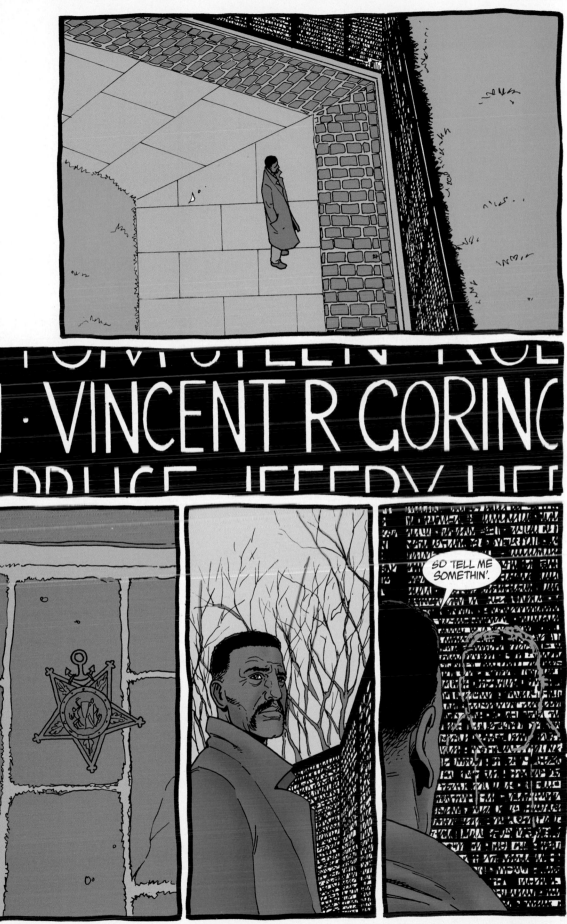

HOW COME YOU SHITHEADS NEVER WRITE?

"Cassidy. Really. This is me."

FREEDOM'S JUST ANOTHER WORD FOR NOTHING LEFT TO LOSE

GARTH ENNIS - Writer STEVE DILLON - Artist

PAMELA RAMBO - Colorist CLEM ROBINS - Letterer AXEL ALONSO - Editor

PREACHER created by GARTH ENNIS and STEVE DILLON

I DON'T NEED THIS SHIT...

WHAT'RE YEH DOIN'?

LEAVING.
WELL SURE HOUL' ON 'TIL DARK AN' I'LL--
FOR GOOD.

WHAT?

I'M LEAVING. I'VE HAD ENOUGH OF THIS SHITTY FUCKING LIFE OF MOTELS AND TAKE-OUT AND TRANQUILIZERS, AND I'M SICK OF YOU AND THE SCUM YOU CALL YOUR FRIENDS. I DON'T NEED IT ANYMORE.

I'M GONE.
LIKE FUCK YEH ARE!!

I'VE BEEN LOOKIN' AFTER YEH FOR SIX FUCKIN' MONTHS! YEH WERE A FUCKIN' WRECK AFTER ARIZONA! YEH'D'VE BEEN LOST WITHOUT ME AN' YEH FUCKIN' WELL KNOW IT, TOO!
YES. THANKS.
AN' WHAT SHITTY FUCKIN' LIFE? I'VE BEEN KEEPIN' US ON THE MOVE, KEEPIN' AHEAD'VE STARR!
STARR COULDN'T GIVE A SHIT ABOUT US WITH JESSE GONE. WHAT YOU'VE BEEN DOING IS VISITING ALL YOUR LOWLIFE PALS UP AND DOWN THE WEST COAST-- AND YES, VERY IMPRESSIVE HOLLY-WOOD CONNECTIONS, CASSIDY. A BUNCH OF JUNKIES AND AN EX-PORNO PRODUCER.
YOU'VE BEEN LIVING LIFE THE WAY YOU LIKE IT, WHICH IS TO LIE ON YOUR DRUNK ASS IN SOME SLEAZEPIT UNTIL THE OWNER COMPLAINS ABOUT THE SMELL. AND YOU'VE BEEN KEEPING ME BOMBED OUT OF MY HEAD SO I WON'T SEE HOW PATHETIC IT ALL IS. SO YOU GET TO KEEP WHAT YOU'VE WANTED ALL ALONG.
ME.
HERE, YOU ASKED ME FOR THAT STUFF, REMEMBER? I NEVER FORCED IT DOWN YER THROAT!
I NEVER SAID YOU DID.
I TOOK THE PILLS. I DRANK THE VODKA. I ASKED FOR THEM.
THEN YOU JUST LEFT THEM LYING AROUND, SO EVERY TIME I LOOKED FOR MORE THEY'D BE THERE. BY THE TIME I DIDN'T NEED THEM I WANTED THEM ANYWAY.
YOU LOOKED AFTER ME FOR SIX FUCKING MONTHS ALL RIGHT.
BUT BAD NEWS: YOU GOT SO FUCKED-UP YOURSELF YOU FOR-GOT TO STOCK UP ON VALIUM ...
NO FUCKIN' WAY ARE YOU WALKIN' OUT ON ME!!

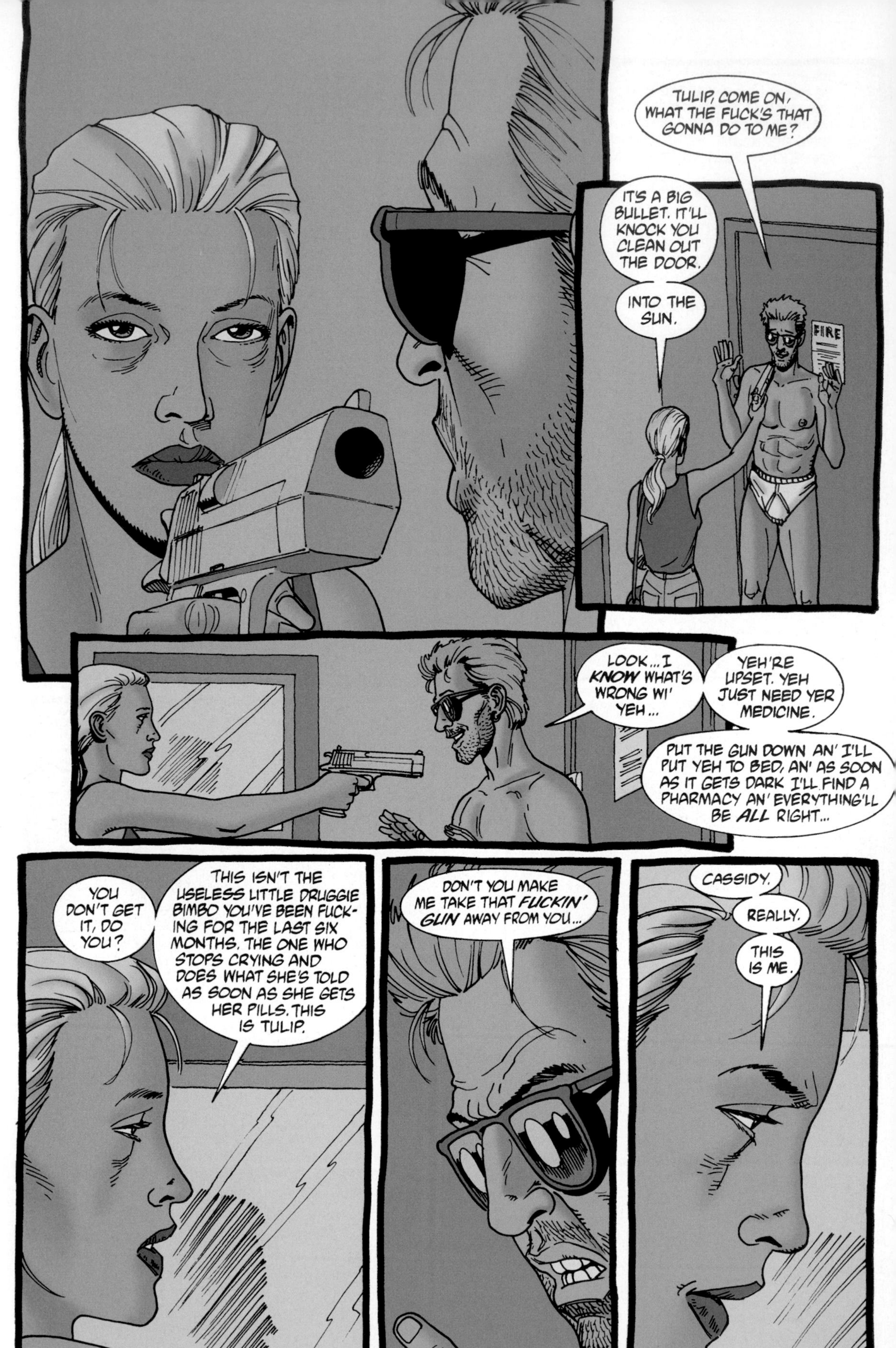
TULIP, COME ON, WHAT THE FUCK'S THAT GONNA DO TO ME?
IT'S A BIG BULLET. IT'LL KNOCK YOU CLEAN OUT THE DOOR.
INTO THE SUN.
FIRE
LOOK... I KNOW WHAT'S WRONG WI' YEH...
YEH'RE UPSET. YEH JUST NEED YER MEDICINE.
PUT THE GUN DOWN AN' I'LL PUT YEH TO BED, AN' AS SOON AS IT GETS DARK I'LL FIND A PHARMACY AN' EVERYTHING'LL BE ALL RIGHT...
YOU DON'T GET IT, DO YOU?
THIS ISN'T THE USELESS LITTLE DRUGGIE BIMBO YOU'VE BEEN FUCKING FOR THE LAST SIX MONTHS. THE ONE WHO STOPS CRYING AND DOES WHAT SHE'S TOLD AS SOON AS SHE GETS HER PILLS. THIS IS TULIP.
DON'T YOU MAKE ME TAKE THAT FUCKIN' GUN AWAY FROM YOU...
CASSIDY.
REALLY.
THIS IS ME.

UHHNNNH

AAAAAHHH

AAAAAAH

AWHH, FUCKIN' JAYSIS--!

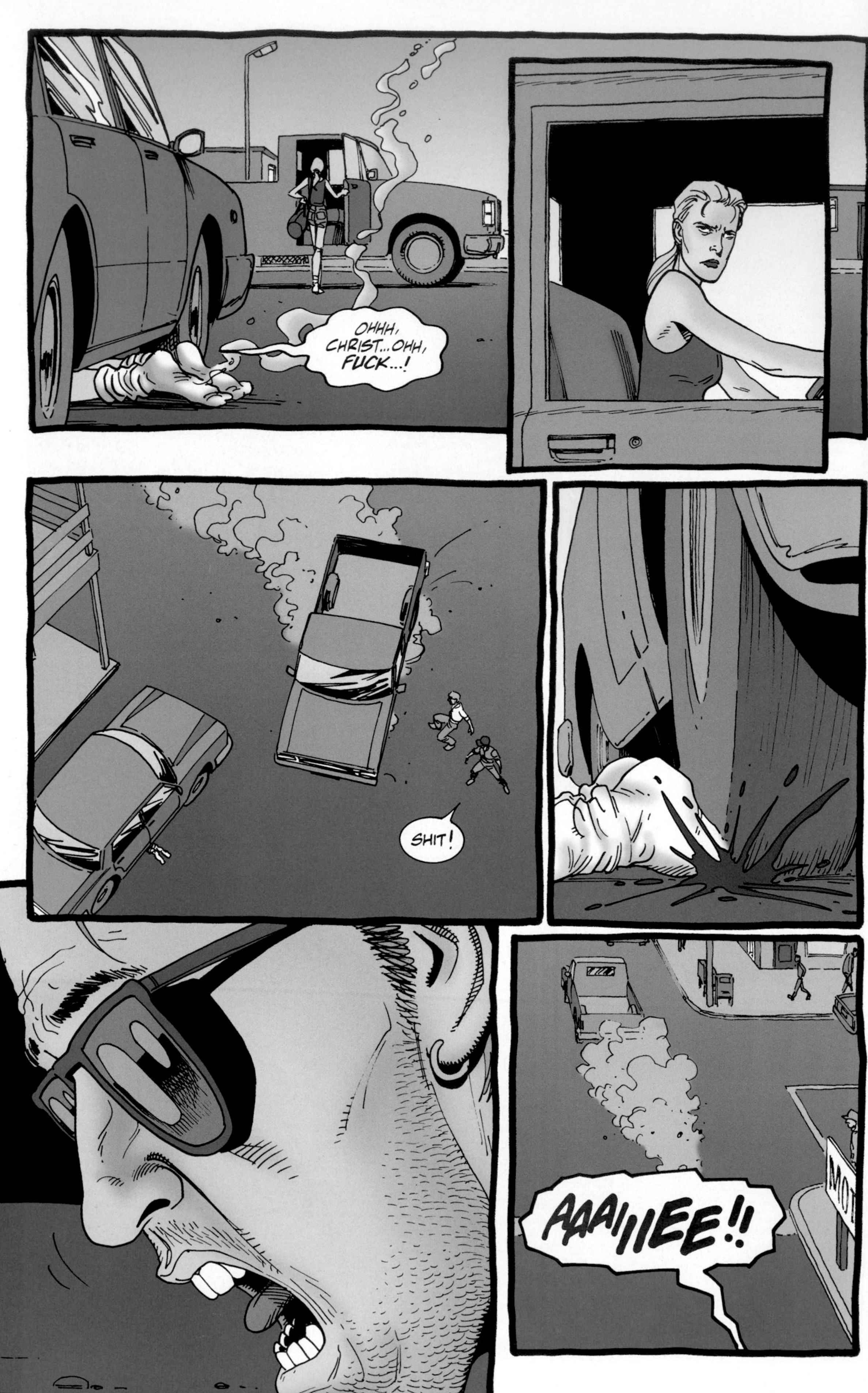
OHHH, CHRIST...OHH, FUCK...!
SHIT!
AAAIIIEE!!

I'LL ALWAYS LOVE YOU.

BUT YOU'RE GONE.

Miller's Tavern
FISHIN' IN THE SUMMER
HUNTIN' IN THE FALL
MILLER'S TAVERN
WATCH HIM PLAYIN' LITTLE LEAGUE
TAKE HIM TO THE GAME
FIRST DAMN SPRING HE'S OLD ENOUGH WE'RE GONNA DRIVE OUT TO THE RIDGE AN' CLIMB MAYNARD'S PEAK, RIGHT WHERE MY DADDY USED TO TAKE ME CAMPIN'. GREATEST DAMN THING IN A BOY'S LIFE, I TELL YOU...
DAMN RIGHT, I SWEAR...
OH YEAH, BUILD A FIRE AN' COOK SOME WIENERS...
HEY, WHAT YOU GONNA CALL HIM, JAKE?
JUNE
HIS NAME IS JOHN WILLIAM GRADY O'HARE.
AND HE IS GONNA MAKE HIS MARK ON THIS DAMN WORLD.

WHAT IF IT'S A GIRL?

HAHAHAHA A GIRL HAHAHA HAHA YEAH, RIGHT HAHAHA

JESUS, CECIL-- Heh! YOU SAY THE DAMNDEST THINGS...!
I DON'T KNOW, BUDDY, THE DAMN WIFE MENTIONED SOMETHIN' JUST IN CASE. SHE LIKES FLOWER NAMES, IF YOU CAN BELIEVE THAT.
A GIRL. I SWEAR.

HOSPITAL FOR YOU, JAKE!
DAMN! LOOKS LIKE THE BOY'S ON TIME!
CIGARS, FELLAS!

TOM, YOU HAUL OUT THAT OL' GRANDAD. DRINKS ARE ON ME.
HELL, JAKE, DRINKS ARE ON THE DAMN HOUSE...
A GIRL, CECIL? YOU BEEN SMOKIN' THAT DAMN WEED LIKE THEM PEACENIKS IN WASHINGTON?

ALL I'M SAYING IS IT COULD HAPPEN...
OH SURE, JAKE O'HARE COULD HAVE A DAUGHTER! WHY THE HELL NOT!
YEAH, AND THEN MAYBE HE COULD VOTE DEMOCRAT, OR--

OR...

DAMN WIFE DIED.
DAMN BABY'S A GIRL.

DAMN.
DAMN.
DAMN.
DAMN.
DAMN.

MR. O'HARE?
UH?
YOU CAN SEE YOUR DAUGHTER NOW.
ROOM
D

I BEG YOUR PARDON, MISS?
YOUR DAUGHTER. YOU CAN SEE HER.

DO YOU THINK I OUGHTA?

WELL-- YES...
OH, OKAY.

THERE SHE IS...
O'HARE, TULIP

ISN'T SHE BEAUTIFUL? HERE, D'YOU WANT TO HOLD HER?
OH--WELL-- I DON'T REALLY KNOW HOW, I MEAN WITH A GIRL...
WHAT'S THE DIFFERENCE? SHE'S A BABY, YOU HOLD HER LIKE ANY BABY...
BUT-- MISS--
HERE.
Gurp
AW HELL.
SO YOU'RE A GIRL.
THAT NEEDN'T BE SO BAD.

HOW WAS SCHOOL TODAY, LITTLE PETAL?

HOR'BLE.

WHY DO I ***HAVE TO*** GO TO SCHOOL, DADDY?

TO LEARN THINGS...

WHAT THINGS?

STILL A MITE HIGH, LITTLE PETAL.

I'M NEVER GONNA BE ANY GOOD...
AW, COME ON NOW. SOME OF THEM WEREN'T TOO FAR OFF!
IT'LL COME TO YOU. YOU'LL GET ALL THE BAD SHOTS OUTTA YOUR SYSTEM AN' YOU'LL START MAKIN' GOOD ONES, SAME AS ANYBODY...

CAN I TRY WITH THE 'MATIC?
WELL NOW, LITTLE PETAL, YOU REMEMBER WHAT DADDY TOLD YOU: AUTOMATIC'S A COMPLICATED WEAPON. FIRES MORE BULLETS, BUT YOU GOT A LOT MORE PARTS TO GO WRONG ON YOU.
LET'S GET YOU SHOOTIN' STRAIGHT FIRST, HUH? THEN WE'LL TAKE A LOOK AT THAT OL' FORTY-FIVE.

MEANTIME... SEEIN' AS IT'S NEARLY CHRISTMAS...

FRONT SIGHT ON YOUR TARGET, LITTLE PETAL. FRONT SIGHT.
FIND YOUR SHOT.
TAKE A BREATH.

FRONT SIGHT. ALWAYS, ALWAYS, ALWAYS.
FRONT SIGHT.

SQUEEEEEEZE..

WAY TO GO, LITTLE PETAL!

LITTLE PETAL?

DADDY, CAN I BE IN THE PARATROOPERS WHEN I GROW UP?
LITTLE PETAL--

WHEN YOU GROW UP, YOU CAN BE WHATEVER THE HELL YOU *WANT*.

...SO I SAID TO THAT DAMN COACH, I SAID--MISTER, MY LITTLE GIRL CAN HIT HARDER AN' RUN FASTER THAN ANY ONE'VE THE DAMN PANSIES YOU'VE GOT ON THIS DAMN TEAM'VE YOURS. WHY THE HELL WON'T YOU LET HER PLAY?
SON OF A BITCH COULDN'T EVEN LOOK ME IN THE EYE. SAID RULES ARE RULES. SAID GIRLS AIN'T ALLOWED TO PLAY BASEBALL AN' THAT'S ALL THERE IS TO IT.
THAT *PRICK*...!
YEAH, WHAT THE HELL'S GOT UP HIS ASS?

JUST ABOUT BROKE HER LITTLE HEART.
I TELL YOU, BOYS: IF A GIRL CAN'T DO THE THINGS SHE WANTS 'CAUSE OF SOME STUPID RULES, IF SHE AIN'T GOT THE SAME CHOICES FELLAS DO--HELL, IF WE AIN'T GOT REAL, GENUINE EQUALITY BETWEEN THE SEXES--
THEN THERE IS ALWAYS GONNA BE SOMETHIN' SERIOUSLY WRONG WITH THIS GREAT COUNTRY OF OURS.
YEAH!
GODDAMN RIGHT!
YOU SAID IT, JAKE!

...HUH?

ROBERT KENNEDY
MEMORIAL
GRADE SCHOOL
EST. 1969

DID YOU GUYS SEE KELLY'S HEROES ON SATURDAY NIGHT? WASN'T IT COOL?
DAVID SOUL

THAT'S A BOYS' MOVIE, TULIP...
YOU'RE WEIRD, TULIP...
WE DON'T WANT TO PLAY WITH YOU...

DID YOU GUYS SEE KELLY'S HEROES ON SATURDAY NIGHT? WASN'T IT COOL?
ROCK

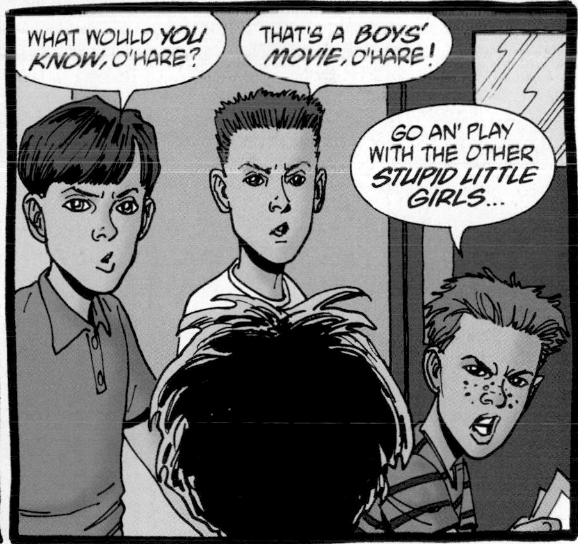
WHAT WOULD YOU KNOW, O'HARE?
THAT'S A BOYS' MOVIE, O'HARE!
GO AN' PLAY WITH THE OTHER STUPID LITTLE GIRLS...

?

NO, MR. O'HARE, I WOULD NOT SAY THAT *ASSAULT WITH A BASEBALL BAT* CONSTITUTES "JUSTICE BEING DONE"...

WELL, MRS. CARLYLE, THE WRIGHT BOY AMBUSHED MY LITTLE GIRL ON HER WAY HOME FROM SCHOOL ON MONDAY. TOOK ALL HER COMIC BOOKS AND CANDY SHE ONLY JUST BOUGHT.

THERE WAS HIM AND *FOUR* OF HIS DAMN GANG, MA'AM--PARDON MY FRENCH. WHAT ELSE WAS SHE S'POSED TO DO, 'CEPT WAIT HIM OUT AN' CRACK HIS SKULL WHEN HIS BACK WAS TURNED?

BUT HUGH AND HIS FRIENDS DENY ALL THIS...

MRS L. CARLYLE PRINCIPAL

ALL DUE RESPECT, MA'AM, BUT HUGH WRIGHT IS NOT TO BE TRUSTED. I SHOULD KNOW, I WENT TO SCHOOL WITH HIS DADDY BILL--
YES--BUT--
AN' HE WAS A LYIN' LITTLE SNAKE JUST LIKE HIS WORTHLESS RAT OF A SON. I USED TO BEAT THE TAR OUTTA HIM ALL THE TIME.

ALL THE SAME, MR. O'HARE, I SIMPLY *CANNOT* LET TULIP OFF WITH THIS. YOU MUST UNDERSTAND--
WELL HELL, CAN'T YOU AT LEAST GET HER ONTO THAT DAMN TEAM NOW? I MEAN HOW 'BOUT THAT SWING, HUH?

PARDON MY FRENCH, MA'AM.

...YES, TULIP IS A VERY INTELLIGENT GIRL--HER GRADES ARE EXCELLENT RIGHT ACROSS THE BOARD, IN FACT--
BUT CAN'T YOU PLEASE ENCOURAGE HER IN SOME SLIGHTLY MORE--MORE FEMININE PURSUITS? AND ATTITUDES?
WELL, MRS. CARLYLE, NO DISRESPECT INTENDED TO YOUR POINT OF VIEW, MA'AM...
MRS L. CARLY
PRINCIPAL

BUT I ALWAYS FIGURED IT WAS BEST TO ENCOURAGE HER IN WHAT SHE LIKED.

...
...
...
YOU CAN DISCIPLINE HER, CAN'T YOU? YOU CAN DO THAT, RIGHT?
SURE.

WHY WERE YOU BEING SO NICE TO MRS. CARLYLE, DADDY?
US FELLAS HAVE TO BE POLITE TO YOU LADIES, LITTLE PETAL. IT'S HOW WE'RE RAISED.
MENU

HOW COME?
HMMM.
I AIN'T EXACTLY SURE, LITTLE PETAL.

IT MIGHT BE TO MAKE UP FOR LADIES GENERALLY HAVIN' LESS FUN.

GOD DAMN!!

DON'T FIGHT HIM, LITTLE PETAL! LET HIM RUN! TIRE HIM OUT!
HOLY JESUS, YOU SEE THEM JAWS? YOU IMAGINE THEM THINGS ON THE WALL OF THE DEN?!
SKIPPER
BAR HARBOR

...SON OF A BITCH FOUGHT US ALL DAY. JUST GET A LINE ON HIM NOW AN' WE'LL HAUL HIM IN.
HELL, LITTLE PETAL, DIDN'T I TELL YOU THIS'D BE MORE FUN THAN SUMMER CAMP?

HE CAN'T BE DEAD!!

--YELLED KRANSKI, FEAR MIXING WITH THE FURY IN HIS VOICE, HE'S OUR SARGE! BUT THE LITTLE ITALIAN MEDIC COULD ONLY SADLY SHAKE HIS HEAD, AND AS THE RAIN FELL SILENCE DESCENDED ON THE BATTERED SQUAD OF G.I.s LIKE A SHROUD.
IT WAS RAFFERTY FROM BROOKLYN WHO BROKE IT. THEN I GUESS WE BETTER GET BACK UP THERE AND KICK THOSE KRAUTS OFF THAT GODDAMN RIDGE, HE SNARLED, HIS KNUCKLES WHITE AS HE GRIPPED THE B.A.R., 'CAUSE THAT'S WHAT SERGEANT DOBERMANN WOULD HAVE WANTED.

SO ONE BY ONE THEY SHOULDERED THEIR M-1s AND STRODE GRIMLY INTO THE NIGHT--
LITTLE PETAL?
YOU ASLEEP?

PRETTY LITTLE THING.
PRETTY AS YOUR MOMMA WAS.

AN' THAT'S SAYIN' SOMETHIN'.

TULIP
GLENN FABRY
·27 APRIL 99·

"It all gets fixed. It all gets fixed and they grow up to be president or something. But you had a gun."

EVEN HITGIRLS GET THE BLUES

GARTH ENNIS - Writer STEVE DILLON - Artist

PAMELA RAMBO - Colorist CLEM ROBINS - Letterer AXEL ALONSO - Editor

PREACHER created by GARTH ENNIS and STEVE DILLON

HOW MUCH LONGER, DADDY?
WHY, 'TIL WHENEVER SOME BIG EIGHT- OR TEN-POINTER STICKS HIS HEAD UP AN' SAYS HELLO...

YOU AIN'T TIRED, ARE YOU, LITTLE PETAL? WE'VE HARDLY EVEN WALKED TWO MILES!
OH DADDY, I'M THIRTEEN! DON'T CALL ME THAT!

HA! THIRTEEN AN' ALL GROWN UP, HUH?
HELL, YOU'RE ALWAYS GONNA BE DADDY'S LITTLE PETAL...!

I GUESS IT WOULDN'T HURT TO REST FOR A MINUTE OR TWO. DADDY'S GOTTA TAKE A DUMP, ANYHOW.

WE GET GOIN' AGAIN AN' WE'LL FIND YOU YOUR FIRST BUCK, LITTLE PETAL. MEAT FOR THE WINTER AN' A NICE BIG SPREAD OF ANTLERS TO GO OVER THE FIRE.
I SWEAR, THERE IS NOTHIN' IN THE WORLD BEATS HUNTIN' SEASON...

BADAMM
FUCK!!

OH NO--
HOLY FUCKIN' JESUS--!

SHIT! MISS, MISS, ARE YOU--
I DIDN'T-- I COULDA SWORN--

I JUST SAW MOVEMENT IN THE BRUSH THERE, AND, AND--
MISS, NO!

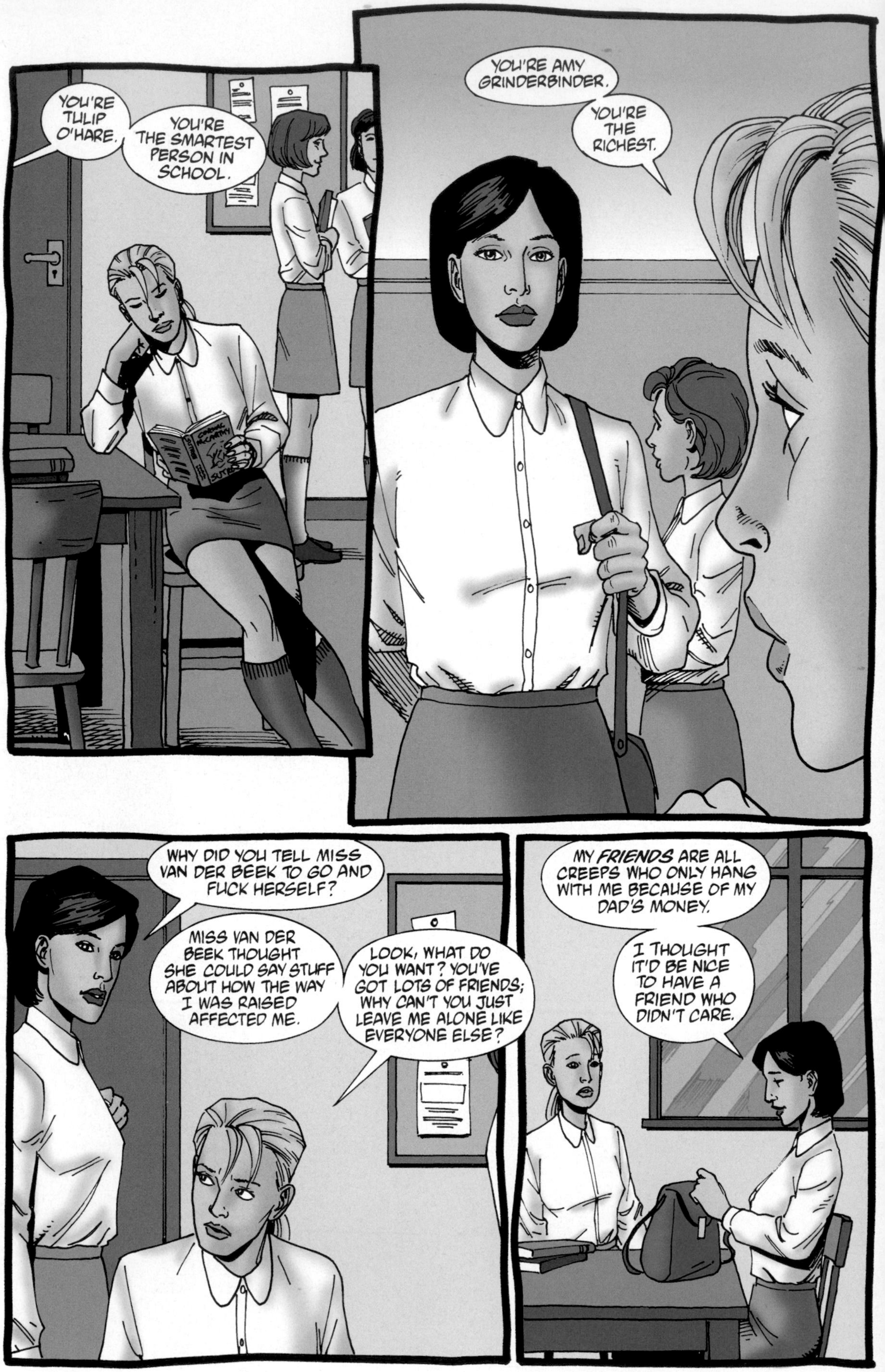

YOU'RE TULIP O'HARE.
YOU'RE THE SMARTEST PERSON IN SCHOOL.

YOU'RE AMY GRINDERBINDER.
YOU'RE THE RICHEST.

WHY DID YOU TELL MISS VAN DER BEEK TO GO AND FUCK HERSELF?
MISS VAN DER BEEK THOUGHT SHE COULD SAY STUFF ABOUT HOW THE WAY I WAS RAISED AFFECTED ME.
LOOK, WHAT DO YOU WANT? YOU'VE GOT LOTS OF FRIENDS; WHY CAN'T YOU JUST LEAVE ME ALONE LIKE EVERYONE ELSE?

MY *FRIENDS* ARE ALL CREEPS WHO ONLY HANG WITH ME BECAUSE OF MY DAD'S MONEY.
I THOUGHT IT'D BE NICE TO HAVE A FRIEND WHO DIDN'T CARE.

...SO MY AUNT SOLD EVERYTHING, THE HOUSE AND ALL MY DAD'S STUFF, ALL OF IT. THEN SHE USED THE MONEY TO SEND ME HERE.
NOBODY ASKED ME WHAT I WANTED, NOT EVEN ONCE.
YOUR GRADES MUST HAVE BEEN AMAZING TO GET IN HERE...

THEY WERE OKAY. I WAS HAPPIER WHERE I WAS.
EVEN WITHOUT YOUR DAD?
YEAH...

TULIP, IT'S REALLY HORRIBLE ABOUT WHAT HAPPENED TO HIM, BUT IT'S BEEN ALMOST TWO YEARS. YOU CAN'T JUST GO AROUND NOT TALKING TO PEOPLE AND BEING SAD FOREVER...
I MEAN SOMEONE AS SMART AS YOU, THINK OF ALL THE STUFF YOU CAN DO AND THE FUN YOU CAN HAVE...

YEAH, I GET THIS A LOT. THAT'S WHY I GO AROUND NOT TALKING TO PEOPLE.

WHAT'RE YOU DOING AT CHRISTMAS?

I'M IN THE CARE OF THE STATE UNTIL I'M SEVENTEEN. ALL THE OTHER BOARDERS GO HOME AT RECESS, EXCEPT FOR ME.
CARE OF THE STATE, IT'S JUST THIS HORRIBLE OLD ORPHANAGE...
YOU WANT TO COME STAY WITH ME?

BUT... WHAT ABOUT YOUR DAD?
WOUND AROUND THIS.

WHAT'RE YOU, CRAZY? IT WORKS, IT'S PERFECT, I TOTALLY KNEW IT'D WORK...!

BUT--

WHEN IN DOUBT: BLACK. NOW, YOUR HAIR...

BUT WHY ARE WE DOING THIS?

SO GUYS NOTICE US.

BUT I DON'T WANT TO MEET GUYS.

EVEN HANDSOME ONES?

IT DOESN'T MATTER HOW HANDSOME THEY ARE. THEY ALWAYS TURN OUT TO BE JERKS.

NO ONE'S EVER GONNA BE AS NICE AS MY--AS--

YOU SEE, HONEY...YOU KNOW HOW MY DAD'S REALLY RICH, OKAY?
WELL, HE KNOWS ALL THESE OTHER RICH GUYS, THESE GUYS WHO OWN BANKS AND SPORTS TEAMS, AND DO BUSINESS ALL OVER THE WORLD AND'VE BEEN EVERYWHERE AND DONE EVERYTHING...
BUT MY MOM TOLD HIM, BEFORE SHE LEFT WITH AUNT MO, SHE TOLD HIM THAT SO LONG AS SHE KEPT HANGING OUT WITH ASSHOLES LIKE THAT HE WAS GOING TO KEEP ON GETTING SURPRISES--
GOD, YOU ARE SO PRETTY, YOU KNOW? LIKE NATURALLY? I MEAN I NEED ABOUT A TON OF THIS STUFF TO BRING OUT WHAT I'VE GOT, BUT YOU HARDLY NEED ANY...
IT DOESN'T MATTER WHERE YOU'VE BEEN OR WHAT YOU'VE DONE OR HOW SMART YOU ARE. NONE OF IT COUNTS FOR SHIT IF YOU DON'T KNOW PEOPLE.
THAT'S WHAT MY MOM SAID.
I KNOW, 'CAUSE I WAS LISTENING OUTSIDE THEIR DOOR.
THERE.

WANNA SEE WHAT MY DAD GOT ME FOR CHRISTMAS?

I THOUGHT WE WERE SITTING IN IT. LISTEN, WHOSE PARTY IS THIS WE'RE GOING TO, EXACTLY?
KIRSTY KENNEDY'S BROTHER, SOME OF HIS FRIENDS...

SO IT'S A FRAT PARTY-- *JESUS!*

DADDY WANTS HIS LITTLE GIRL TO BE SAFE FROM PERVERTS... *BABOOM!*
AMY, PUT IT AWAY!
RELAX, WILL YOU? I'VE GOT A LICENSE... *BABOOM!*
AMY, I'M NOT FUCKING JOKING! *I HATE GUNS!*

OH HONEY, I'M SORRY...! I *TOTALLY* FORGOT--
LET'S JUST GO.

DO WE KNOW ANYONE HERE?
THIS IS SO COOL!
MY, MY! AND WHAT CAN I GET FOR TWO SUCH RAVISHING YOUNG LADIES AS YOU THIS EVENING?
WELL WHAT'S GOOD?
THE PUNCH. THE PUNCH IS EXCELLENT.
AND HOW ABOUT YOUR FRIEND--OH, THERE'S A BOTTLE OF THAT OPEN ALREADY...
THIS ONE'S FINE.
WELL FUCK YOU, BABY.
HEY, YOU WANT SOME MORE PUNCH THERE?

ISN'T THIS AMAZING? LOOK AT THAT GUY! WHAT IS THIS MUSIC? ISN'T HE GORGEOUS? HOLY SHIT!
ARE YOU OKAY?

YEAH, I--
ACTUALLY--
NO, I'M NOT...

AMY, THIS PARTY FUCKING SUCKS, OKAY? I'M GOING TO GET OUR JACKETS. YOU STAY HERE.
STAY. HERE.

...SHIT.

AMY?

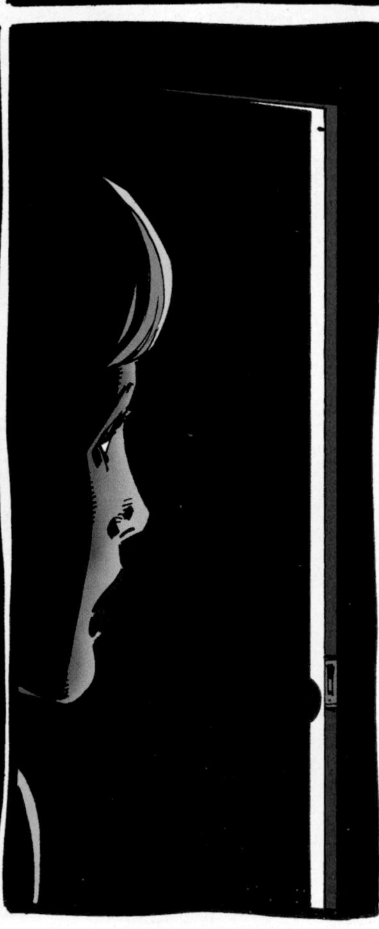

WANT SOME TOO, YOU FUCKIN' WHORE?

WHAT THE FUCK--
CLOSE THE FUCKIN' DOOR--

FUCKIN' HOLD THE BITCH!
NAAAHHHH!
FUCK-- FUCK--
YOU FUCKIN' FUCKIN' COOZE, YOU DON'T FUCKIN' QUIT IT I'LL FUCKIN' KNOCK YOUR FUCKIN' TEETH OUT!

WHAT THE FUCK?!
FUCK
NO
JESUS

AMY--
GET--
GET IN THE FUCKING TRUCK--

COCKSUCKIN' FUCKIN' SLUTS.

T-TULIP--
IN THE TRUCK.

KLIK

WHOA. WELL.
THAT WAS FUCKING *AMAZING*.
WHAT WAS?

YOU WERE! YOU TOTALLY FUCK-ING SAVED ME!
YOU WERE FUCKING INCREDIBLE, TULIP, YOU HAD THE GUN AND YOU WERE LIKE, LIKE *UNSTOPPABLE*--
AMY, WE COULD BE IN SHIT UP TO OUR EYEBALLS HERE!

OH COME ON, WHAT ARE THEY GOING TO SAY? "OFFICER, OFFICER, THIS CRAZY GIRL BLEW THE SHIT OUT OF OUR FRATHOUSE! *WE WERE SO SCARED WE NEVER EVEN GOT TO RAPE HER FRIEND!*"
TULIP?

IT ISN'T FUNNY, AMY! I ALMOST KILLED THAT GUY, I FUCKING WOULD HAVE IF THE GUN WAS LOADED! AND THAT'S THE KIND OF THING YOU *NEVER* GET AWAY FROM!
I FUCKING HATE GUNS, AMY! **OKAY?!**

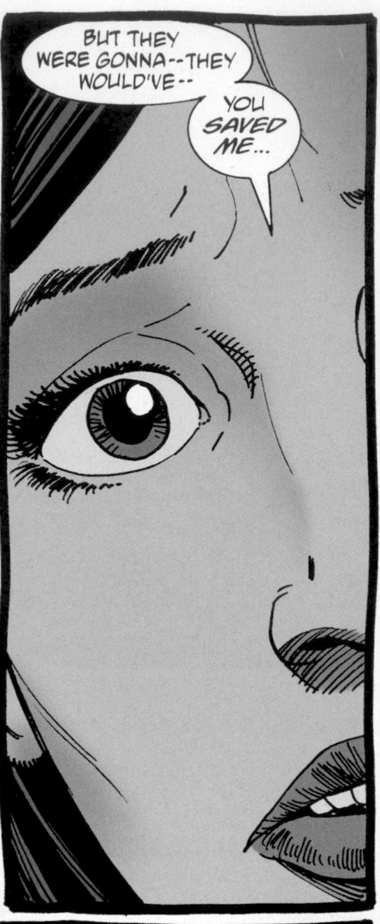
BUT THEY WERE GONNA--THEY WOULD'VE--
YOU SAVED ME...

OH AMY, I'M SORRY...!

G-G-GUYS LIKE THAT--
THEY DON'T GO TO JAIL, TULIP.

THEIR DADS CAN BUY JUDGES. I SHOULD KNOW.
THEY DO WHATEVER THEY WANT AND ANYONE WHO STANDS UP TO THEM'S A SLUT OR A TEASE, OR WAS PROBABLY JUST ASKING FOR IT. IT ALL GETS FIXED.
IT ALL GETS FIXED AND THEY GROW UP TO BE PRESIDENT OR SOMETHING.

BUT YOU HAD A GUN.

HEY.
MM.
BOSTON HERALD
SPORT
SEN. GRINDERBINDER
'CHOKED ON CLAM' - AIDE

SO HOW DID IT GO?
OH, FINE. MOM'S NOT CONTESTING IT. THEY GAVE ME A GREAT BIG CHECK FOR MILLIONS AND MILLIONS OF DOLLARS.

BUT YOU'D RATHER HAVE YOUR DAD BACK, HUH?
YEAH.
YEAH.

DO YOU WANT TO GO TO COLLEGE?
OR DO YOU WANT TO TAKE A YEAR OFF AND SEE THE COUNTRY ON THIS GREAT BIG CHECK OF MINE?

YEAH...
LET'S TAKE A YEAR OFF.

LET'S TAKE TWO.

WHERE THE HELL WERE YOU?
SAM'S
BAR

I WAITED FOR YOU ALL NIGHT, I MEAN I WAS REALLY FUCKING WORRIED! JESUS CHRIST, TULIP, WE'RE--I DON'T EVEN *KNOW* WHERE WE ARE!
WE'RE IN TEXAS. LOOK, I KNOW YOU'RE MAD, OKAY? BUT LISTEN.

I WAS WAITING RIGHT HERE FOR YOU, JUST LIKE I PROMISED, WHEN ALL OF A SUDDEN THIS *GUY* WALKED IN--
SO WE GOT TALKING AND IT WAS LIKE THERE WAS THIS--THIS--I'VE NEVER FELT ANYTHING LIKE IT, BUT THERE WAS THIS EXPLOSION OR SOMETHING INSIDE ME AND I KNEW HE COULD *SEE IT*--

AND THEN HIS GIRL-FRIEND--I MEAN HIS EX-GIRLFRIEND--TRIED TO SCRATCH MY EYES OUT IN THE LADIES' ROOM--
AND THEN...

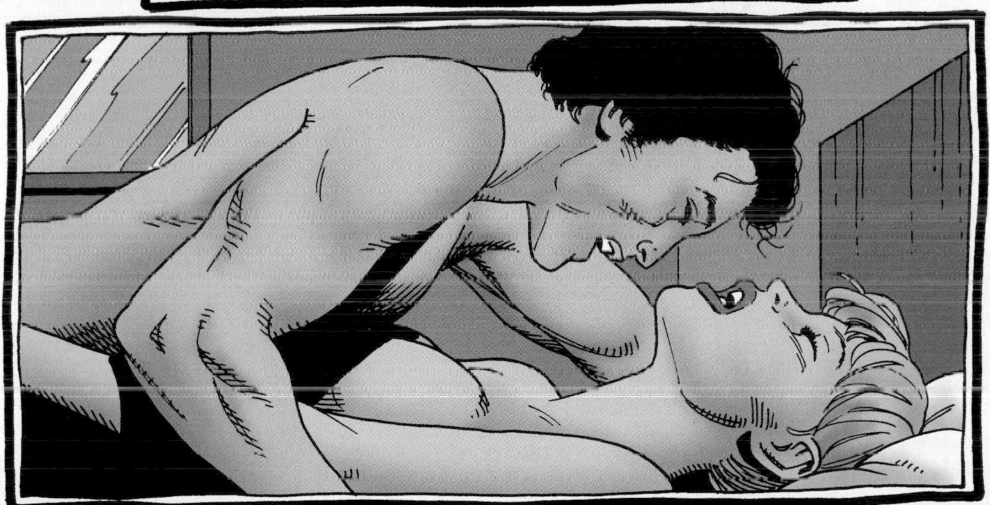

SO YOU--
YOU FINALLY--
HOLY SHIT!

SO WHO IS THIS GUY?

HE'S GONE.

I'LL ALWAYS LOVE HIM, AMY.
BUT HE'S GONE.
18

TULIP... HONEY, WHERE'VE YOU BEEN?
WHO'S GONE?

JESSE. HE'S GONE. HE'S DEAD.
HAVE YOU GOT ANYTHING TO DRINK, AMY? FOR CHRIST'S SAKE DON'T GIVE ME ANYTHING TO DRINK...

GIRLFRIEND--
WHAT'S HAPPENED TO YOU?

IT'S JUST A LITTLE HOT CHOCOLATE. C'MON.
OKAY, SO YOU DROVE ALL THE WAY HERE FROM NEVADA, IS THAT RIGHT? WHAT WERE YOU DOING IN NEVADA?
HAVING...A BAD TIME...
AND WHAT'S THIS ABOUT JESSE BEING DEAD?
IT WAS THAT THING IN ARIZONA. THE BOMB.
WE WERE... HE FELL...
HE'S DEAD...
TULIP... LISTEN TO ME, OKAY?
JESSE IS NOT DEAD.
I DON'T KNOW WHAT HAPPENED IN ARIZONA, BUT JESSE CALLED ME ABOUT A MONTH AFTER ALL OF THAT. RIGHT AFTER YOU DID, IN FACT, THAT TIME WHEN YOU SOUNDED SO WEIRD.
THEN HE CALLED ME AGAIN THREE DAYS AGO. FROM TEXAS.
HE'S COMING HERE, HONEY.
HE SAYS HE WANTS ME TO HELP HIM LOOK FOR YOU.

NO--
TULIP--
NO!
HE'S DEAD, AMY! HE FELL OUT OF A FUCKING AIRPLANE, HE COULDN'T HAVE SURVIVED!
YOU'RE SUPPOSED TO BE MY FRIEND, JESUS, WHY ARE YOU FUCKING WITH ME LIKE THIS?!
HONEY, NO, NOBODY'S FUCKING WITH YOU! HE SAID HE WAS ON HIS WAY, HE'S GETTING HERE LATER TONIGHT OR TOMORROW! REALLY!
I SWEAR TO GOD, TULIP! I AM YOUR FRIEND! OF ALL THE PEOPLE IN THIS FUCKING WORLD, WHY WOULD I WANT TO FUCK WITH YOU?!
BZZZZT
BZZZZT
BZZZZT

YOU HAVE TO LISTEN TO ME!
GLENN AND STEVE 99
DUHH DUHH!!

"Er... I want cock too..."

TOO DUMB FOR NEW YORK CITY AND TOO UGLY FOR L.A.

GARTH ENNIS - Writer STEVE DILLON - Artist

PAMELA RAMBO - Colorist CLEM ROBINS - Letterer AXEL ALONSO - Editor

PREACHER created by GARTH ENNIS and STEVE DILLON

...'CAUSE I'M S'POSED TO BE DEAD, SKEETER. I WANNA STICK TO THESE HERE BACK ROADS WHERE THERE'S LESS CHANCE OF GETTIN' PULLED OVER.
COULD LEAD TO ALL KINDSA COMPLICATIONS...

WUFF...
HELL NO, I WANNA PUSH ON AN' MAKE NEW YORK TONIGHT. AMY'S EXPECTIN' ME AN' I WANNA START LOOKIN' FOR TULIP 'SOON AS I CAN.

SAY, NOW WHY DON'T WE JUST HELP OUT THIS FELLA HERE...

WUFF! WUFF!
C'MON, SKEET, I'M TIRED AN' I WANNA TALK TO SOMEONE. WE PRETTY MUCH EXHAUSTED YOUR OPINIONS ON AMERICAN POLITICS A WHILE BACK.
I'M SURE HE WON'T BE NO PSYCHO.

"WHY, MISTER HAUER, IMAGINE MEETIN' YOU ALL THE WAY OUT HERE..."

HI THERE! TRYING TO GET TO CINCINNATI?
WELL, I'M HEADED NORTH, BUT... I CAN TAKE YOU AS FAR AS HAGERSTOWN. YOU COULD GET A BUS FROM THERE.
SOUNDS GOOD!

MARTY STRAUSS. PLEASED TO MEET YOU, REVEREND--?
JESSE CUSTER.

YOU WORKIN' IN CINCINNATI?
OH NO, I'M JUST... WELL, I GREW UP THERE. FIRST TIME BACK FOR YEARS.
JUST GOING HOME, I GUESS.

THANK YOU, REVEREND.
SAY, MAYBE YOU'VE HEARD OF ME. I USED TO DO PORNO FILMS UNDER THE NAME *TOM COOZE*?

...DON'T RING NO BELLS...
'COURSE IT DOESN'T! STUPID OF ME! HOW WOULD A *MINISTER* KNOW ABOUT PORNO?
STUPID, STUPID ME...

YOU DON'T DO THAT NO MORE, HUH?
NO...NO, IT WAS MY FIFTEEN MINUTES OF FAME, I GUESS. WELL, MORE THAN THAT, I DID QUITE A FEW FILMS...

BUT, YOU KNOW, I KILLED A BUNCH OF PEOPLE IN A VIBRATOR ACCIDENT. I WAS SORT OF BLACKLISTED AFTER THAT.

HECK, THERE I GO AGAIN--! I'M SORRY, REVEREND, YOU DON'T WANT TO HEAR ABOUT THINGS LIKE THAT!
OH NO, MARTY, YOU CAN TELL ME. YOU GO AHEAD AN' GET IT OFF YOUR CHEST IF IT'LL MAKE YOU FEEL BETTER.
HELL, CONFESSIN' YOUR SINS, THAT'S WHAT PREACHERS ARE S'POSED TO BE THERE FOR...

ISN'T THAT PRIESTS?

PREACHERS TOO.

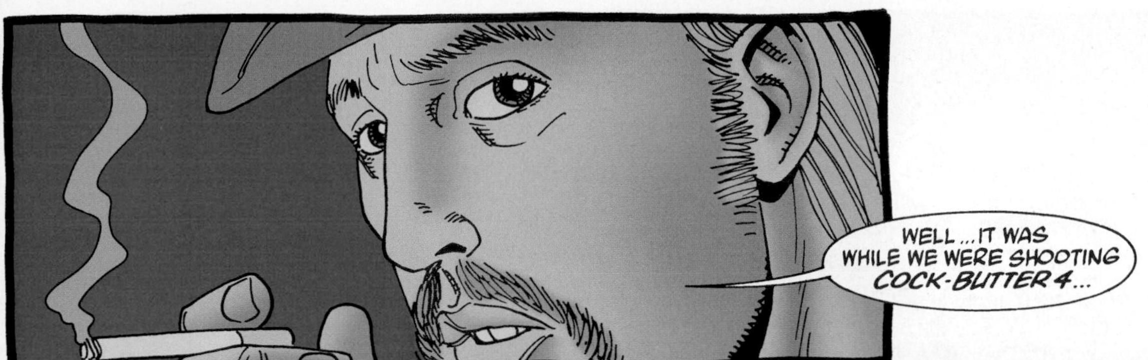
WELL ... IT WAS WHILE WE WERE SHOOTING *COCK-BUTTER 4*...

I WAS RESTING BETWEEN SCENES, SEE, AND I WAS WATCHING THEM SHOOT THIS JACUZZI SEQUENCE WITH NINA NORKS AND FIONA FUNBAGS, OKAY?
SO I GET A LITTLE BORED AND I'M WANDERING ROUND THE SET, AND I FIND THIS PLUG-IN DILDO THEY'RE GOING TO BE USING LATER ON-- YOU EVER SEEN ONE OF THOSE THINGS?
NOT UP CLOSE.

THEY GO LIKE A DAMN JACKHAMMER! I MEAN THE *SPEED* YOU CAN GET THEM UP TO!
DDRRR! DDRRRR!

SO I'M SORT OF FOOLING AROUND WITH IT, YOU KNOW, SEEING HOW FAST IT'LL GO-- BUT MY HANDS ARE STILL COVERED IN K.Y. FROM THE LAST SCENE, AND--WELL--
I DROP IT AND IT ROLLS INTO THE JACUZZI AND IT'S STILL PLUGGED IN, AND...

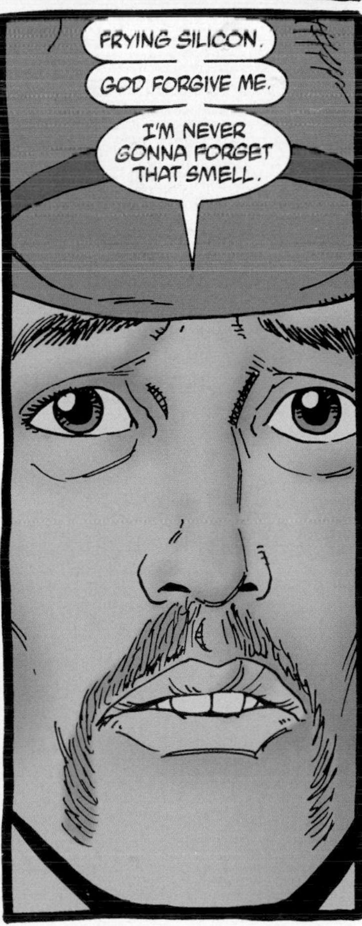
FRYING SILICON.
GOD FORGIVE ME.
I'M NEVER GONNA FORGET THAT SMELL.

SO THAT-- HHEM! THAT WAS WHEN YOU QUIT?
PRETTY MUCH. WELL, ONCE SOUTHPAW NELSON GOT THROUGH WITH ME.

MM?
SEE, THE PRODUCER OF THE FILM WAS QUITE A HEAVILY CONNECTED GUY. HE AND HIS BACKERS HAD A LOT OF MONEY INVESTED IN THIS PROJECT, AND IN THOSE TWO GIRLS, AND... WELL, THEY WANTED ME TO KNOW IT...
SOUTHPAW NELSON IS THIS GUY WHO... HE KIND OF...

BEATS HELL OUTTA FOLKS FOR THIS PRODUCER FELLA?
OH, MAN. HE WORKED MY BALLS LIKE A SPEED-BAG.

I MEAN HE'S ONLY THREE FOOT ELEVEN, BUT WHAT A LEFT HOOK...!
ANYHOW, BETWEEN THAT AND WORD GETTING OUT ABOUT THE DILDO INCIDENT, I WAS PRETTY MUCH FINISHED IN THE INDUSTRY. TIME TO HANG UP THE LEATHER COCK-RING AND MOVE ON TO PASTURES NEW, YOU KNOW?

YOU BITTER ABOUT IT?
HECK, NO! THIS IS AMERICA, REVEREND!

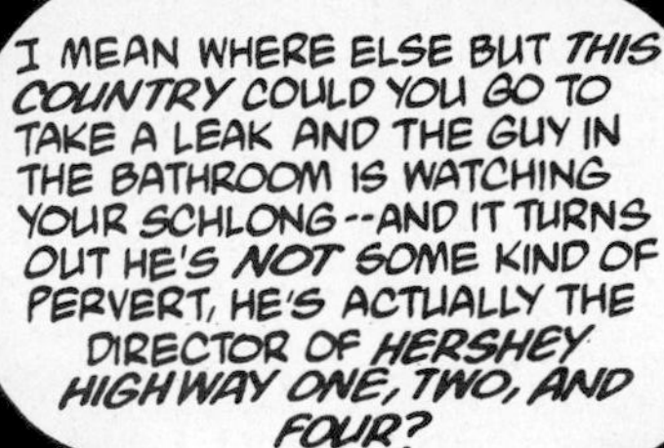
I MEAN WHERE ELSE BUT *THIS COUNTRY* COULD YOU GO TO TAKE A LEAK AND THE GUY IN THE BATHROOM IS WATCHING YOUR SCHLONG--AND IT TURNS OUT HE'S *NOT* SOME KIND OF PERVERT, HE'S ACTUALLY THE DIRECTOR OF *HERSHEY HIGHWAY ONE, TWO, AND FOUR?*

ONLY IN AMERICA, REVEREND. ONLY IN THIS GREAT COUNTRY OF OURS DO YOU GET TO *LIVE THE DREAM*.

GOD BLESS US ALL, REVEREND!
AND GOD BLESS THE UNITED STATES OF AMERICA--!

I'M SORRY...
HELL NO, MARTY. YOU GO ON AN' LET IT OUT. ONLY NATURAL.

NO, I SUPPOSE IT WAS MY TIME IN THE SUN, AND I ENJOYED IT--BUT I DON'T MISS IT ALL THAT MUCH. I NEVER LIKED THE SWEARING.

NO?
NO. I MEAN HAVING SEX WITH PEOPLE ON CAMERA, THAT WAS FINE. BUT TALKING DIRTY WHILE YOU'RE DOING IT?

I ALWAYS FOUND THAT KIND OF CRUDE.

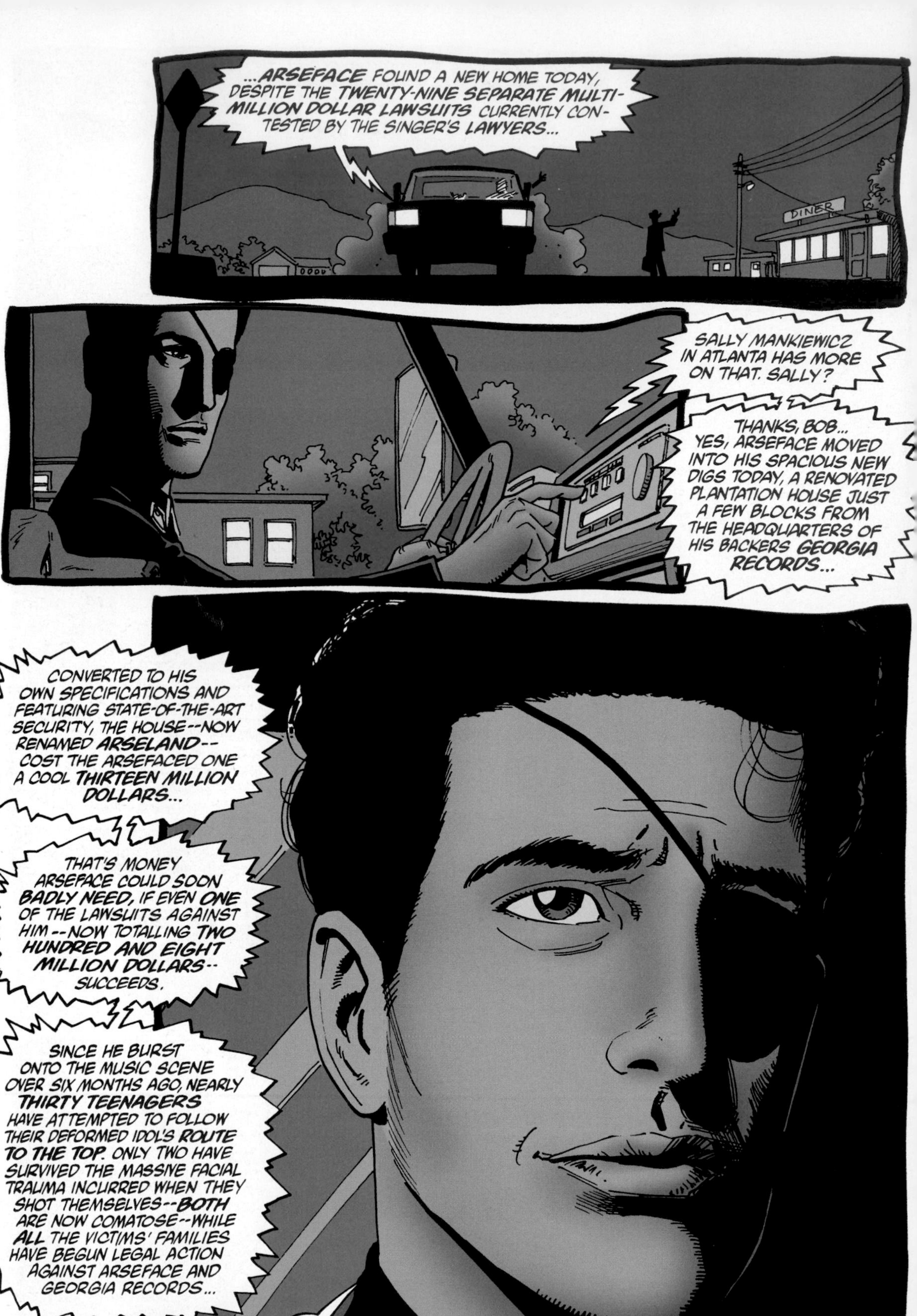
...ARSEFACE FOUND A NEW HOME TODAY, DESPITE THE TWENTY-NINE SEPARATE MULTI-MILLION DOLLAR LAWSUITS CURRENTLY CONTESTED BY THE SINGER'S LAWYERS...
DINER
SALLY MANKIEWICZ IN ATLANTA HAS MORE ON THAT. SALLY?
THANKS, BOB... YES, ARSEFACE MOVED INTO HIS SPACIOUS NEW DIGS TODAY, A RENOVATED PLANTATION HOUSE JUST A FEW BLOCKS FROM THE HEADQUARTERS OF HIS BACKERS GEORGIA RECORDS...
CONVERTED TO HIS OWN SPECIFICATIONS AND FEATURING STATE-OF-THE-ART SECURITY, THE HOUSE--NOW RENAMED ARSELAND--COST THE ARSEFACED ONE A COOL THIRTEEN MILLION DOLLARS...
THAT'S MONEY ARSEFACE COULD SOON BADLY NEED, IF EVEN ONE OF THE LAWSUITS AGAINST HIM--NOW TOTALLING TWO HUNDRED AND EIGHT MILLION DOLLARS--SUCCEEDS.
SINCE HE BURST ONTO THE MUSIC SCENE OVER SIX MONTHS AGO, NEARLY THIRTY TEENAGERS HAVE ATTEMPTED TO FOLLOW THEIR DEFORMED IDOL'S ROUTE TO THE TOP. ONLY TWO HAVE SURVIVED THE MASSIVE FACIAL TRAUMA INCURRED WHEN THEY SHOT THEMSELVES--BOTH ARE NOW COMATOSE--WHILE ALL THE VICTIMS' FAMILIES HAVE BEGUN LEGAL ACTION AGAINST ARSEFACE AND GEORGIA RECORDS...
OH, LORD.
LIFE IMITATES ARSE.

THANK YOU... WHILE WE AT GEORGIA RECORDS DEEPLY REGRET THESE TRAGIC ACCIDENTS, WE CAN IN NO WAY ACCEPT RESPONSIBILITY FOR THEM OCCURRIN'. AS MAH OL' PAPPY USED TO SAY: YOU STICK YOUR HAND IN THE FIRE ON SOMEONE ELSE'S SAY-SO, SCREW YOU. AH'M SURE THEY'LL HOLD YOUR JOB SLINGIN' BURGERS 'TIL YOU GET OUTTA THE HOSPITAL.

WUFF.

THIS WAS JUST THE LATEST IN A STRING OF INFLAMMATORY STATEMENTS BY GENE SERGEANT, ARSE-FACE'S FREQUENTLY CONTROVERSIAL MANAGER. AS THE STORM OVER ARSEFACE AND HIS SUICIDAL WANNABES CONTINUES TO RAGE, WE CAN ONLY WONDER:

WHO ARE THE ARSES? WHAT SHADOWY COMPULSIONS MOTIVATE THEM?

BOB?

TFFF
TFFF

TFFF
TFFF
TFFF
BY 'ECK, FREDDY LAD, WE WERE FOOKIN' LUCKY TO GET OUT OF THERE ALIVE. IF IT 'ADN'T BEEN FOR ME TRADEMARK FAST-TALKIN' BANTER, WELL, I FOOKIN' DREAD TO THINK...

YOU ALMOST KILLED THE PAIR OF US, BOB! HITCHING A RIDE WITH A FUCKING ENGLISH RUGBY TEAM! RIPPING THEM OFF FOR GAS MONEY!
I'M THE ONE GOT US OUT OF IT, DOWN ON MY KNEES LIKE A FUCKING CIRCUS SEAL WITH THE FIFTEEN OF THEM LINED UP IN FRONT OF ME, JESUS, I'LL NEVER GET RID OF THE FUCKING TASTE!

WELL, I TOLD YOU TO TAKE YOUR TEETH OUT FIRST! COME ON, IT WAS AN ARRANGEMENT WORKED OUT BEST FOR ALL CONCERNED. LEAST SAID, SOONEST MENDED.
AN' LOOK, 'ERE'S SOMEONE COMIN' NOW. WE'RE SORTED.

I'LL DO TALKIN'...
TFF
TFFF
TFFF

EY-OOP! GOIN' ANY-WHERE NEAR PHILLY, ARE YOU?
NOPE, NEW YORK. TAKE YOU AS FAR AS BETHLEHEM, IF YOU WANT.

AW, LOOK AT THIS LITTLE FELLA--!
MUCH OBLIGED, REVEREND. I'M BOB GLOVER, THIS BIG LONG STREAK O' MISERY'S CALLED FREDDY ALLEN. WE'RE SEXUAL BOUNTY HUNTERS.
WUFF!

...
WE MET BEFORE?
DON'T THINK SO.
IT'S JUST...
WELL, MY MEMORY AIN'T ALL IT USED TO BE, I GUESS.

YOU DON'T PLAY RUGBY, DO YOU?
NOPE.
OKAY.

SO I SAID, "I'M AN ENGLISHMAN, AND A YORKSHIRE-MAN. I TAKE IT OOP SHITTER AN' I'M NOT ASHAMED TO SAY SO..."

"...DAD."
SO WHY DON'T YOU TELL US WHAT HAPPENED NEXT, BOB...

WELL HE FOOKIN' LATHERED THE SHITE OUT'VE ME, DIDN'T HE? BEAT ME ALL ROUND HOUSE WITH COAL SHOVEL, BROKE BOTH ME FOOKIN' LEGS CHUCKIN' ME OUT OF TOP FLOOR WINDOW, TOLD ME NEVER TO DARKEN HIS DOOR AGAIN!
SO I WENT DOWN TO THAT NIGEL AT THE UNIVERSITY, I SAID "NIGEL, I TOLD ME DAD LIKE YOU SAID I SHOULD, AN' LOOK WHAT HE FOOKIN' DID TO ME!" AN' DO YOU KNOW WHAT HE SAID? HE SAID, "OOOH, HOW STRANGE, MUMMY NEVER OBJECTED WHEN I CAME OUT TO HER AND QUENTIN!" *THE NONCE!*

SO WITH DISGUSTIN' LEVEL OF 'OMOPHOBIA THEN PRESENT IN SOUTH YORKS PIT VILLAGES, AN' WHAT WITH MOTHER'S STROKE AN' FATHER HIRIN' LADS TO DUFF US OOP, I THOUGHT--I'VE 'AD ENOUGH SHEFFIELD TODGER. I'M OFF TO CALIFORNIA.
I 'AD THIS *DREAM*, SEE...

SEXUAL INVESTIGATION... A WHOLE NEW FIELD OF DETECTIVE WORK, A BULGIN' PURPLE VEIN JUST ASKIN' TO BE MINED! AN' WHERE BETTER TO BEGIN THAN THAT GRAND MODERN-DAY BABYLON, SAN FRANCISCO! THAT'S WHAT I RECKONED!
IT ALL FELL INTO PLACE ONCE I MET YOUNG FREDDY HERE. WITH MY EXPERIENCE I COULD 'ANDLE MOST OF THE BUGGERING WORK WHILE FREDDY DID THE FELLATIN'. DIDN'T WIN U.S. NAVY COCKSUCKIN' CHAMPIONSHIP THREE YEARS IN A ROW FOR NOTHIN', DID YOU, LAD!
er... heh-heh...
IT WEREN'T SO LONG BEFORE MY DREAM WERE REAL...
THAT YOUR DREAM TOO, FREDDY?
NO... NO, NOT REALLY.
BUT YOU LEARN TO SETTLE FOR WHAT YOU CAN GET, DON'T YOU?
PBBT

OH! BETTER OUT THAN IN!
I GUESS YOU DO.

THE SEX DETECTIVE AGENCY... JUST CAN'T SHAKE THE FEELIN' I'VE COME ACROSS YOU BOYS BEFORE...

WELL YOU WOULDN'T BE THE FIRST, LAD! BOOM-BOOM!
NAY, I'D REMEMBER. I NEVER FORGET A FACE. THAT'S WHY THIS QUARRY OF OURS'LL NOT ESCAPE HIS FATE MUCH LONGER.

THAT RIGHT?
OH AYE. CHAP WE'RE AFTER STOLE 'ALF A MILLION DOLLARS FROM 'IS FORMER EMPLOYER AFTER A DISPUTE OF SOME KIND, WENT ON THE RUN WITH IT. THERE'S TEN GRAND ON THE FOOKER'S 'EAD, AN' WE AIM TO COLLECT IT.
LAD BY THE NAME OF TOM COOZE...

HE'S 'AD SOME LUCK, BUT NO ONE ESCAPES JUSTICE FOREVER...
JUSTICE? IS THAT WHY WE'RE WORKING FOR ONE OF THE BIGGEST SLEAZE-BAG PORNOGRAPHERS ON THE WEST COAST?
SHUT UP, YOU!

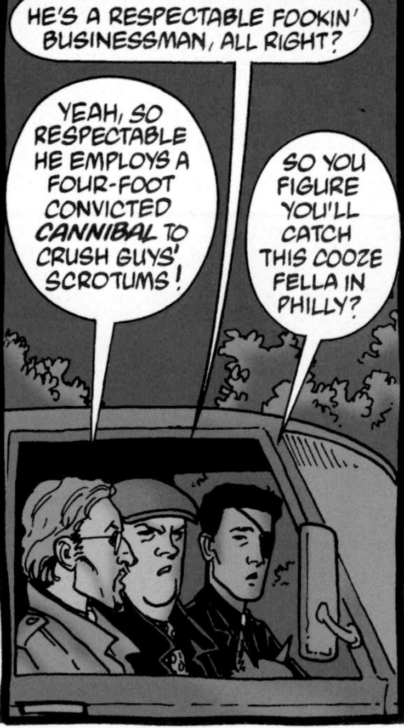
HE'S A RESPECTABLE FOOKIN' BUSINESSMAN, ALL RIGHT?
YEAH, SO RESPECTABLE HE EMPLOYS A FOUR-FOOT CONVICTED CANNIBAL TO CRUSH GUYS' SCROTUMS!
SO YOU FIGURE YOU'LL CATCH THIS COOZE FELLA IN PHILLY?

OH AYE, SEX CAPITAL OF THE EAST COAST ACCORDING TO OUR INFORMATION. WE'LL FIND HIM THERE OR MY NAME'S NOT BUGGERY BOB.
HE CAN RUN--BUT HE CAN'T HIDE...

...SO WE OPEN THE DOOR AN' THERE HE IS SITTIN' WITH NOTHIN' ON BUT HIS POINTY EARS AN' AN ERECTION, HOLDIN' A LIVE GOPHER IN ONE HAND AN' A SYRINGE FULL'VE HUMAN ADRENALINE IN T'OTHER--NOT THAT YOU'LL FIND *THAT* MENTIONED IN HIS FOOKIN' AUTO-BIOGRAPHY...
OH, WE'RE 'ERE.
WELL MUCH OBLIGED, REVEREND.
SAY, Y'ALL DON'T FIND THE COOZE BOY IN PHILLY, I HEARD THEY GOT A LOTTA SEX IN BOSTON. COULD BE WORTH A TRY.
OR I DUNNO. TORONTO.
NAY LAD, YOU LEAVE IT TO THE PROFESSIONALS. WE'VE AS GOOD AS GOT THE BASTARD.
Y'KNOW...I'M ALWAYS TELLIN' FREDDY 'ERE: YOU YANKS DON'T KNOW 'OW FOOKIN' LOOKY YOU ARE, DO YOU?
NEXT YANKEE I MEET, I'LL BE SURE AN' ASK HIM.
NAY, 'COURSE YOU DON'T! YOU DON'T KNOW WHAT IT'S LIKE TO COME 'ERE AS *OUTSIDER!*
TO COME SAILIN' INTO NEW YORK AFTER CROSSIN' ATLANTIC...I 'AD TO WORK MY PASSAGE, AN' I THINK YOU KNOW WHAT I'M TRYIN' TO SAY...
YOU LOOK OOP AN' YOU SEE THAT LIBERTY LASS WAVIN' HER BIG LIT-OOP DILDO USHERIN' YOU INTO BRAVE NEW WORLD OF OPPORTUNITY AN' OPULENCE, AN' YOU THINK--IT ALL STARTS 'ERE. *ME SECOND CHANCE AT LIFE.*

AN' BELIEVE ME, REVEREND: TWENTY YEARS GRABBIN' YER ANKLES ROUND BACK OF BARNSLEY TOWN 'ALL, YOU'D BE READY FOR A SECOND FOOKIN' CHANCE--
YOU'RE A HELL OF AN AMERICAN, BOB.
Y'ALL TAKE CARE NOW.

WHAT A PLEASANT LAD!
I SUPPOSE YOU HAD TO MENTION THE COCKSUCKING TROPHY...?

CHEER UP, LAD! BE THERE SOON!
COME ON, I'LL BUY YOU A CUP OF TEA AN' A BUN AN' WE CAN SING ONE O' THEM TORCH SONGS YOU'RE ALWAYS ON ABOUT...

HELL, I KNOW WHERE I SEEN THAT FAT BOY BEFORE! IT WAS IN SAN FRANCISCO AT THAT DAMN PARTY!

THERE WAS THAT FELLA WITH THE SHEEP AN' THE SEX DWARF AN' THE BIG CHOCOLATE FIST, AN' I JUST GOT THROUGH BEATIN' HELL OUTTA THAT JESUS PERVERT WHEN THE BAD BOYS TRIED TO KIDNAP TULIP-- AN' I HAD TO TAKE THAT CAR TO CHASE 'EM--
AN' OL' BOB THERE WAS UP ON THE ROOF WITH HIS PECKER OUT, THAT'S IT...!

ALWAYS DID WONDER WHAT HAPPENED TO HIM.

INTO THE MIDNIGHT HOUR WITH WKBX PHILADELPHIA'S BEST, AND TONIGHT I HAVE WITH ME TWO GUESTS WHO'VE BEEN SHARPENING THEIR KNIVES ALL WEEK: MR. ULYSSES GETT, WHOSE LATEST BOOK HIDDEN AGENDA: FINGERING MODERN FEMINISM IS RIDING HIGH ON THE BESTSELLER LISTS--
AND MISS MARTHA MOORE-- LECTURER AT YALE AND EDITOR OF TRUE CLIT, AN ANTHOLOGY OF RADICAL WOMEN'S WESTERN POETRY.
HELLO, TOM.
HELLO, TOM. IT'S MS., ACTUALLY. AND I RESENT THE KNIFE REFERENCE; IT'S THIS KIND OF CASUAL, EVERYDAY PHALLIC SYMBOLISM THAT THRUSTS THE TRADITIONAL MASCULINE POWER STRUCTURE INTO SOCIETY'S FACE. IT'S LINGUISTIC FASCISM, REALLY.
HMMMM... ANY THOUGHTS ON THAT, ULYSSES?
HEH! JUST TWO, TOM. HOG AND WASH.
WELL, I FAIL TO SEE THE HUMOR IN THIS SITUATION...
NO KIDDING.
IT'S ONLY NATURAL YOU SHOULD RESORT TO CHEAP DERISION AND PUERILE HUMOR. THE OUTWARDLY IMPRESSIVE BUT UNSUSTAINABLE ERECTION THAT IS THE GYNOPHOBIC MALE PSYCHE CAN ONLY EVER OFFER SUCH FEEBLE SPURTINGS IN ITS DEFENSE BEFORE ITS INEVITABLE COLLAPSE...
HEH! SOUNDS TO ME LIKE A CERTAIN UPTIGHT COMMIE CONSPIRACY NUT IS STARTING TO SEE HER DAMN PHALLIC SYMBOLS EVERYWHERE!
I CAN CERTAINLY SEE ONE IN FRONT OF ME NOW.
OH YES, WELL, THAT'S TYPICAL! TYPICAL SNEERING FEMINAZI, TAKING CHILDISH POTSHOTS AT ANYONE WHO REMINDS THEM OF THE AUTHORITY THEY KNOW THEY NEED, OF EVERYTHING THAT MADE THIS COUNTRY GREAT--
AND ONCE AGAIN WE SEE AMERICAN MILITARY-INDUSTRIAL IMPERIALISM REVEALED IN ITS TRUE COLORS: THE STARS AND STRIPES WRAPPED AROUND A THROBBING, UNSTABLE POWER-TOWER WHOSE PARANOID DEFENDERS CANNOT BEAR TO HEAR IT DERIDED--IN CASE ITS ULTIMATELY SELF-DESTRUCTIVE NATURE IS REVEALED...
WOULD YOU LISTEN TO THIS CRAP? THIS IS WHAT YOU GET WHEN... PEOPLE STRAY FROM THEIR TRADITIONAL ROLES AS HOMEMAKERS. I MEAN WHAT, IF I MAY BE SO BOLD AS TO ASK, IS SO BAD ABOUT THE KITCHEN ANYWAY?
WHAT WOULD YOU KNOW ABOUT HOMEMAKING? YOU LIVE ALONE IN THAT BROWNSTONE IN BOSTON, THE ONE YOU COULDN'T HELP SHOWING OFF IN YOUR STUPID PAUL REVERE DOCUMENTARY!
THIS IS SILLY, WE'RE GETTING COMPLETELY OFF THE POINT. TOM, CAN'T WE GO BACK TO THE ORIGINAL TOPIC?
THERE WAS NO ORIGINAL TOPIC, ULYSSES.
UH... COME AGAIN, TOM?
NO NEED WITH YOU TWO. MY, MY, WHAT A LOT OF CALLERS WE'VE GOT...!

WARREN FROM THE CITY, YOU'RE THROUGH TO WKBX!
FUCKERS! FUCKERS! FU--

...SAY AGAIN THERE IS NO PLACE FOR THAT KIND OF SICKENING PROFANITY ON TALK RADIO. WE'RE TRYING TO INSPIRE OPINION AND DEBATE HERE; WE ARE NOT IN THE BUSINESS OF PROMOTING RABBLE-ROUSING FILTH.

NOW, WE'VE GOT JESSE FROM TEXAS ON LINE TWO. JESSE, YOU'RE THROUGH TO WKBX, PHILADELPHIA'S BEST...
HEY, TOM. GOT KIND OF A QUESTION FOR ULYSSES AN' MARTHA.
THEY'RE LISTENING, JESSE.

WELL WHAT I ALWAYS WONDER 'BOUT PEOPLE LIKE THEM IS, CAN THEY QUIT YELLIN' SLOGANS AT EACH OTHER LIKE A COUPLE OF GODDAMN PARROTS AN' JUST TELL US WHAT THEY REALLY WANT?

WELL THAT'S... THAT'S AN INTERESTING QUESTION, JESSE...

ANY THOUGHTS, MARTHA?
I...I... OH GOD--!
MARTHA...?
COCK! COCK, COCK, I NEED COCK! OH CHRIST, POETRY'S NOT ENOUGH ANY-MORE! IT'S GOT TO BE COCK!
I WANT COCK, DAMMIT! I WANT COCK!!
...WELL, ISN'T THAT A SURPRISE! HOW ABOUT YOU, ULYSSES?
MM?
ULYSSES?

THANGYUH VERRMUCH...

YOU LIVE LOCAL?
UH-HUH, THANGYEW. YEAH, IF YOU COULD JUZ TAKE ME DOWN THE ROAD A LIDDLE BIT...

NOZZIR, NOT ROUND HEAH. JUZ WALKIN' THE LAND, YOU KNOW.
JUZ TAKIN' CARE AHBIZNESS.

UH, NO THANGYEW. NO THANGYEW MA FRIEND.
SUTHAN BOY, HUH?
YEP.
YEAH ME TOO.
YEAH THIZZ A GREAT COUNTRY. A GREAT COUNTRY, YEAH...
LIKE THIZ BOY ON THE RADIO HEAH I KEEP HEARIN', THIZ BOY DON' SPEAK TOO GOOD, GOT IZ FACE ALL MEZZD UP LIKE THAT? ONLY 'N 'MERICA. ONLY 'N 'MERICA.
AH WUZ WHERE HE IZ ONCE.
LONG TIME 'GO.
HAD THE WORL' AT MA FEET, YESSIR. KINDA LIFE EVER'BODY DREAMSA LIVIN', BUT IT ALL GOTTA BE TOO MUCH.
AH HEARD ALL KINDSA STORIES 'BOUT ME SPOSEDA BE TRUE--'CEPT THEY AIN'T, NOSSIR. NEVER HUNG OL' MAN PARKER'S WALKIN' STICK OFF MASELF AT NO ORGY, UH-UH. NEVER EVEN HAD NO ORGIES. AN' THAT CROOL, CROOL ONE 'BOUT YELLIN' OUT SORRY MOMMA WHEN AH'S BEIN' INNIMATE WITH A LADY, THAT AIN'T TRUE NEITHER. AIN'T NONE OF IT TRUE.
DON' THING SO, ANYHOW.
SO NOW'DAYZ AH JUZ LIVE MA OWN DREAMZ, 'STEADA WORRYIN' ALLA TIME 'BOUT EVER'-BODY ELSE'S.

YOU KNOW...
I BEEN HEARIN' A LOT ABOUT DREAMS THIS PAST WHILE. 'BOUT SECOND CHANCES AN' SUCH, AN' WHAT FOLKS EXPECT FROM THIS PLACE AN' THE HOPES THEY INVEST IN IT.
AN' I DO KNOW THIS IS A GREAT, GREAT COUNTRY, EVEN IF SOMETIMES ITS FUTURE LIES IN THE HANDS OF FOOLS--
BUT I WORRY IT MIGHT NOT STAND THE WEIGHT OF ALL THEM GODDAMN DREAMS.
WELL YORE CONCERN IS TOUCHIN', MIGHTY TOUCHIN'... DAMN, LOOKIT THAT...
BUT THIZ HERE'S THE GREATES' AN' FINES' COUNTRY EVER WAS OR WILL BE, YESSIR. AIN'T NO NEEDA BE AFRAID FOR HER.
JUZ 'CAUSE SHE OPENZA GATES TO TH' STARS, THAT DON' MEAN EVER'MAN STEPS THROUGH EMZ GONNA CLIMB THAT HIGH. ALL 'MERICA DOES IS SHOW TH' WAY.
WHOLE POINTA THIZ COUNTRY, 'CEPT MOST FOLKS'RE TOO BLINDA SEE IT.
UH-HUH-HUH.

BBZZZZZZTT
HELLO?
AMY, HONEY, I'M SORRY IF I WOKE YOU...
BZZZZTT
JESSE? JESSE, GET UP HERE NOW.
WELL I GOT MY DOG HERE. I DUNNO IF--
JESSE, WILL YOU PLEASE JUST COME ON UP? RIGHT NOW, OKAY?
SHE'S HERE.

GLENN
FABRY
·99·

"You know what this is tonight? Snowing like this?
On the streets of New York?"

...HOWDY.
HI.

BROOKE'S
187

Da-dee-dee-da-da-dum,
dee-dee-dee-dee-dee...
♫ da-da-dum-da-da...

SHE'LL ALWAYSH, BE A WOMAN, TO MEEE... ♪
AHUH--! AHUH-HUH-HUH!

SAME AGAIN?
HIT ME.

I WAS IN HELL WITHOUT YOU.

HONEY?
WHAT HAPPENED TO YOUR *POOR* EYE?

I MEAN-- I MEAN WHAT HAPPENED TO YOU, ANY-WAY?
TULIP-- HONEY--
WHY WEREN'T YOU KILLED WHEN YOU FELL OUT OF THE PLANE? WHAT HAVE YOU BEEN DOING? I MEAN IT'S BEEN MONTHS AND MONTHS AND MONTHS!

JESSE, WHERE HAVE YOU **BEEN**?

YECH.
LASER-SOUND
PRETTY BAD, ISN'T IT? I REALLY WANT TO CHANGE IT'ROUND A BIT.

OH, THANKS... ARE YOU SURE IT'S OKAY FOR HIM TO BE HERE?
NO PROBLEM AT ALL. HE SEEMS LIKE A SWEET-NATURED LITTLE GUY.

NO, I'D LIKE TO PUT SOME JOHNNY CASH OR WILLIE NELSON ON THERE. BUT THE GUY WHO OWNS THE PLACE HATES COUNTRY.
DO YOU KNOW THAT WILLIE NELSON SONG *TIME OF THE PREACHER*?

MM-HMM-*HMMM HMMM*, HMM-HMM-HMM ...YES, ISN'T THAT A WONDERFUL SONG?
I LIKE IT BECAUSE IT REMINDS ME OF A FRIEND OF MINE, THIS GUY WHO'S KIND OF A PREACHER.

KIND OF A PREACHER?
YEAH. HE'S CURRENTLY BANGING HIS GIRLFRIEND'S BRAINS OUT ON THE FLOOR OF MY APARTMENT.
KIND OF A PREACHER.

I SUPPOSE A LOT OF MODERN CHURCHES ARE TAKING A MORE PROGRESSIVE STANCE ON THAT SORT OF THING...
OH, THEY JUST HADN'T SEEN EACH OTHER IN A LONG TIME.
PLUS SHE THOUGHT HE WAS DEAD, AS A MATTER OF FACT.
BUT ANYWAY, THEY MET UP AT MY PLACE AND BEFORE YOU KNEW IT THEY JUST JUMPED ON EACH OTHER AND STARTED TEARING THEIR CLOTHES OFF. SO ME AND THE POOCH HERE DECIDED TO DISCREETLY WITHDRAW.
DISCRETION IN DECEMBER... YOU MUST BE FOND OF THESE TWO. IT'S TEN BELOW OUT THERE.
WHAT'S THE LITTLE GUY'S NAME?
I DIDN'T HAVE TIME TO ASK.
WUFF!
HMH.
IT'S NICE, ISN'T IT? WHEN TWO PEOPLE ARE THAT DEVOTED TO EACH OTHER?
YEAH, IT IS...
BUT SOME-THING BAD'S HAPPENED.
AND I THINK I MIGHT KNOW WHO'S BEHIND IT.

YOU SAW US TOGETHER?
AND YOU LEFT ME WITH HIM?

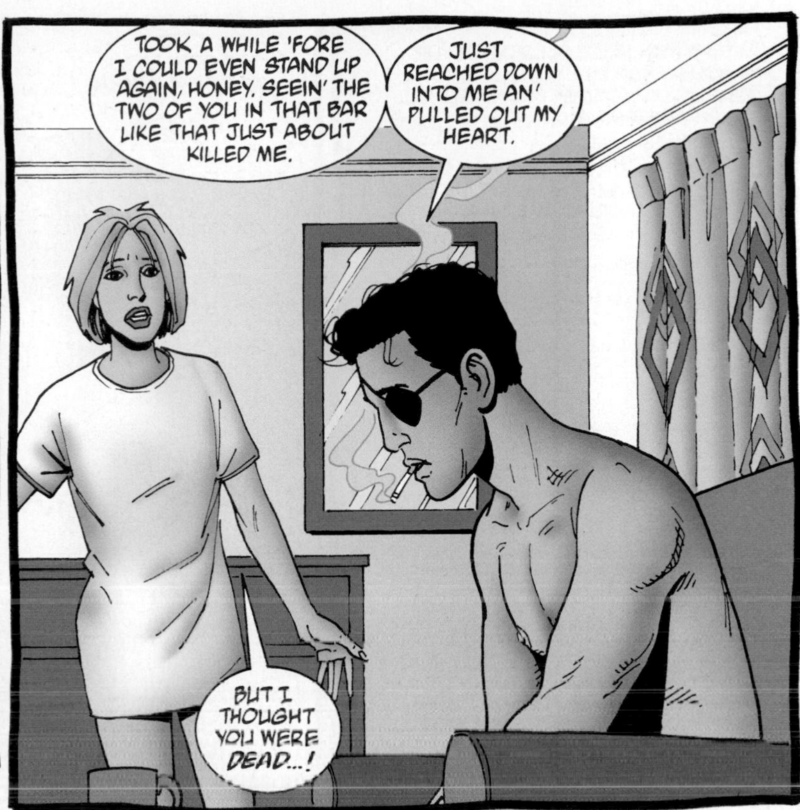
TOOK A WHILE 'FORE I COULD EVEN STAND UP AGAIN, HONEY. SEEIN' THE TWO OF YOU IN THAT BAR LIKE THAT JUST ABOUT KILLED ME.
JUST REACHED DOWN INTO ME AN' PULLED OUT MY HEART.
BUT I THOUGHT YOU WERE DEAD...!

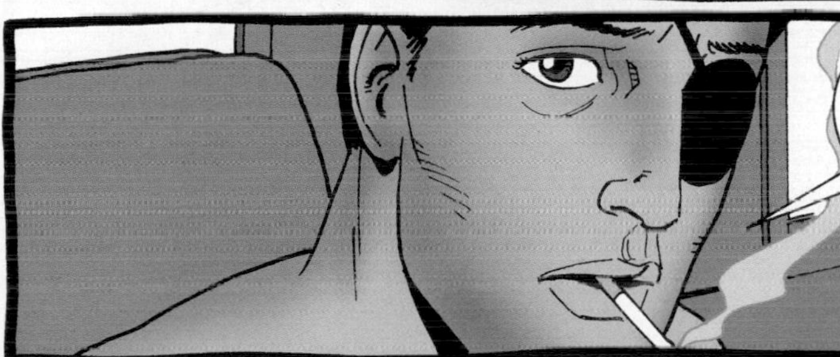
YEAH. AN' WHEN I DID STAND UP I FELT DEAD. FELT LIKE THE LAST GOOD THING IN MY LIFE WAS GONE: THEY TOOK YOUR MOM AN' YOUR DADDY AN' NOW THEY GONE AN' TOOK HER TOO.
SO I...I GOT LOST, I GUESS.

AND YOU THINK I WANTED THAT?
DID YOU HATE ME? BLAME ME? IS THAT WHY YOU DIDN'T COME AFTER US?
HATE YOU? HONEY, THAT IS CRAZY...!

NO, ALL I THOUGHT WAS THAT'S IT. SHE THINKS YOU'RE DEAD AN' SHE'S MOVED ON. THERE AIN'T NO BLAME IN THAT...
AN' THEM DREAMS I HAD OF BEIN' WITH YOU FOREVER, WELL, I FIGURED DREAMS WAS ALL THEY'D BEEN.

YOU THOUGHT THAT?
FOR A WHILE.
YOU IDIOT.
YEP.

I KNOW YOU WERE ALL FUCKED UP AND YOU WEREN'T THINKING STRAIGHT-- I MEAN YOU'D ALMOST BEEN KILLED, I UNDERSTAND ALL THAT--
BUT WHAT I DON'T GET IS HOW YOU COULD JUST WALK AWAY AND LEAVE ME WITH HIM...
CASSIDY?
CASSIDY! WHY, JESSE? WHY?!
WHY DID YOU LEAVE ME WITH THAT EVIL FUCKING MONSTER?!
...?
TULIP...
CASSIDY AIN'T-- HELL, I AIN'T EXACTLY SURE WHAT I THINK OF HIM RIGHT NOW, BUT HE AIN'T NO MONSTER...
YOU MEAN YOU DON'T KNOW? HOW COULD YOU NOT KNOW? THE WAY HE IS, THE THINGS HE DID...
YOU DON'T KNOW--
BECAUSE I
NEVER
TOLD YOU.

TULIP AND JESSE WERE BORN TO LOVE.

YOU SEE THOSE TWO TOGETHER AND YOU KNOW WHY THE STARS ARE SHINING.
YOU KNOW WHAT TIME IT IS.

WHEN THEY FIRST MET IT WAS ALL FULL THROTTLE; IT WAS HEARTS AND GUNS AND CAR CHASES AND SWEATY SEX WHENEVER THEY FELT LIKE IT, AND LOTS OF STARING INTO EACH OTHER'S EYES AT SUNDOWN AND *I'LL DO ANYTHING FOR YOU*...
AND THEN THEY GOT SPLIT UP, AND THAT WAS A LONG, DARK, COLD, BAD TIME.

AND THEN... PRESUMABLY BECAUSE THE WORLD *IS* A GOOD PLACE AND IT *IS* WORTH FIGHTING FOR AFTER ALL...
THEY FOUND EACH OTHER AGAIN.

SAME AGAIN?
OH YEAH.

I'M SORRY. THIS MUST BE REALLY DULL FOR YOU. YOU PROBABLY HEAR STORIES LIKE THIS ALL THE TIME.
TRUE.
BUT I ALWAYS LIKE THE NICE ONES.

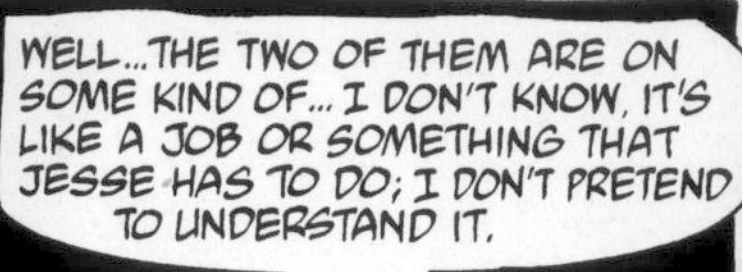

WELL... THE TWO OF THEM ARE ON SOME KIND OF... I DON'T KNOW, IT'S LIKE A JOB OR SOMETHING THAT JESSE HAS TO DO; I DON'T PRETEND TO UNDERSTAND IT.
THERE'S ALL SORTS OF WEIRDNESS INVOLVED, BUT TULIP CAN TAKE CARE OF HER-SELF--AND NO ONE IN THEIR RIGHT MIND WOULD WANT TO FUCK WITH JESSE. HE'S A SOUTHERN BOY, YOU KNOW? TEXAN.
BIG ON HONOR.

i.e., BIG ON BREAKING YOUR NECK IF YOU SO MUCH AS LOOK SIDEWAYS AT HIM... THANKS...
BUT SOME-WHERE ALONG THE WAY THEY PICKED UP THIS GUY CALLED CASSIDY.

NOW I DON'T QUITE KNOW WHAT HIS STORY IS, I ONLY MET HIM FOR A SECOND. BUT IT'S LIKE TULIP TOLD ME HE'S THIS REAL 24/7 PARTY GUY, HUNDRED PERCENT ATTITUDE, OKAY?
AND ALL I COULD SEE WAS THIS NERVOUS LITTLE BOY.

WELL, IT WAS ONLY FOR A SECOND.
I MEAN HE HAD GOOD REASON TO BE NERVOUS, BECAUSE HE'D JUST MADE A PASS AT TULIP WHEN JESSE'S BACK WAS TURNED. AND I TOLD HER TO TELL HIM, BECAUSE THAT KIND OF THING ALWAYS ENDS IN TEARS, RIGHT?
FLOODS.

SO THE NEXT THING YOU KNOW TULIP CALLS ME SOUNDING REALLY WEIRD, AND JESSE CALLS TO SAY SHE THINKS HE'S DEAD FOR SOME REASON, BUT HE'S ON HIS WAY TO FIND HER... AND THE MONTHS GO BY AND SUDDENLY SHE SHOWS UP LOOKING JUST AWFUL, AS IF SOMETHING TERRIBLE'S BEEN DONE TO HER--
AND THE WHOLE DAMN THING'S GOT CASSIDY WRITTEN ALL OVER IT.

IT MUST BE HARD FOR YOU TO BELIEVE THIS ABOUT HIM.
NO, HONEY.
YOU SAY IT, IT'S TRUE.
HE WAS GOING TO STAY IN NEW ORLEANS AND I THOUGHT FINE, PROBLEM SOLVED. BUT HE CAME WITH US AFTER ALL, AND HE BEGGED ME FOR A LAST CHANCE AND I JUST COULDN'T TELL YOU AND--AND WRECK EVERYTHING...
I WAS SO FUCKING STUPID.
PLEASE DON'T SAY THAT.
YOU COULDN'TA KNOWN IN A MILLION YEARS.
I WAS STUPID. I SHOULDA PULLED MY HEAD OUTTA MY ASS AN' WALKED RIGHT IN THERE AN' GOT YOU AWAY FROM HIM.
INSTEAD I FUCKED UP AN' YOU WENT TO HELL.
AN' FOR SIX MONTHS HE--
I DON'T WANT TO THINK ABOUT IT--!

WHO THE HELL
IS THAT GUY?

LET'S
GO OUT.

YOU SEEM SO PREOCCUPIED WITH YOUR FRIENDS' TROUBLES, MISS. DON'T YOU EVER FIND TIME FOR ROMANCE YOURSELF?
MM?

AH... LOOK...
NO OFFENSE OR ANYTHING, BUT EVEN IF WE HADN'T ONLY JUST MET I'M REALLY NOT-- I MEAN YOU SEEM LIKE A NICE GUY, BUT--

OH! OH NO, MISS! OH, I AM SORRY!
NO, IT WAS A GENUINELY INNOCENT INQUIRY. I'M HONESTLY NOT HITTING ON YOU OR ANYTHING LIKE THAT.
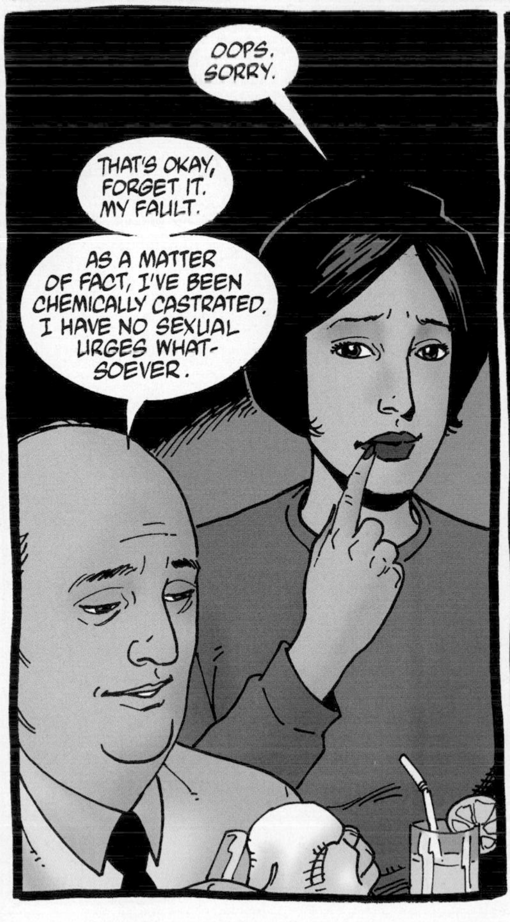
OOPS. SORRY.
THAT'S OKAY, FORGET IT. MY FAULT.
AS A MATTER OF FACT, I'VE BEEN CHEMICALLY CASTRATED. I HAVE NO SEXUAL URGES WHAT-SOEVER.
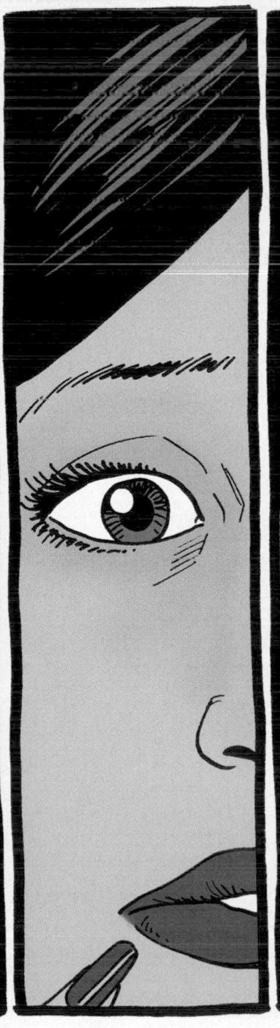

OH NO, RELAX. I DIDN'T ACTUALLY DO ANY-THING.
IT WAS JUST AN ACCIDENT, REALLY.

YOU WERE CHEMICALLY CASTRATED BY ACCIDENT?
IT'S QUITE AN INTERESTING STORY, ACTUALLY.

IT WAS A YEAR OR TWO AGO.
I'D GONE DOWN TO MY LOCAL POLICE PRECINCT TO SORT OUT A DISPUTE OVER SOME PARKING TICKETS--IT LATER TURNED OUT I'D BEEN RIGHT, AND THEY'D BEEN ISSUED TO ME BY MISTAKE...

SO I WAS WAITING FOR THE OFFICER CONCERNED OUT BY THE FRONT DESK, SITTING WITH ALL KINDS OF PEOPLE, AND A PLAINCLOTHES FELLOW APPEARED AND SHOUTED JOHN SOAP!
BUT I THOUGHT HE SAID JOE SOAP, WHICH IS MY NAME, YOU SEE, SO I PUT MY HAND UP AND HE GESTURED FOR ME TO COME WITH HIM...

I GOT SOME VERY ODD LOOKS ON MY WAY OUT, BUT I DIDN'T THINK ANYTHING OF THEM, AND THE OFFICER TOOK ME INTO AN OFFICE AND GAVE ME A FORM TO SIGN...

YOU JUST... SIGNED?
I ASSUMED IT WAS STANDARD PROCEDURE.

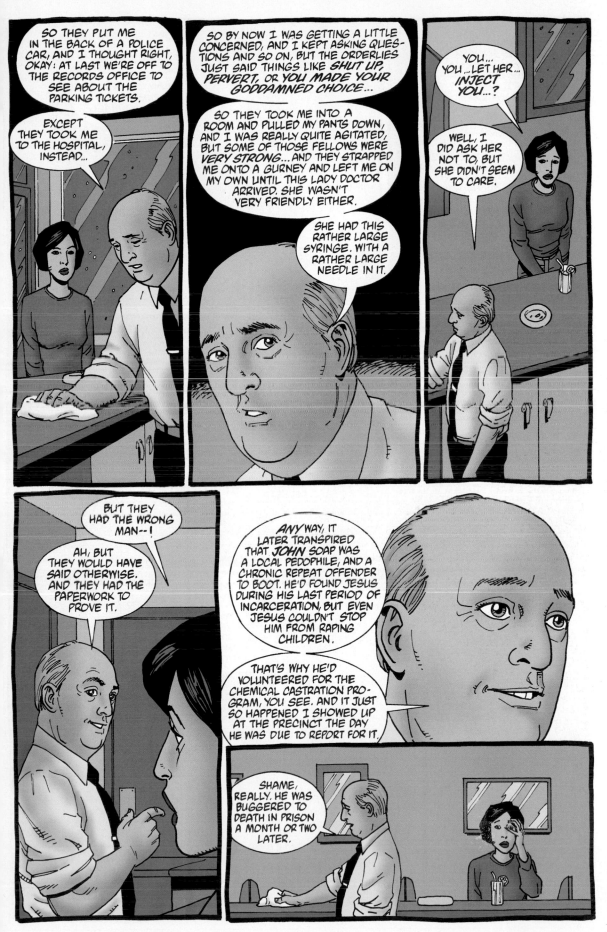

SO THEY PUT ME IN THE BACK OF A POLICE CAR, AND I THOUGHT RIGHT, OKAY: AT LAST WE'RE OFF TO THE RECORDS OFFICE TO SEE ABOUT THE PARKING TICKETS.

EXCEPT THEY TOOK ME TO THE HOSPITAL, INSTEAD...

SO BY NOW I WAS GETTING A LITTLE CONCERNED, AND I KEPT ASKING QUES-TIONS AND SO ON, BUT THE ORDERLIES JUST SAID THINGS LIKE *SHUT UP, PERVERT,* OR *YOU MADE YOUR GODDAMNED CHOICE...*
SO THEY TOOK ME INTO A ROOM AND PULLED MY PANTS DOWN, AND I WAS REALLY QUITE AGITATED, BUT SOME OF THOSE FELLOWS WERE *VERY STRONG*... AND THEY STRAPPED ME ONTO A GURNEY AND LEFT ME ON MY OWN UNTIL THIS LADY DOCTOR ARRIVED. SHE WASN'T VERY FRIENDLY EITHER.
SHE HAD THIS RATHER LARGE SYRINGE. WITH A RATHER LARGE NEEDLE IN IT.

YOU... YOU...LET HER... *INJECT YOU...?*
WELL, I DID ASK HER NOT TO, BUT SHE DIDN'T SEEM TO CARE.

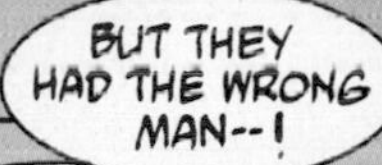
BUT THEY HAD THE WRONG MAN--!

AH, BUT THEY WOULD HAVE SAID OTHERWISE. AND THEY HAD THE PAPERWORK TO PROVE IT.
*ANY*WAY, IT LATER TRANSPIRED THAT *JOHN* SOAP WAS A LOCAL PEDOPHILE, AND A CHRONIC REPEAT OFFENDER TO BOOT. HE'D FOUND JESUS DURING HIS LAST PERIOD OF INCARCERATION, BUT EVEN JESUS COULDN'T STOP HIM FROM RAPING CHILDREN.
THAT'S WHY HE'D VOLUNTEERED FOR THE CHEMICAL CASTRATION PRO-GRAM, YOU SEE. AND IT JUST SO HAPPENED I SHOWED UP AT THE PRECINCT THE DAY HE WAS DUE TO REPORT FOR IT.

SHAME, REALLY. HE WAS BUGGERED TO DEATH IN PRISON A MONTH OR TWO LATER.

MR. SOAP... THESE PEOPLE DISSOLVED YOUR GENITALS. YOU MUST HAVE GOTTEN A A FORTUNE IN COMPENSATION.
CALL ME JOE.
YES, I GOT A COUPLE OF MILLION ONCE EVERYTHING WAS STRAIGHTENED OUT. THE ONLY TROUBLE WAS I COULDN'T SATISFY MY WIFE SEXUALLY ANYMORE, AND SHE DECIDED TO SUE FOR DIVORCE.

...AND SHE GOT THE FUCKING MONEY...
EVERY PENNY, I'M AFRAID-- OH, PLEASE DON'T HURT YOURSELF, MISS!

CALL ME AMY, JOE.
PLEASED TO MEET YOU, AMY.
YEAH.

I SUPPOSE THAT'S WHY I LIKE HEARING ABOUT PEOPLE LIKE THOSE FRIENDS OF YOURS. BORN TO LOVE, WASN'T THAT WHAT YOU SAID? THAT'S SO WONDERFUL...
MM?
OH, JUST IGNORE ME.

I'M A HOPELESS ROMANTIC.
BUT A STORY LIKE THEIRS, IT SURELY GIVES YOU HOPE IN A MEAN OLD WORLD LIKE THIS ONE.

JESUS--! WHAT THE HELL-- 'OU SCARED THE LIVIN' SHIT OUTTA ME, WHAT THE HELL YOU WANNA DO THAT FOR--?

HA HA HA HA HA! FUN!!

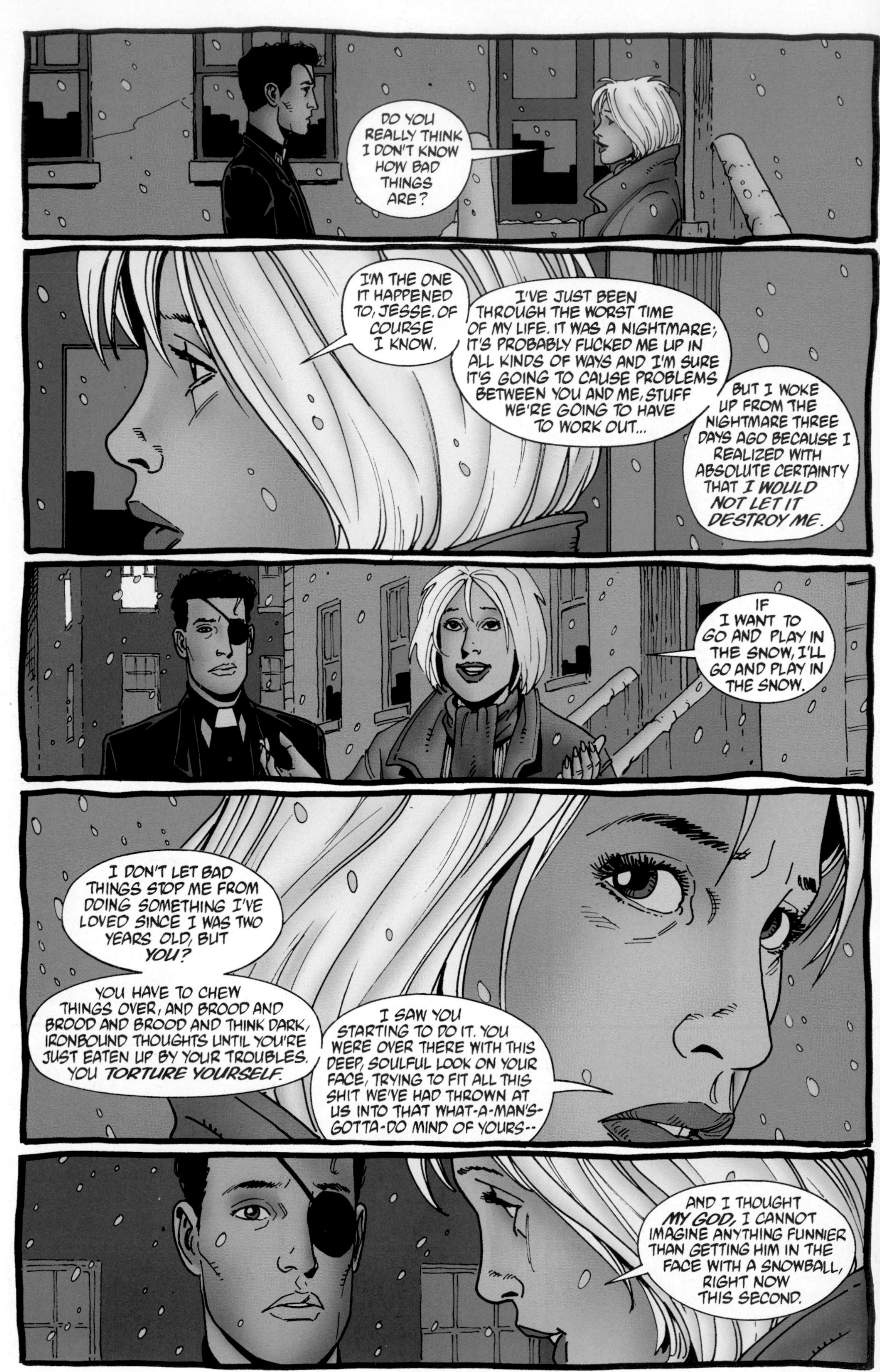
DO YOU REALLY THINK I DON'T KNOW HOW BAD THINGS ARE?
I'M THE ONE IT HAPPENED TO, JESSE. OF COURSE I KNOW.
I'VE JUST BEEN THROUGH THE WORST TIME OF MY LIFE. IT WAS A NIGHTMARE; IT'S PROBABLY FUCKED ME UP IN ALL KINDS OF WAYS AND I'M SURE IT'S GOING TO CAUSE PROBLEMS BETWEEN YOU AND ME, STUFF WE'RE GOING TO HAVE TO WORK OUT...
BUT I WOKE UP FROM THE NIGHTMARE THREE DAYS AGO BECAUSE I REALIZED WITH ABSOLUTE CERTAINTY THAT I WOULD NOT LET IT DESTROY ME.
IF I WANT TO GO AND PLAY IN THE SNOW, I'LL GO AND PLAY IN THE SNOW.
I DON'T LET BAD THINGS STOP ME FROM DOING SOMETHING I'VE LOVED SINCE I WAS TWO YEARS OLD, BUT YOU?
YOU HAVE TO CHEW THINGS OVER, AND BROOD AND BROOD AND BROOD AND THINK DARK, IRONBOUND THOUGHTS UNTIL YOU'RE JUST EATEN UP BY YOUR TROUBLES. YOU TORTURE YOURSELF.
I SAW YOU STARTING TO DO IT. YOU WERE OVER THERE WITH THIS DEEP, SOULFUL LOOK ON YOUR FACE, TRYING TO FIT ALL THIS SHIT WE'VE HAD THROWN AT US INTO THAT WHAT-A-MAN'S-GOTTA-DO MIND OF YOURS--
AND I THOUGHT MY GOD, I CANNOT IMAGINE ANYTHING FUNNIER THAN GETTING HIM IN THE FACE WITH A SNOWBALL, RIGHT NOW THIS SECOND.

YOU THOUGHT THAT, HUH?
YEP.

TELL ME WHY YOU CAME TO FIND ME.

NOT HOW LONG YOU AGONIZED OVER IT, OR HOW YOU DECIDED, OR ALL THE DIFFERENT FEARS AND POSSIBILITIES THAT WENT THROUGH YOUR MIND. JUST *WHY*.
...

'CAUSE LIVIN' WITHOUT YOU AIN'T REALLY LIVIN'.

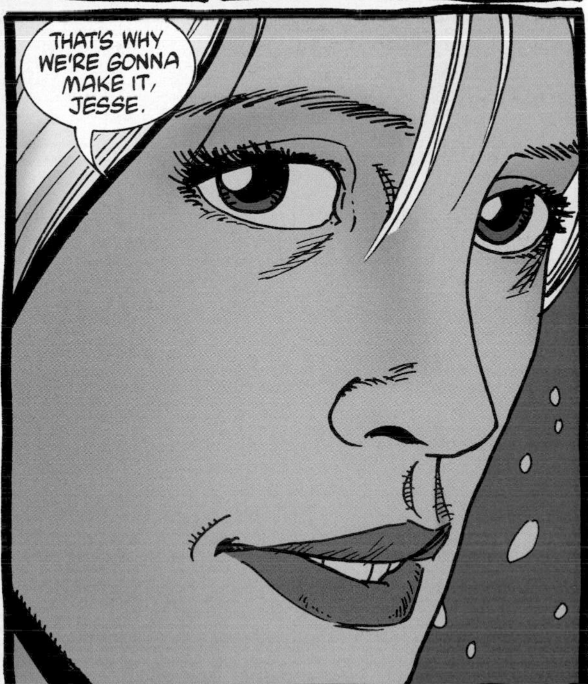
THAT'S WHY WE'RE GONNA MAKE IT, JESSE.

I KNOW IT WON'T BE EASY, BUT GOD, WHERE'S THE POINT IN MAKING IT HARDER ON YOURSELF...
AW, YOU KNOW GUYS LIKE ME, HONEY. LIFE AIN'T S'POSED TO BE SIMPLE.
JUST HOW WE'RE RAISED, I GUESS.

SAY THAT AGAIN.
HUH...?
THAT THING YOU JUST SAID. SAY IT AGAIN.

GUYS LIKE ME... IT'S HOW WE'RE RAISED?
THAT?

THAT'S IT, JESSE.

GUYS LIKE YOU.

I MEAN THEY TOOK YOUR BALLS, JOE, I CAN'T BELIEVE YOU CAN STILL FEEL ROMANTIC AFTER SOMETHING LIKE THAT...
AND HOPE? HOW DO YOU FIND HOPE IN ANYTHING, AFTER WHAT'S HAPPENED TO YOU?

I HAVE TO.
LOOK AT THESE FRIENDS OF YOURS, THE PREACHER AND HIS YOUNG LADY. DON'T YOU SEE HOW THEY KEEP ON FINDING EACH OTHER?

THEY GET SPLIT UP BUT THEY'RE REUNITED, AND THEN THEY GET SPLIT UP AGAIN-- AND EVEN THOUGH ONE THINKS THE OTHER'S DEAD, EVEN WITH ALL THIS CASSIDY FELLOW CAN DO TO THEM, THEY FIND EACH OTHER AGAIN...
BECAUSE AS YOU YOURSELF SAID, THE WORLD IS NOT AN IRREDEEMABLY BAD PLACE, AND IT'S THINGS LIKE THIS THAT PROVE IT.
AND IF YOU DON'T BELIEVE ME, ASK YOURSELF THIS: WHAT KEEPS THEM TOGETHER? WHY DID JESSE COME LOOKING FOR TULIP AFTER ALL THIS TIME?

OKAY, JOE. 'CAUSE THERE'S HOPE.
'CAUSE IN THE HALLS OF HIS MEMORY STILL ECHOED HER EYES.

I SHOULD QUIT WORRYING ABOUT THOSE TWO, SHOULDN'T I?
THAT YOU SHOULD.
THANK YOU, NOEL. ARE YOU SURE I CAN'T CALL YOU A CAB?
ASH 'KAY, JOE... JUSH COUPLA BLOCKSH...
YA KNOW SHOMETHIN'?
WHEN YA KIN JERK OFF TA THE THOUGHTA YER WIFE, AN'...AN' NOT JUST SHUM BLONDE INNA SHTROKE-BOOK?
ASH WHEN YA KNOW ISH *LOVE*.
...SAME AGAIN?
SAME AGAIN.
AND HAVE ONE YOURSELF.

YOU KNOW WHAT THIS IS TONIGHT?

SNOWING LIKE THIS?

ON THE STREETS OF NEW YORK?

IT'S OUR FAIRYTALE.

I BUILT MY DREAMS AROUND YOU

GARTH ENNIS - Writer **STEVE DILLON - Artist**

PAMELA RAMBO - Colorist CLEM ROBINS - Letterer AXEL ALONSO - Editor

PREACHER created by GARTH ENNIS and STEVE DILLON

Cover art for the first trade paperback edition of PREACHER VOL. 7: SALVATION by Glenn Fabry

Cover art for the first trade paperback edition of PREACHER VOL. 8: ALL HELL'S A-COMING by Glenn Fabry